AT THE EDGE

I SHOULDN'T BE HERE

N E I L B U O N O C O R E

authorHOUSE®

AuthorHouse™
1663 Liberty Drive
Bloomington, IN 47403
www.authorhouse.com
Phone: 833-262-8899

Published by AuthorHouse 03/18/2022

ISBN: 978-1-6655-5419-0 (sc)
ISBN: 978-1-6655-5418-3 (e)

Library of Congress Control Number: 2022905078

Print information available on the last page.

Any people depicted in stock imagery provided by Getty Images are models,
and such images are being used for illustrative purposes only.
Certain stock imagery © Getty Images.

This book is printed on acid-free paper.

DISCLAIMER

This is a work of non-fiction. The events and experiences I describe are true and have been faithfully rendered as I have remembered to the best of my ability. I have changed some of the names and omitted some details in places. Some dialogue has been re-created and most dialogue is verbatim and unchanged.

To the best of my ability and memory, I have recreated the events, people, locales, organizations portrayed in this book. Some events have been compressed. All characters and incidents are real and are not products of the author's imagination.

The author has made every effort to insure, that the information was correct at press time. The author and the publisher do not assume any liability and hereby disclaim any liability to any party for any loss, damage, or disruption by errors or omissions resulting from negligence, accident or any other cause.

AUTHOR'S NOTE

A life changing event occurred after eleven years of marriage causing a rift between my family and the immediate and extended family. While writing the book I learned that the fallout did not occur after eleven years of marriage but started when I was a child.

Since childhood I had more than fifteen near death experiences and only one was related to my law enforcement career. I do not know if I survived those experiences do to my belief in God, or was it good luck.

The book was written where some chapters were fast forwarded in time to provide background information to keep the reader engaged.

1

THANKSGIVING

I awoke early in the morning while everyone was still asleep; my thoughts on a getaway. While driving eastbound on Sunrise Highway, I lapsed into deep thought for several miles.

Sometime later, I found myself at the edge of a dock staring out into the water on a foggy night. Time had passed, and suddenly I realized that I didn't know where I was. I appeared to be in a daze, not knowing how I arrived there or I possibly had a breakdown. I felt like I had been crushed and then ripped apart by years of emotional torment and rejection by the people who should have loved me. Familial love is supposed to be mostly unconditional, but my family believed that loyalty was more important than love. The abandonment and rejection by my family was pushing me over the edge.

While I sat on the dock, the sun rose, and it suddenly became clear to me that I had a wife and children. I needed to get in touch with them. Surrounded by boats and water, I scurried frantically to find a phone and called my wife.

I said. "Hello Joann."

She answered. "Are you all right?

I replied. "I'm OK."

She asked. "Where are you?"

I paused and looked around. "I'm not sure."

Suddenly, I realized that I was in the area where we had fished one summer.

She uttered. "Stay there. I'll pick you up."

I replied. "No, no, give me some time. I'll be all right. I'll be home."

I had a constant lump in my throat, a tightness in my neck, and an emptiness in my heart that plagued me every day. For the past four years, we lived as outcasts, rather than submit to intimidation by my immediate family. To battle coercion, we sacrificed a normal lifestyle for survival.

I was born to the parents of first- and second-generation Italians, in a family of humble beginnings. We were raised as Catholics, and I attended parochial elementary school. Since my parents were unable to afford the tuition for parochial high school, I attended public high school.

Raised to be independent, I worked since the age of nine. In our family, if you wanted something, you needed to work for it. The age difference between my older brother and younger sister created an atmosphere where we were rarely around one another, so we did not have common interests.

I graduated community college with an applied science associate's degree in mechanical engineering technology, and I worked in the engineering department at Grumman Aerospace Corporation. While there, I was assigned to the lunar module program, which landed men on the moon.

After a round of layoffs, I searched for a more secure profession and was hired by the federal government as a sky marshal. When the program ended, I was absorbed by the Customs Patrol Division.

Years later, I was promoted to supervisor, then tour-commander, and eventually to special agent. During the late seventies, I returned to college, graduating with a Bachelor's of Science Degree in criminal justice with a behavioral science minor.

During their lifetime, most people can recall a close call, a few near-death experiences while driving in a car or otherwise. From the age of eight, I survived fifteen near-death experiences. Only one was related to my career in law enforcement.

In 1974 at the age of twenty-eight, I acted as my own contractor and built the house where my wife and I raised our children. The house was in a small South Shore community on Long Island, adjacent to the town where my brother and his family lived. I was thankful every day that I could raise our children in a better environment than I had growing up in the Bronx.

To awaken every morning and gaze out over the waters of the Great South Bay and to the horizon and the barrier beaches of Fire Island was a dream come true. Sometimes after dinner, we'd walk to the bay and sit on the beach watching small fishing boats and cabin cruisers cut through the water. When the fish were running, I'd drive the seventeen-foot runabout to the Fire Island Inlet and fish for striped bass. On the weekends, we loaded the boat with fishing equipment and traveled across the bay to fish, crab, swim, and bask in the sun.

After I was married, when visiting my parents in the housing projects in the Bronx, I feared for their safety. I noticed the heroin addicts nodding off at the strip mall in a half state of euphoria, self-contained and unaware of their surroundings. While walking toward the apartment building, I frowned at the sight of a variety of unsavory characters hanging around the building. Upon entering the apartment building, I walked up the stairs, where a hypodermic needle lay on the steps; the stench of urine and garbage attacked my senses, evidence of social degradation.

During the mid-seventies, after repeated suggestions, I convinced my parents to move out of the housing projects and into the suburbs of Long Island. We were relieved that they now lived in suburbia, a safer environment. Some years later, when the crack epidemic emerged in the Castle Hill Projects, gunfire from roofs and windows became commonplace. The residents became accustomed to bloodshed, and children and the elderly were afraid to leave their apartments.

In 1979, together with my wife and children, we returned from New Jersey after visiting my sister-in-law. A few days later my mother phoned me. She sounded surprised and upset. "Why didn't you come to our house on Thanksgiving?"

I paused for a moment. "I spoke with you weeks earlier that we were spending Thanksgiving with my sister-in-law, and then we would visit with you on Christmas."

Mom said. "We always see you on Thanksgiving."

I replied. "Ma, weeks earlier I explained to you our Thanksgiving arrangements. Why are you surprised?"

She said, "We want to see you!"

I remarked. "Come over for dinner on Saturday."

She stated. "OK, we'll see you then."

I thought that my parents' imminent visit was an opportunity for my mother to apologize for her anger regarding our Thanksgiving plans.

A few days later, Aunt Mary my father's sister called me on the phone. "I'm sorry that your children were sick and I didn't get to see all of you at your parents' home on Thanksgiving."

I said. "I was surprised to hear you say that because on Thanksgiving we were invited to my sister in-law's home in New Jersey,"

She replied, "Your parents told me that your wife was sick."

I was puzzled. "I don't understand why my parents would say that because we were visiting my sister-in-law in New Jersey."

She sounded confused and said, "Oh well, anyway, it's been nice talking to you."

I said. "Same to you, goodbye."

I did know what to make of make of my aunt's understanding of my Thanksgiving visit to my in-laws.

My wife was cooking in the kitchen and yelled to me, "Get the door. Your parents are here!"

I greeted them as they walked in, their expressions sullen, and their demeanor odd. We stood in the dining room, as they were unwilling to remove their winter coats.

My mother glared at me. "We were all at the house on Thanksgiving, and the family was expecting you to be with us!"

I looked at her and said. "I explained to you weeks earlier that we were committed to visiting my sister in-law on Thanksgiving and that we'd spend Christmas with you."

My mother insisted. "You're supposed to be with your family!"

Now I was getting upset and uttered. "My wife has a family too."

My mother raised her index finger in the air as her eyes opened wide. "I'm the mother, you don't question me, I have an imagination!"

As a thirty-three-year-old married man and the father of two children, it reminded me of being scolded as a child. I stood there speechless. Out of the corner of my eye, I observed my children seated on the steps, quietly watching, staring at Grandma.

I lowered my voice. "I'll respect you, but you need to respect me, Respect is mutual."

My mother stood there silently.

I walked into the kitchen and looked at my father. "What's going on here? You didn't come here for a visit, so why did you come?"

My father moved closer cornering me and spoke in a loud voice. "You better obey us, or we'll have your children taken away from you!"

As an adult, I'd never been involved in a serious disagreement with my father such as this. I was surprised by his behavior, thinking that what he said was a slip of the tongue.

I looked at him and said, "What are you talking about?"

Speaking loudly, he repeated. "You heard me. We'll have your children taken away!"

My wife immediately picked up the wall phone. Her tone tense, she said. "I'm dialing 911."

My parents lapsed into silence as they looked down, then they briskly walked toward the stairs, stepping down as they ignored their grandchildren and exited the front door. I looked at my wife bewildered. "What just happened here? I do not understand their behavior. We visit your sister and all hell breaks loose. My parents were invited here for a visit, and they came here prepared for an argument."

My wife said. "So much for all the food I made for them."

When I walked into the living room, I sat on the sofa, my jaw slack, attempting to comprehend my parents' behavior. When my mother emphasized that she had an imagination I worried about her rant. Imagination is the formation of a mental image or a concept of that which is not real or present and the ability to deal creatively with reality. It allows one to explore ideas of things that are not in our present environment or perhaps not even real. When someone tells you that they have an imagination, it's somewhat frightening. I thought about them and their lives. They were raised in families of humble beginnings, and now they were enraged because we supposedly snubbed them in favor of my wife's family.

I was unable to understand how my parents' visit came with a threat to have my children taken away. It made me realize that there was much more to this incident.

While sitting there, I stared out over the bay, recalling my continued pleas to my parents a few years earlier to move out of the housing projects, away from the drugs and crime. They bought a house on Long Island closer to us, providing the opportunity for us to spend more time together.

In 1980, one month after the incident with my parents, on the second day of January, we received hang-up and annoyance phone calls on a daily basis. The phone calls continued into the months thereafter and were unlike anything we had experienced before.

2

HOUSE

In 1973, when the rent increased in our apartment in Baldwin, my wife and I decided to buy a house. After combing Nassau County, we learned that housing prices were not within our budget. While looking through the newspaper we located a plot of land for sale in Suffolk County near the water in Oakdale. My brother lived a few miles away and this was an opportunity for us to get to know each better and share our lives. The property was located in a waterfront community that was quiet until the boating season. The only drawback was the Vanderbilt Tea House, which operated as a serene restaurant at the end of the street. The neighbors reported that the restaurant activity was minimal, and not a concern.

After five years of marriage, we drained our savings account, cashed our U.S. savings bonds and purchased the property. It was somewhat frightening to tie-up everything we saved in a small piece of land.

The housing cost to build a house on our property exceeded our budget. My wife looked at me.

"Why don't you find the trades and hire them directly, you can be the builder?"

I said. "But I don't have any experience in that area."

She looked at me. "I think you can do it."

I paused for a moment and said. "I'll think about it."

I realized that building a house was our only option to reduce the cost to meet our budget, since purchasing an existing house or hiring a builder was not affordable.

I spent four years attending a technical high school. During that time, the curriculum focused on design and construction. The technical courses focused on drafting/design and practical shop classes. The design classes consisted of two periods a day for four years learning how to draw blueprints.

In order to get the house built, I first contacted relatives and friends, searching for anyone with building construction knowledge that might guide me through the process, but I was unsuccessful. There was a friend of the family that was an engineer but he lived too far away from us.

After months of phone calls, visiting building supply companies and word of mouth references I selected the building trades. We met our budget. The bank approved the building loan and we started excavation.

Every day for the next four months, at six in the morning I traveled twenty-five miles to Suffolk County and met with the building trades. In the afternoon, I returned home, showered, ate and reported for duty at JFK Airport.

I hired an excavator to clear the land and dig the hole for the footing.

Since the house was located near the water, I asked the mason to add steel rods in the entire concrete footing for reinforcement. The plans didn't call for it, but my research told me different.

After the framing lumber was delivered to the jobsite, I noticed the next day that lumber was missing. I checked with the neighbors but no one had seen any activity at the site. Our budget was tight and I couldn't afford a shortage of any materials. As a result, I decided to keep an eye on the materials at night. At the end of my shift at JFK, I drove forty-five miles east to the jobsite and parked at the end of the street. Maintaining a bird's eye view of the lumber I sat patiently in my car. Sometime past midnight, a van slowly drives by the property, turns around and backs up next to the lumber. The driver proceeds to load lumber into the cargo compartment. I started up the car, headed down the street, and parked in front of the van.

I walked over to the driver. "Can I help you?"

The guy looks at me and in a casual voice. "I'm just looking for a two by four."

I looked at him. "This is not a lumber yard. Put back the wood and get out of here!"

The van displayed the company logo of a local heating and cooling company. I pointed to the company logo on the van.

I asked him. "You work for this company?"

He replied. "Yeah."

I said. "If I call your boss and told him you were stealing lumber, what would he do?"

The guy's eyes opened wide and said. "Please, don't do that, don't do that, I'll get fired!"

I looked at him. "I'll tell you what; return the lumber that you took last night and I won't call your boss!"

He nodded yes. "I'll have it for you later."

I said. "I'll be waiting."

After the footing/foundation was completed I hired two carpenters to frame the house. When the second floor was framed I walked around in awe admiring the view of the bay from the back of the house and the vast acreage of serene undeveloped land viewed from the front. We couldn't wait to move in.

My brother and I worked together and wired the house. Being strapped for money, I paid my brother for his work but not nearly electrician's wages. During the first electrical inspection, I was informed by the inspector there were wiring locations that needed to be corrected. The wiring areas in question were fixed. The inspector returned for the final inspection and noted additional wiring locations that he failed to notify me about on the first inspection.

I looked at him. "The current areas that you're noting were not part of your previous inspection, why didn't you inform me at that time?

He locked eyes with me. "You need to correct the areas!"

I was adamant. "Why didn't you tell me at the same time of the first inspection? I fixed the areas you designated, did you not see them? You're creating an endless inspection process!"

He said. "Look, just fix these two locations and you're done. We'll send you the underwriters certificate."

I replied. "Okay."

Charlie, a neighbor stopped by the house as he walked his dog. "Looks good, Neil, ready for plumbing?"

I said. "Yeah, the electrical inspector just finished the final inspection looking to return for an additional inspection. He pointed out areas of concern but he did not request that I make corrections. He nit-picked and waited for my response. I felt uncomfortable during the inspection process as if he was looking for a payoff."

He replied. "Neil, I've been working in the trade my whole life, it's not a bribe, you're paying him for his knowledge."

I said, "The inspector didn't ask for money, but the implication was there. He attempted to delay the construction!"

Charlie stated. "Neil, that's what they do. The inspector can look and look until they find something wrong delaying your progress for several weeks."

I replied. "Bribery is not part of what I am."

The next day the plumber walked on the side of the house looking at the new trench location for the city water line. "Neil, the excavator will be here in a few days to fill in the old trench and dig a new one to re-route the water line; and the plumbing inspector will be here next week. He gets five, but I'll take care of him."

I replied. "I'm sorry about the change, Tom, since I just learned that the water cost is cheaper if we connect up to the main road instead of the side street."

Tom looked at me with a smile on his face, shaking his head. "Neil, I'll cover the cost of the new trench."

My jaw dropped. "Are you serious?"

Tom replied, "I've never seen anybody as young as you, build a house." How old are you?"

I said. " I'm twenty- seven.

Smiling at him I thanked him for his generosity and compliment. Tom's comment made me stop and think about the responsibility associated with building a house. At that time, I was consumed with every aspect of the project and focused daily on a future home for us to live, a roof over our heads. Tom's comment meant a lot to me especially from a contractor that worked many years in the construction trade.

A few days later the roofing contractor nailed down the shingles as I watched from the ground. When I walked toward the side of the house, the roofer's helper accidentally stepped off the roof. He plunged toward the ground with his arms stretched out, flying like Superman yelling, "Ah…………splash!" He hit the water in the full- frontal position, in perfect alignment with the open trench that was no more than five feet wide. Living near the bay, the trench had filled up with ground water and it had been topped off after a recent heavy rain storm. The water absorbed the impact of the roofer's fall. God must have been with him, because the odds of him falling thirty feet and landing in perfect alignment with the trench were a million to one. I rushed over and pulled the roofer out of the water. He stood there in shock, not saying anything, soaked and with a blank look on his face.

I asked. "Are you alright?"

He didn't respond.

I asked again. "Are you hurt? Are you alright?"

There was not a scratch on him. It must have been divine intervention. I offered, "I'll take you to the hospital?"

He said. "Take me home, take me home!"

I replied. "Are you sure, I can take you to the hospital!"

He demanded. "No, take me home!"

I said. "Okay."

When I rolled up in front of the roofer's house, he said, "Wait here, I'll be right out."

I replied. "Okay."

A few minutes later he returned to the car wearing dry clothing. "Take me back to the job."

I raised my eyebrows a bit. "Are you sure?"

He said. "Yes, yes, I'm sure, it's okay." At the house he exited the car, climbed up the ladder and he worked on the roof the rest of the day as if nothing had happened.

Nick called me today. "Neil, I know money is tight for you during construction. If you need to borrow money let me know?"

I replied. "Well, if I can borrow money to buy the cesspools and septic tank I could save a few hundred dollars."

He asked. "How much do you need?" he asked.

I said. "I'd need a thousand to buy the cesspools and septic tank."

He said. "When you're ready, stop by the house for the money."

I mentioned. "If you can do that I would really appreciate it," I said?

He replied. "Sure thing."

Next week Jimmy the excavator pulled up in front of the house at 7 am. He sat inside a ten-wheel dump truck towing a flatbed trailer with a lowered crane. Jimmy was a middle-aged guy, average height, ruddy complexion and a dark heavy mustache. Wearing a black skull cap pulled down over his head he yelled in a raspy voice, "Hey, you gotta move that car!"

As the diesel engine roared on the truck. I yelled back.

I replied. "I'll take care of it."

Jimmy set up using the crane to move the soil around the property. He called to me. "Look at the bog (poorly drained soil) in here, its gotta come out, and replaced with bank run before I can drop- in the pools!"

I said, "Do what whatever you have to do to get the job done."

After several hours of digging, Jimmy replaced the bog with clean sand for better drainage. While he raised the septic tank with the crane, a car entered the driveway bearing a Health Department decal on the door. Jimmy exited the crane and met with the inspector. While the engine idled, the inspector repeatedly pointed to the ground. I couldn't hear what he was saying but Jimmy immediately walked over to me. "Listen, the Inspector's here and he gets ten!"

I said. "I don't have any money to give him."

He glared at me. "Look, he can make it hard for you!"

I said firmly. "Jimmy, I'm a federal officer, I can't give him a bribe."

His jaw dropped. "Don't worry, don't you worry, I'll take care of it!"

I wondered how to avoid placing myself in jeopardy if every building inspector needed to be bribed to move the construction process along. With additional inspections required before completion, I wondered if I'd ever complete the house on time. I would not risk bribing any inspector to move the project forward. Weeks later, the building inspector arrived and introduced himself as Mr. Lament. I made up a story to try to thwart any implied or suggested proposal for a bribe. I said, "We have a guy named Lament that works with us in the Treasury Department. Is he related to you?"

He said. "No, I don't have anyone working there." He looked at me with a smirk on his face. The inspector never looked around at the framing.

He said. "Everything looks good here, you're clear to proceed."

I replied. "Thanks."

During the final inspection, I used the same technique on a different inspector and he approved the house for occupancy. A year later, on the front-page of the Long Island newspaper displayed a group of town of Islip building inspectors, exiting their office in handcuffs. I wondered what took so long.

After the spackling was completed, together with my mother-in law we painted the interior of the entire house. She liked me and we had a good relationship. She worked as a seamstress and a clothing designer who custom made wedding dresses in her basement. She worked until all hours of the night to support her family. I don't know where she found the time to work with me but she sacrificed for us.

We moved in four months later in February 1974.

Several months later my mother-in law passed away at the age of fifty-four. She had inspired us to build our house. She was the glue that held her family together.

At her wake, the viewing room was filled with many people that they were bumping into each other paying their respects. When my mother arrived at the funeral home she was in awe of the crowd of people in the viewing room. She asked, "Who are all these people?"

My wife looked at her and said, "My mother did a lot of work in the community, for the church, for friends and the VFW."

My mother was silent at the wake. At the funeral mass, the priest presented the eulogy summarizing my mother in law's contribution to the church, where she provided the material and fabricated curtains for the entire performing stage in the school auditorium. While I listened to the eulogy, I broke down and cried. I was close to my mother in law and her death was a loss to me, a far greater loss to her family. My mother looked over at me with an anger on her face. I don't know what she was thinking, but I did not feel her response to my mother-in law's death was compassionate. After all, my wife lost her mother after a short battle with cancer. I felt that my mother's lack of compassion and anger toward my feelings for my mother in law meant trouble ahead.

3

THE BRONX

I was born in St Francis Hospital, in 1946. We lived on Pugsley Ave. in a five-story orange brick building on the third floor with no elevator. Our one-bedroom apartment faced the fairly busy street in the south-central section of the Bronx. Dad worked for the New York City Housing Authority, and he moonlighted for a court transcribing service. Mom didn't work. She was the family disciplinarian; she was the law.

One of my earliest recollections was when mom and I rushed into the bedroom as the air raid siren sounded. We slid under the dusty bed. I hit my head on the wooden slats that held up the mattress. My best recollection was I must have been four years old. My older brother and I slept in the bedroom and shared the bed while my parents slept in the living room on a Castro convertible sofa.

I asked Mom, "How long do we have to stay under here?"

She said. "A little while until it's safe."

I replied. "Okay."

The air raid was my most vivid recollection of my life living in the Bronx. Since that time, I have possessed the ability to recall situations that occurred during the early years of my life because they were important to me. As far back as I can remember, I had a habit of repeating any important situations, including the dialogue, over and over in my mind. It's impossible to remember everything that occurred in your life, but I vividly recall the situations that I am writing about.

At times while growing up, I wondered why I dwelled on different situations. I think I was just born that way. "A good memory can be a blessing or a curse." In my case, I feel it's a blessing.

After the air raid, I stood up and looked out of the window at the Top Hat Bar across the street. When the bar closed, the drunks filtered out. Many times, on weekends the drunks yelled to each other as they walked outside, awakening Dad. He jumped out of bed and rushed into the bathroom. He rapidly opened the window. As it scraped in the frame and the sash weights rumbled in the wall, he yelled at them. "Shut-up, we're trying to sleep." If I wasn't awoken before, I was after he yelled at them.

On a cool autumn day, Mom registered me late in the term for the kindergarten class at the public school. The following morning, we approached the front of the dirty gray building surrounded by a tall black iron fence. Mom struggled to open the rusty brown steel door as the hinges squeaked. We entered the hallway as the loud, echoing voices traveled throughout the halls. While we walked toward the classroom, the noise increased, and I became frightened. I stood in the doorway of the dimly lit classroom in awe of the high ceiling and tall windows that were covered with metal grating. Children played with wooden blocks, while others ran between small tables and chairs. I called to Mom as she walked away, "I don't like it here."

She replied. "It's okay. I'll be in the hallway, while you're in class."

I said. "I don't know anybody!"

She pointed out. "It'll be alright; you'll make friends."

When the school day ended, I couldn't wait to go home.

On the second day of kindergarten, Mom released me in the hallway. I walked a short distance into the classroom, turned around and walked out yelling, "Ma, Ma, come back!"

She returned to me. "What is it?"

I moaned. "I wanna go home!"

She said. "You have to stay in school!"

I replied. "I don't like it here!"

She insisted. "You have to go to school!"

I started to cry.

I moaned. "I don't like it here, I wanna go home, I wanna go home!"

We entered the principal's office as Mom made eye contact with her. "My son does not like being in class."

"Well, I understand; he's probably better off at home." After that day, I never again attended kindergarten.

Since I did not attend school, I was always with Mom. Weeks later we walked together on Gleason Ave. to visit her friend Helen.

After the visit, I ran into the park across the street on Noble Ave. Mom pushed me on the swing. I yelled, "Push me higher, push me higher."

The motion made me feel like I was flying. When I tired of the swings, I ran toward the monkey bars and climbed as high as possible, watching the dried leaves on the ground blown around by the wind. Then bored with the monkey bars, I ran toward the children's slide and climbed to the top where I lost my balance and fell hitting my head on the pavement. I cried loudly. "Ma, Ma, Ma!"

A man nearby quickly helped me up. Stooping down, he asked, "Are you alright? Are you alright?"

I continued to cry. Yelling from a distance Mom ran toward me.

She insisted. "What did you do, what did you do?"

She looked down at me angrily. "You almost cracked your skull!"

I continued crying. I don't know why Mom yelled at me for falling down. Maybe she was upset that I fell. I don't know why she wasn't nearby while I climbed up the slide? We sat on the bench until I calmed down, and then we walked home.

A few weeks later I held Mom's hand as we crossed Hugh J. Grant Circle on our way to Parkchester. The self-contained, planned middle-class community of Parkchester, consisted of 171 apartment buildings and nearly one hundred stores. I looked at Mom. "Where are we going?"

She said. "We're going to Macy's."

I replied. "What are you going to buy?"

She mentioned. "We're just window shopping."

We walked up and down the aisles at Macy's for what? I don't know.

After window shopping we headed up the street toward the Oval Cafeteria, where we met Aunt Ester for lunch. I sat at the table for the first time in a public place. The tables were close together and made me feel as though everyone watched me. I turned to Mom and said, "I don't like it here!"

She replied, "Sit quietly and behave yourself."

Moments later, I slid off the chair and sat on the floor under the table. Aunt Ester said. "He's so shy."

Mom replied. "Yeah he's quiet."

I became self-conscious when I heard them speak about my shyness. I didn't know how to cope with it. Being easily embarrassed, I guess I was born that way. After a while Mom peeked her head under the table. "Get up and sit on the chair. "

I said. "No, I don't want to!"

She replied. "If you don't sit on the chair, you can't eat."

I moaned. "I don't wanna eat; I wanna stay here!"

I sat under the table until they finished eating. When we walked outside, I was relieved. At the age of five, I realized I was afraid of people and things that were unfamiliar to me.

In the spring, Mom and I walked on the sidewalk along the swamps on Chatterton Ave., while the swamp reeds swayed in the wind. Upon our arrival at the semi-attached two- story brick house on Bruckner Boulevard, we entered the hallway. The door opened on the first floor. "Hi, how are you, come in." Aunt Rose stood there well dressed in her shoulder length dyed platinum blonde hair, wearing heavy makeup and large earrings. I think she modeled herself after Jean Harlow an American film actress and sex symbol of the 1930's, but not as pretty. While we stood there, her mixed breed Shepard stood next to her and stared at us. I loved animals, but we didn't own a dog. I tried to pet the dog.

The dog growled and lunged toward me biting my lip. I looked at Mom crying. "He bit me!"

Aunt Rose rushed the dog into the bedroom. Mom examined the bite on my lip. Aunt Rose returned and looked down at me.

She said. "When you pet the dog, you have to make nice to him."

I had tears in my eyes.

I moaned. "I just wanted to pet him."

Mom spoke with her for a while and then we returned home.

The next morning Dad stood next to me while I ate cereal. He looked down at me. "I'm taking you to the doctor for rabies shots for the dog bite."

I said. "Why?"

Dad advised. "You have to get the shots for protection against the rabies disease."

I moaned. "Do I have to?"

Dad advised. "Yes, you do."

While Dad drove the car, all I could think about was the pain from the shots. I hated shots. We entered St. Barnabas Hospital and sat on a wooden bench, inhaling the hospital antiseptic odor that filled the air. The nurse walked over and looked at Dad. "Your son is here for the rabies shots?"

"Yes."

"Please come with me." We entered a room where I lay on my back on the examination table. I stared at the high ceiling, blinded by a huge bright light from above as I nervously waited.

The doctor walked in and his presence frightened me. He looked down at me. "Now pull up your shirt." My heartbeat increased. The nurse handed the doctor a large needle. He pointed it upward. "I'm going to insert this needle into your stomach, so don't move." The needle looked long enough to pass through the other side of my body. I screamed from the pain.

Dad looked at me. "It'll be alright; you'll be alright; just lie there."

I lay there for what seemed like a long time. We walked toward the car. I looked up at Dad. "It still hurts."

Dad remarked. "It'll go away."

The pain remained with me throughout the day.

While driving home Dad rather matter-of-factly said, "We need to come back here every day for thirteen days- until you to receive the series of rabies shots."

I moaned. "Why do I have to get more shots, they hurt?"

Dad advised. "You need to get protection against rabies so you don't get sick."

I told him. "I don't like the shots, they hurt."

Dad pointed out. "You'll get used to it."

Later on, I heard that Aunt Rose had her dog put to sleep. Until this day, I don't know if the rabies shots were for prevention or a precaution.

The following year, we visited Aunt Rose at her new apartment on Burr Ave. in Pelham Bay. I stood in the middle of the living room next to Mom while her miniature Chihuahua named Quito circled us. The dog barked and nipped at my ankles. I refused to pet the dog. Unbeknownst to me, the dog sat down behind me. Feeling tired of standing, I stepped back with one leg to relax for a moment. My foot made contact with the dog. The dog barked. Aunt Rose yelled, "Oh my God, what did you do, what did you do?"

I looked at her crying. "I didn't know the dog was there." I learned later, that dog suffered a broken leg. I felt so bad.

In September 1951, I sat the one-piece metal framed desk with a wooden writing table and seat as they were- lined up like soldiers. The one room cottage was the first- grade class at St. Helena's Elementary School. Sister Cecile walked up and down the aisles handing out papers. The boys sat at their desks wearing white shirts, blue pants and ties, while the girls wore white blouses with green jumpers. The classroom was a much better experience for me than kindergarten at PS 119.

We hid under our desks as the air raid siren sounded with our heads turned away from the windows until it was over. The drills were strictly observed and very common in the 1950s. The Russians had exploded their first hydrogen bomb, so whenever the siren activated, I always hoped it was just a drill.

A few years later on Halloween, I met with my friends after school, outside my apartment building. Dressed as a hobo wearing worn out clothes, I dirtied my face, smearing on dark watercolor paint.

In preparation for trick or treating, we poured baking flour into a sock and tied a knot at the end. We used the socks to hit each other as we trick-or-treated. We walked without our parents up and down the six flights of stairs in the ten apartment buildings in the neighborhood. We knocked on every apartment door. Sometimes we ran into other groups of kids in the hallways. Groups of us yelled at each other, as the noise echoed throughout the building. Most people gave us candy corn, while others filled a bowl with dried cereal. A real treat was a small bar of chocolate or an apple. At times, we became unruly especially when people ignored the doorbell. We'd strike the door in anger with the flour filled sock, as the mystique of the white dust lingered in the air.

My parents didn't buy candy and I had a sweet tooth, so Halloween was a day when I overdid it. After trick-or-treating, I returned home. Mom told me, "You're late for dinner, and everybody has- eaten. You're being punished, and if you have any candy in that bag, you'd better get rid of it!"

I looked up at her. "Can't I have some of it?"

She ordered me. "We don't keep candy in this house!"

I moaned. "Why?"

Mom had told me that years earlier, she worked in a candy factory and she did not feel that mass produced candy was sanitary.

I never thought we were poor because we always had food to eat, clothing to wear and a place to live. On Thanksgiving morning, I knocked on doors in the neighborhood begging for treats. Thanksgiving was not as popular as Halloween. I enjoyed Thanksgiving more because a costume was not- needed, and I had a chance to collect money instead of candy. People gave us pennies, maybe a nickel, very few treats or nothing. At the end of the day, I collected almost a dollar and an appetite big enough to eat a horse.

Mom walked into the bedroom. "Try on these pants."

My eyes questioned her. "Whose are these?"

Mom pointed out. "I got them from your cousin." The light gray pants with dark stitching running up and down the seams were too flashy for my taste.

I moaned. "I don't like them," I whined. "They don't fit."

Mom remarked. "Nobody has to know; I'll take up the hem. They're dress pants."

"Okay." Mom never said anything, but I knew that she bought them in a second-hand store. I often wore hand–me-downs from my brother, which I thought was cool. If they were good enough for him, they were good enough for me. Once I was over the fact that the pants were- worn by someone else, she was right, nobody knew the clothes were preowned.

4

THE FARM

In late August of 1955, my parents prepared for a vacation at Aunt Ida's farm in upstate New York. We loaded the 1949 faded blue Plymouth with suitcases, supplies and headed north on the Taconic State Parkway. As we drove up and down the mountains; we admired the sweeping views of farmland, green grass and an occasional wildlife specimen. When Dad noticed an animal, he pointed to it as we passed. Dad ate an apple and threw the core out of the window onto to the grass. "I'll grow an apple tree there," he smirked. I sort-of believed him or maybe it was just his way to validate littering.

I looked at Dad. "When are we going to get there?"

"Not much longer, Highland is ninety miles from the Bronx." My oldest recollection of the farm was when I was about four-years-old. Nellie, an old plow horse, lived in the barn. I stood close to her admiring her size and dad lifted me up onto her bare back. While I sat there, holding her mane. I knew riding her exceeded my ability. I loved the feeling, sitting on top of giant warm animal. The sensation remained with me forever.

Seated in the car, I couldn't wait to arrive at the farm. The thought of exploring, fishing and picking fruit every day, was a dream come true. I didn't know the magnitude of fifty acres of land, but it was large enough for me to get lost.

Dad turned into the dirt driveway off Vineyard Ave, and kicked up dust as it drifted as a cloud through the corn- field. He continued up a gently sloping hill toward the farmhouse that was comfortably set back from the road. Entering the rundown two story white building, with green trim and a wrap-around porch, was like being in another world. Aunt Ida rented out the rooms to friends and family.

I couldn't wait to explore fifty acres of low rolling hills, dominated by apple trees, surrounded by acres of corn and strawberries.

While we unloaded the car, I stopped to admire the mountain across the road. Anticipating one day, I might explore the emerald green pastureland surrounded by birches, willows and spruces, where a few black cows grazed. The magnificence of the mountain captivated me, as if God had placed it there. I focused on that mountain many times during the day.

We carried the suitcases up to the second floor and walked into the faded painted bedroom, with a lumpy worn-out linoleum floor. Mom unrolled the moldy smelling mattress and spread it out on top of the dusty, rusted, coiled bedsprings. She struggled to open the misaligned drawers in the dark wooden chest where we stored our clothes.

Ida's son Angelo slept in the bedroom across the hall. Whenever I passed by his bedroom it was empty, until the evening when the door was closed. Angelo was his name, but everyone called him Honey. He tended the crops, seeding, cultivating, repairing farm equipment, and doing anything required to keep the farm going. He rose at 4 a.m. and was sleeping by 9 p.m. seven days a week. Honey was a man of few words, but he was totally involved in running the day-to-day operations of the farm. He came from the old school, 'well done is better than well said.' I heard he married later in life.

On my way to the dining room, I watched Ida cooking on the gas stove. Ida appeared to be in her sixties, slightly overweight with shoulder-length gray hair and crooked teeth. She looked older than her age. While Ida stirred the simmering tomatoes in a large pot on the stove, she wiped her hands on the white apron. The aroma traveled throughout the house. Every day Ida walked through her victory garden, weeding, watering and picking ripe produce. When the crop came in, Ida simmered raspberries and strawberries. With mason jars lined up on the table, she poured the jam into the jars and sealed the top with liquid wax.

The next morning, Dad awakened me. "Get dressed; we're going fishing." I walked into the dining room where two rows of white metal tables were- lined up against the wall, separated by wooden iceboxes. Seated at the table, I ate a bowl of Frosted Flakes, as I watched the flypaper sway back and forth near the screened door. After eating, I dropped the bowl into the sink and ran outside toward the car. I asked Dad, "Where's the fishing rods?"

Dad advised. "They're already in the car."

I uttered. "Okay."

Dad drove the car about a mile to a local fishing hole where we unloaded our equipment. "Should I put the rods in the boat?" I asked.

"No, I'll take them. You carry the tackle box and be careful getting into the boat."

Dad rowed the boat into the open water. He looked at me. "While I'm casting, you use this rod. I'll put a hook and sinker on the line, and you slide a worm onto the hook, and let the end wiggle. Now, slowly lower the hook and sinker until you hit bottom, and when you feel a nibble, raise the rod to set the hook in the fish's mouth."

"Okay." Sometimes it seemed like hours passed without a bite. It's the anticipation and the nibbling on the line that keeps your interest. When fishing, if you don't learn anything else, you learn patience.

We returned to the farm where we strung out the catch, and Dad photographed the fish. Whatever fish we didn't eat, we planted in Ida's garden. Dad loved to take photographs. He was constantly taking pictures of our family. He'd, write the date and location on the back of the photos and stored them with the negatives in expandable legal portfolios where he maintained his own filing system at home.

The next day I decided to explore the dirt road toward the wooden bridge that crossed over the slowly flowing stream. While I lay on the bridge timbers and dropped stones between the spaces into the crystal- clear flowing water, I hoped to hit a fish and knock it out. While walking with my head down toward the pond, I found small pieces of slate protruding through the dirt. The slate may have been used by the Indians to make arrow- heads. I scaled them across the water counting the number of times they bounced.

On the other side of the pond, I watched bull- frogs seated on lily pads, some of them up to seven inches long. They lay in wait for unsuspecting prey. When it was quiet, you could hear them croaking in a low frequency jag-o-rum to each other under the low hanging brush. I scaled flat rocks across the water trying to hit them. Later on, I heard gunshots at the pond where my brother and cousin Sandy shot at the bullfrogs. I ran back to the farmhouse fearing gunfire.

The picturesque landscape of the farm across the road drew me in like a magnet. Crossing the road, I walked through the brush under the trees toward the clearing. A short distance away, I noticed a rundown wooden shed without windows. As I moved closer, several hundred rabbits grazed in a fenced in area. When I approached the shed, the rabbits ran inside. I'd never been close to a rabbit, let alone hundreds of rabbits. Fascinated by their presence, I opened the shed door and walked inside. The interior was empty except for several hundred rabbits nestled together. Looking at the rabbits, I said to myself, "Here's my chance to pet one of them." When I approached them, they scurried into the corner of the shed. A frightening sound of hundreds of feet pounding on the wooden floor was astonishing. They nestled in the corner tightly together forming a giant ball of fur. Each time I approached them, they moved into another corner of the shed, snuggling together. After a few attempts to pet them, I quit. The rabbits were very fast and agile, even in a confined area. I felt as if I was doing something I shouldn't be doing, so I decided to return to the farmhouse.

The following morning, while I ate breakfast, Dad walked over to me. "Did you go over to the rabbit farm yesterday?"

I nodded. "Yes."

Dad remarked. "You scared them so much that some of them died!"

I cried as I looked at him. "I didn't hurt them; I just wanted to pet them and they wouldn't let me!"

Dad ordered. "You stay away from there and stay on this farm, do you understand!"

I nodded. "Okay."

On the side of the farmhouse, I discovered Ida's victory garden where zucchinis, string beans and tomatoes grew in abundance. Adjacent to the vegetables stood a short fence covered with green leaves bearing clusters of red berries. I picked one, then another and another savoring a flavor that I had never experienced before. Seated on the ground, I gently removed each berry from the plant one by one not crushing them. I became addicted to them. The tart flavor had a sweetness, unlike any other fruit. Having never eaten a raspberry, I hit that patch every day whenever I was hungry, unaware that I severely affected Ida's jam supply. Fruit of this quality was not available in the Bronx. I was unable to stop eating them until my stomach was full. The quality of these raspberries has never been duplicated until this day. Other times when I was hungry, I'd walk into the strawberry fields and eat the largest berries in the patch. I was in heaven.

The tractor roared, as Honey sprayed the apple trees with the chemical DDT. He wore a respirator that looked like he was from outer space. Before I ate an apple, I wiped off the insecticide, shining it on my tee shirt. Little did I know that once the fruit is sprayed with insecticide, it has already penetrated into the fruit.

Mom watched me and yelled, "Don't eat those apples, you'll get diarrhea!" I ignored her and walked out of her sight eating four or five apples in succession. The flavor outweighed her instructions. My appetite for a fresh picked apple was addictive since they were firm, without bruises, no specs, scuffs or decay. Freshly picked farm apples are the sweetest and crunchiest, with an underlying tartness that has been unsurpassed until this day.

My brother and Cousin Sandy stood on the side of the farmhouse. I tried to hang out with them, but they weren't interested since they were much older. I idolized my brother and Sandy; they were cool guys.

A few years later, Sandy was part of a Rock 'in Roll vocal group called the Indigos. They cut a few records. I cherished the professionally produced photo of Sandy's vocal group that he had given to me. They dressed up in bright plaid blazers with their neatly trimmed slicked back hair.

Whenever the topic of Rock 'in Roll surfaced among my friends, I couldn't wait to tell them about Cousin Sandy. Years later, I traveled to the Times Square Record Shop in Manhattan on 42nd Street, below the ground in the subway arcade. That's where I bought Sandy's record. The record shop was an iconic place. They stocked every 45 RPM Rock and Roll record produced. The walls inside the store were- covered from floor to ceiling with records in the original vibrant colored paper sleeves covering every wall as if it was wallpaper.

Richard and Sandy walked toward the back of the farm property and I wanted to tag along. I followed them across the wooden bridge and up the hill. Richard yelled to me, "Stop hanging around us pinhead!"

Sandy glared at him. "That's not nice, Richard, leave him alone." The top of my head was not rounded which I thought was the result of the fall from the slide years earlier.

As I continued to follow them, Richard yelled back, "Stay away from us 'neckie'!" My brother nicknamed me 'neckie,' since I maintained a slender build, having a thin neck.

Richard and Sandy walked briskly up the hill where the dirt road ended and continued into the brush until they were out my sight. Running in their direction, I was not paying attention and fell into a deep hole. I stood up, surprised and shaken up. Weeds had grown and covered the hole opening. Unable to reach the top, I grabbed the weeds that hung down to pull myself out. Grabbing onto the weeds, I fell down, since the roots were not strong enough to hold my weight. Looking around inside the hole, it appeared that heavy equipment had dug out this ditch years earlier and weeds had grown covering it up. After a few minutes, I realized that getting out would not be easy. While I stood in the middle of the ditch for a while, I listened for a noise from farm equipment or people and not hearing anything I started to worry. I realized it would be useless to yell for help since the farmhouse was too far away.

I sat down on the ground and waited, hoping that my brother and cousin would return in the same direction. It seemed like hours had passed and not hearing anything, I wondered how long before somebody would start to look for me.

Looking at the top of the hole it was beyond my reach. I decided to use a flat rock and dig out dirt in the vertical portion of the ditch to create a groove to insert my foot. Digging persistently, I created grooves at different levels. With a running start, I placed my foot into the lowest groove and my hand into the higher groove and fell back onto the ground. In need of height, I dug-out some buried rocks and stacked them on top of each other to gain height. Starting at one end of the hole, I ran, stepping onto the top the rocks with one foot and placed my other foot into the groove. I fell back onto the ground. After stabilizing the rocks, I launched myself with all of my might and gained the height needed to grab a branch that held me. Unconcerned if the branch was poison ivy or sumac, I dragged my body far enough to clear the hole and laid on the ground with a sigh of relief while my heart beat like a drum.

Dirty and scratched up, I rushed toward the farmhouse to get cleaned up. When I approached the farmhouse, Aunt Ester, sat on a lawn chair in front. She asked. "Neil, what happened to you, your Mother is looking for you?"

I put my head down. "Ah nothing." I kept walking. I didn't want to say anything to her because she would tell my mother and I would be in trouble for being somewhere that I shouldn't be, doing something that I shouldn't be doing. Punishment would have followed and I didn't want that to happen. Running into the bathroom, I removed my dirty clothes, washed and slipped on long pants to cover up the scratches.

The next morning at breakfast, I told Mom, "I'm itchy, I'm scratching a lot."

She looked at my arms. "You have poison ivy, where did you get that?"

I shrugged. "I was in the woods."

Mom advised. "I'll put calamine lotion on it and stay out of the woods!"

I uttered. "Okay."

5

NO MONEY

At the age of nine I recalled running into the kitchen where Mom was cooking. "Could I have a quarter to go to the movies on Saturday?"

Mom declared. "No, there's no money for that. You'll have to go to work if you want money."

I moaned. "But, my friends get an allowance. Why can't I?"

Mom remarked. "We don't have any money."

I pointed out. "But, Mom, when you need groceries, I shop for you."

Mom looked away. "You help the family by doing your chores."

I ran into the bedroom and sat down on my bed, angry that my parents were unable to afford a quarter. My friends received a weekly allowance from their parents. I did chores for Mom, whatever she asked me to do. How much more did she expect me to do? I thought that my chores and helping Mom were worth an allowance.

The next morning, I awoke at five thirty. It was a dreary, drizzly day while everybody was asleep. I tiptoed into the kitchen and ate a bowl of Frosted Flakes. Opening the closet, I held the bright red shoeshine box, by the cast iron foot rest. I struggled to close the door quietly not to awaken anyone. While walking toward the train station, I fought to wake up, rubbing my eyes and yawning.

At the Parkchester train station, the regular shoeshine guy worked on the busy downtown side. Holding up a sheet of paper, 'Shoe Shine 15 cents'. I set up on the uptown side. There was a constant flow of people, with hurried looks on their faces. They scurried to the entrance steps of the elevated subway as the frequent rumblings of the rush hour trains vibrated above.

As I held up my sign, a tall well-dressed man in a trench coat holding a folded newspaper walked over to me. "Shine, kid?"

"Sure, mister." Anxious to do a good job I focused only on his shoes. After I removed the liquid cleaner, I applied the shoe polish gasping from the odor of the wax. Brushing off the polish, I buffed the shoes with a flannel rag and topped it off with a spit shine.

"Thanks, kid, here you go." He handed me a quarter.

I looked up at him smiling. "Gee thanks, mister."

I raced home, changing into my school uniform and walked to school. Whenever I needed money, I'd head out to Parkchester, hoping to earn cash.

Across the hall lived Alan Silver, my best friend. His family was Jewish and we were Catholic. Religion was never an issue during our friendship. We respected one another, as we grew older. I knocked on Alan's door. "Hey, you want to go to the movies?"

He looked at me. "What's playing?"

I said. "'Son of Sinbad' and 'The Day the World Ended.'"

Alan replied. "Let's go."

We walked to the Circle Movie Theater, and I spent the money I earned for the admission fee. Kids were running up and down the aisles while we searched the theater for an undamaged fold-down seat. We sat waiting for the show to start as we inhaled the odor from spilled soda, popcorn and crushed candy that seemed to be embedded into the floor. Alan returned with candy at intermission. "Hey, want some?"

"Okay, thanks."

During the winter months and when the weather was stormy, Alan and I played war on the linoleum floor in his bedroom. We built forts, houses and corrals with Lincoln Logs. After we stocked the structures with the men and artillery, we shot toothpicks out of metal cannons at the toy soldiers. We played war for hours. It was as if we were in another world, unaware of time, until Alan's mom yelled from the kitchen. "Alan… he has to go home, it's time to eat." I hated when his mom ended our playtime. We could have played forever.

When the weather improved, Alan and I headed to PS 119 playground and fast pitched to each other with a spaldeen (rubber ball) using a broomstick handle for a bat. We pitched and hit against each other throwing at the concrete handball wall as a backstop. Alan played shortstop for the little league and I played first base on a different team.

After school one afternoon I removed the school uniform and changed into my street clothes. Outside, Alan and Paul were playing stoop-ball. I looked at them. "Can I play?"

"Okay." Alan threw the ball against the bottom step as the ball scooted past me into the street. I chased it between the parked cars and into the traffic lane without looking. Car tires screeched on the pavement as I watched a giant chrome bumper stop inches away from my head. My heart beat like a drum while escaped severe injury or death. I ran toward the building, up two flights of courtyard steps without looking back. The car door slammed. The driver yelled, "Hey you, hey you!" He left the car in the middle of the street. Any normal guy would have quit. Struggling to open the entrance door, I needed to increase my speed. With the fear of God in me, I slapped my hands on the white limestone stair treads to gain speed running up the steps. At the third floor, I heard the driver below and hoped that the apartment door was unlocked. If he caught me, I feared he'd hurt me for what I had done. At the apartment, I swung open the door and immediately locked it behind me. Mom must have been in another room. My heart pounded like a drum. Unable to calm down and barely catching my breath, I sat on the floor, with my ear pushed against the door, as I listened for the driver. After what felt like several minutes, it became quiet. A car started up and I peered out the window as the driver left the area. I lay on the bed trying to calm down. The thought of escaping serious injury or being killed haunted me for years thereafter. I knew that running out into the street without looking was wrong, so for fear of punishment, I never explained the incident to my parents.

Routinely, Mom handed me a grocery list. "Go shopping. Be sure to squeeze the bread to make sure it's fresh."

I said. "Okay."

While I pulled the two-wheel metal carrier to the supermarket, it made me feel good to shop for the family. As I had done many times before, I walked across the Cross- Bronx Expressway overpass as the cars sped by below. It reminded me of the construction of the roadway a few years earlier. Crossing over the highway every day on my way home from school with my friends, we'd throw dirt balls at the cars below. One time after throwing a dirt ball at a car that passed under the overpass, the driver pulled over onto the shoulder and yelled at me as I stood on the footbridge. The dirt ball must have contained a rock that damaged the car's windshield. I knew I had done wrong and I was afraid that the driver would come after me, so I ran all the way home. That was the last time I threw a dirt ball.

During construction of the Cross- Bronx Expressway when it snowed, I'd ride my sleigh like a rocket down the big hill in front of the A& P Supermarket. Sleigh riding in a construction zone was almost heaven, since we didn't worry about traffic. In our neighborhood, a steep hill was hard to find. The completion of the Cross -Bronx Expressway ended the best sleigh riding in the area.

Mom's shopping list consisted of mostly canned vegetables, soup, canned fruit, a bag of potatoes, bread, milk and eggs. Mom didn't trust me to buy foods that required close scrutiny, like meats and fresh food. Shopping was easy today since I didn't have to wait in line at the meat counter for bologna. I raced home as the rain poured drenching the shopping bags. The worst part of food shopping was lugging the carrier up three flights of stairs without breaking the eggs.

Mom hid a box of candy that remained after her friends visited. Very little had been eaten and she hid it to keep it away from my sweet tooth. When I found the candy, I'd swiped a few pieces now and then.

Months later while I sat at the kitchen table, Mom looked at me. "Did you eat the candy I was hiding?"

I said. "I had a couple of pieces."

Mom declared. "The box is almost empty."

I moaned. "Maybe my brother ate some."

Mom declared. "Your brother doesn't do that; he doesn't snoop and get into things like you. You're being punished, go to your room."

I moaned. "Okay."

Everyone finished their dinner while I sat at the table alone, staring at the steamed chicory on my plate. Mom turned to me as she stood at the sink. "Finish your food, we're all members of the 'clean plate club' here!" Reluctantly I put a small amount of chicory into my mouth, which seemed to satisfy her for the moment. Mom had cooked the chicory in water, without seasoning which I found to be barely edible.

My parents grew up during the 'Great Depression' and rarely threw any food away. Leftover food was a rare occurrence. Mom's cooking style for us was plain, rarely seasoned, not at all like traditional Italian cooking. I never walked away from the table hungry. When uneaten food remained on my plate, Mom yelled out. "Finish your food; there're children starving in other countries." That made sense to me, except when the dinner contained cooked kale or chicory. Mom looked at me with rage. "You better eat your food or you'll be punished; now finish your food!"

I moaned. "I can't eat this, it tastes like iron!"

Mom ordered. "That's too bad; everybody ate dinner, so you'll stay at the table till you're done!" She walked out of the kitchen. My brother and Father were not home.

Mom returned to the kitchen and looked at the uneaten chicory. "Don't defy me! You're being impudent! You'll be sorry!" A moment later, she rifled through the utensil drawer, a familiar sound to me. I knew what was coming so I pushed back my chair and raced towards the bedroom just as the rolling pin bounced hitting my leg. My heart beat fast, but I escaped without being hurt.

My failure to cry during Mom's punishment always enraged her. Tears would have been proof, that I learned a lesson. My silent submission to her heaviest forms of punishment intensified her fury as she followed me continuing to yell. If she had been a man, she would have continued with physical punishment and make me weep for mercy.

While in the bedroom, I sat on the bed next to the homemade blue wooden stand-up record player with a red- hinged top. When my brother wasn't home, I played his 45 RPM Rock and Roll Doo-Wop records over and over, memorizing the words and never getting tired of the melody.

The records kept me out of Mom's way, helping me forget about her punishment. The music brought me to a place that made me feel really good about myself. It was a time when I could have privacy and enjoyment. Rock and Roll Doo-Wop lyrics, melodies and harmonies from the 1950s helped me identify and shape my personal values: honesty, integrity, and appreciation for the love that I was willing to give.

The songs have an honest and open form: boy meets girl, boy and girl fall in love. Boy and girl walk down the aisle, boy and girl start a life, start a family and have a boy and girl of their own. The music explained to us the things that our parents could not and shaped our hopes for the future. Rock and Roll was the music for the adolescence ushering us into adulthood, meaningfully teaching us the lessons of life contained in the lyrics.

The songs were every kid's guide to psychology and anatomy and helped me grow into a responsible, proper, respectful adult. The music helped me get in touch with my inner feelings and expressed in a "cool" way what was going on with my emotions and hormones. The songs always left me feeling good at the core and hopeful about the world around me and the world ahead of me.

Till this day, I listen to Doo Wop songs because the music is timeless. I enjoyed Motown and Disco music, but I never quite understood the themes of Rap music.

The following year my sister was born. Now we were five people living in a one- bedroom apartment. My parents slept on a Castro convertible sofa in the living room and my brother, sister and I shared the bedroom. The quarters were tight which didn't leave much room for privacy, but I was not bothered by it.

In 1955, my parents bought a 17-inch RCA table top TV. Mom never missed watching soap operas. Fascinated, I watched my favorite heroes: Superman and the Lone Ranger, where I learned that the good guys win. When I watched shows like, 'Danny Thomas' and 'Father Knows Best' I learned the show's message that life is fair and if you followed the rules you would be safe and happy. The fifties were the age of innocence and naiveté where every day was predictable and nothing was ever going to change. As I grew older I learned later that life is not fair.

Since I was very involved in sports and activities, I did not make much use of the library. I didn't want to be cooped up in the apartment reading books. Sports kept me away from Mom's rule; but, I always found time to read a Superman comic book from cover to cover. While asleep I dreamed that I flew through the air like Superman, feeling a chill running up and down my spine, trying to make the dream last as long as possible.

At the age of nine, I believed Santa Claus delivered gifts to our apartment through the dumb waiter shaft. My friends were not home, so I searched for a lost toy behind the sofa. During the search, I found a box that was partially open. Being unfamiliar to me, I peeked inside and noticed a blue corduroy shirt. I called out, "Ma, what is this?"

She walked into the living room and looked at me as her jaw dropped. "That's not for you, give that to me!" As she angrily removed it from my hands, she snapped, "You're not supposed to go snooping around the house."

I looked at her forgivingly. "I'm sorry."

Christmas is the most exciting holiday of the year for children. A time of the year when I'd write letters to Santa Claus asking for gifts that I wanted, but in I knew it was long shot. Christmas was memorable that year. The corduroy shirt turned out to be my Christmas gift along with a slinky and a ball. Christmas was a humbling experience that year. That was the last year I believed in Santa Claus.

6

CARPENTRY

Dad carried a large piece of plywood into the apartment and rested it against the wall in the foyer. The odor from the plywood permeated the air. He removed a dark wooden tool box from the hall closet and unlocked the brass spring-loaded latches. Looking inside the toolbox, I noticed a black metal tool with a red wheel and hand crank. I looked at him. "What's that?"

Dad said. "That's a hand drill."

I asked him. "Can I see it?"

Dad nodded. "Okay but don't put any bits in it."

I uttered. "Okay."

As I watched Dad draw lines and cut wood, I turned the crank on the hand drill fascinated by the gears, and I hoped to use it someday. Much time had passed and I asked Dad, "Can I cut the wood?"

Dad advised. "Okay, but let me start the cut."

I moaned. "I'm not strong enough to push the saw."

Dad said. "When you get older you'll be able to do it."

While Dad cut the wood, Mom yelled from the kitchen, "You're making a lot of dust in there!"

Dad yelled. "Don't worry, I'll clean it up when I'm done. "

At the edge of the living room floor, I sat and watched for hours while Dad sanded and assembled the wood completing the storage box. He installed the hinges and outside metal corner molding. While he cleaned up, I crawled inside the box and closed the lid lying in complete darkness. I could have slept in there. Later on, I placed my Erector Set, Lincoln Logs and the remainder of my toys inside of it, with plenty of room to spare.

Dad stored the tool box in the closet and I couldn't wait to get my hands on his tools to build something.

The weather was bad outside, so I decided to break out the Erector Set. I sat on the oak floor for hours in the living room using the bolts and nuts to connect metal beams together constructing buildings, bridges, and trucks. When I completed a project, sometimes I called out. "Look at this, Ma."

She simply replied, "It's nice."

After I showed the project to my parents, I'd take it apart and start all over again. Sometimes while in the middle of a project, I'd turn to my parents and say, "I want to build bridges when I get older." They just looked at me.

Dad opened the tackle box and turned to me. "We're going fishing on Sunday. Why don't you go out and catch some night-crawlers?"

I responded with joy. "I'll go out tonight."

Dad said. "Okay."

When it turned dark, I left the apartment carrying a flashlight and an empty coffee can. The majority of the private homes in the neighborhood did not contain grassy front yards. I searched up and down the neighborhood for a yard with a lawn. A few blocks away, I located a good-sized lawn. I shined the light on edge of the property. Unable to find any crawlers, I walked further onto the property. I knew I was trespassing, but if I caught a crawler, it would be worth the risk. Prepared to run if I heard a door or window open.

Slowly walking on the lawn, I noticed a slimy brown worm stretched out under the blades of grass. I made a stab at it with my fingers, but it got away. You need to be fast; they don't stray far from their hole. Using my index finger and thumb in one quick motion I tried to grab their body. The first few times I missed. Their slimy bodies slipped through my fingers, but I eventually caught them.

Two hours later, I collected half a can of night crawlers. At home, I walked into the kitchen. "Dad, look at these worms I caught."

Dad asked. "Let me see them. That's good."

I uttered. "What should I do with them?"

Dad advised. "Put them in the refrigerator and I'll add some coffee grinds for them to eat."

I replied. "Okay."

The next morning, Mom opened the refrigerator, and in a high-pitched voice, demanded, "What are those worms doing in here?"

I babbled. "I caught them last night for fishing."

She looked down at me. "Get them out of here right now, the refrigerator is only for food!"

I moaned. "Okay."

Without hesitating, I picked up a discarded wooden crate at the produce market. With my toy hammer and saw, I pieced together the wood to make a box. By adding soil and thin strips of newspaper, I hoped to recreate a home for the worms. Anxious to see the worms squirming around, I dumped them onto the soil, as they scurried around searching for a new home. Later on, I sprinkled coffee grinds on top, hoping to keep them alive for fishing. Outside my bedroom window, I stored the worms on the fire escape, checking and watering them every day.

I walked in and out of the kitchen bored to death. Mom seemed annoyed. "Why don't you go find something to do outside?"

I looked at the floor. "O...kay" I walked downstairs and met my friend Pete, while he bounced a ball in front of his attached brick home. I looked at him. "Hey, let's go play down at the swamps."

He said. "Okay."

A few blocks away from the apartment, rainwater collected on low-lying vacant land creating a swamp. Over the years, the land became a dumping ground for discarded furniture, bicycles, wood, paint cans, anything except household garbage. While searching through the debris, I yelled to Pete. "Hey why don't we build a raft and float it here?"

Pete agreed. "Yeah."

We collected pieces of wood and carried it home.

Rushing into the apartment, I opened the closet door and quietly removed a hammer, crow bar and a saw from Dad's tool box. Outside Pete and I disassembled the wooden pallet. I looked at him, "I don't know how to measure."

I said. "Me neither. Let's cut the pieces about a little larger than a wooden pallet."

When we finished, the raft was about three feet by five feet.

I looked at Pete. "That looks good enough."

He agreed. "Yeah I guess so. We don't have enough nails for the top part."

I advised. "We'll take out the old ones and use them."

Pete said, "Let's put it in my garage overnight so nobody steals it."

I ordered. "Lift, it up."

Pete moaned. "It's too heavy to carry to the swamp?"

I looked at Pete. "I know, we'll attach my metal skates to the bottom and we'll roll it there."

Pete remarked. "Good idea."

Quietly I sneaked into the apartment carrying Dad's tools. Mom spotted me. "What are you doing with those things?"

I wined. "I'm building something."

Mom ordered. "You better put those things back where you found them and wait till I tell your father."

I uttered. "Okay."

The next day I ran across the street holding my metal roller skates. Pete opened the garage door, and we attached the skates to the bottom of the raft. We rolled it toward the swamps. Over time, clusters of tan swamp reeds multiplied and surrounded the lots, creating an atmosphere of privacy, away from the busy traffic and buildings. As the wind blew, the swamp reeds swayed back and forth creating a feeling of tranquility.

We removed the skates from the bottom of the raft. I said to Pete, "Hand me that stick. I'll use it to push the raft around in the water."

Pete glanced at me. "I'll push you off now. Then use the stick to move into deeper water."

I pointed out. "Okay, it's floating but it's not gonna hold two of us."

Pete said. "Yeah, it's barely above water." In the middle of the swamp, the raft started to sink slowly to the bottom. While I stood in waist high water, I worked my way back to shore. "Pete, good thing you weren't on there with me."

Pete declared. "Well I guess that's the end of the raft."

I nodded. "Yeah."

I walked into the apartment with my wet clothes. Mom looked at me. "Where were you; you're all wet!"

I moaned. "I fell in the water in the swamps."

Mom ordered. "Get out of those wet clothes and wash the dirt off of them before you put them in the hamper; you're not going out again!"

Looking down I wined. "Okay,"

The next day I sneaked out of the house hoping Mom forgot about the incident in the swamp. I needed to find my brother's bicycle that he had outgrown. The building superintendent unlocked the door to the basement storage room. The odor from the garbage seeped into the room. After dinner, the super collected the tenants' garbage using the dumbwaiter and stored it temporarily in the basement.

I pulled the string on the ceiling light that barely lit the storage room. The light reflected off the spider webs that laced the room, as heavy dust distorted the colors on carts and bicycles that had been there forever. Some items were- covered with blankets. Underneath a dismantled bike, I located the faded brown, single speed bicycle, with worn balloon tires. I pulled it out. My brother had outgrown it, and I was anxious to use it.

After pumping up the tires, I pushed the bicycle up the wooden ramp and started to pedal through the streets.

After I became confident, I'd coast down a hill with no hands. I pumped the pedals on the Belgium Block (Cobblestone) road underneath the elevated subway on Westchester Avenue, as the handle bars vibrated incessantly. The cobblestone pavement was the original roadway that was used by the old cable cars over a hundred years ago. Quickly, I steered onto the newly paved Cross Bronx Expressway service road, pedaling up and down the gentle sloped hill on Powell Ave. When I picked up speed and pedaled downhill, the acceleration was exhilarating. I experienced a feeling of freedom as a chill ran up and down my spine.

I stopped to watch the neighborhood teenagers who stood in front of the corner candy store. The boys remained in one group and the girls in another. The boys wore blue jeans with rolled up cuffs, white T-shirts, with rolled up sleeves and black shined shoes or engineer's boots. Their hair was slicked back around the sides, DA style like the 'Fonz,' and the top front curled down to toward the nose, held in place by heavy Brylcreem or Vitalis hair cream.

The girls sported short hair with curls and bangs, pedal pusher pants and thin form-fitting blouses. A few teenagers parked their cars near the candy store to show off their rides. Sometimes when I passed the crowd, my brother stood there with his friends. He occasionally acknowledged me by nodding his head while they talked and smoked cigarettes. My brother was handsome with a medium build, 5'10" height, curly brown hair, DA style with a curled down hair drop. A cool looking guy, he fit in with his group of friends. I looked up to him as a role model and wanted to be just like him. I was impressed when he taught me how to spit shine shoes.

On the way home, I rode in the street on Gleason Ave. as I watched an older kid at a distance sitting on the steps in front of an unattached brick house. As I moved closer, he stood up and ran into the street. He yelled at me, "Get the hell off my block and stay away from here!" He pushed me down onto the pavement, for what reason, I don't know. The guy wore blue jeans with his tee shirt sleeves rolled up over his shoulders and slicked-back brown hair. I didn't know him. He angrily kicked me in the ribs, stomped on my legs and bicycle. Trapped underneath the bike as the frame pressed against my leg, I lay there helplessly in shock. My only thought was to get away from him before he caused me any further pain. I looked for a way out. He stepped back toward the curb and yelled at me. "Don't come near this block again!" While he stood on the sidewalk with his hands on his hips, he sneered at me. Ignoring the pain, I stood the bike up. Unable to ride it, since the bent front tire rubbed against the frame. I lifted it off the ground, rolled it home on one wheel and into the basement storage room.

Inside the apartment, Mom stood in the kitchen. Ignoring her, I headed for the bathroom. I removed the torn clothes and threw them into the hamper. The scrapes on my arms ran along my elbows, so I washed them applying mercurochrome and covered up with a long sleeve shirt. The shock of the attack bothered me more than the injuries. Living in the Bronx, you learn quickly to be on your guard and always expect the unexpected.

As I lay on the bed staring at the ceiling, I wondered why this guy, out of the blue, who I did not know, would inflict harm on me. The memories of the attack remained with me for some time.

7

REJECTION

In the early part of 1981 my father sent this letter to me.

Neil

>*A couple of weeks ago, we went to a dinner reunion for the neighbors and friends of St. John Vianney. We were seated at a table next to Father Whelan. He greeted us all, and I refreshed his memory with our names. I sat down at his table and reminded him that he came out to Long Island twelve years ago to marry you. He smiled and asked for you and your wife and then I told him with a fairly quick rundown of what is going on and how we are treated. The poor man shook his head and took my hand and said, "I'll pray for them at mass tomorrow." Also, at this affair was Tom O'Neill and his wife Lillian. Being friends at the time, we were at their table and I found out he is with Customs. I learned quite a few things about your job that I never knew; it was quite interesting.*
>
>*It's a small world.*

I was somewhat surprised to receive the letter from my Father. While growing up I had more of a connection with him than with my mother. Dad was a good man, but he always took direction from mom since she was the matriarch of the family and she conveyed her version of events to him. Once he heard what my mother had to say my father wasn't interested in anything I had to say. What concerned me, was that my parents were now spreading their version of the story to make my wife and I look bad in the community.

After I received the letter from my father, I called Father Whelan on the phone. He was well acquainted with me since he chaperoned the Friday night church dances and conducted confraternity classes, which I attended. He immediately recalled performing our marriage ceremony eleven years earlier. I mentioned to Father Whelan that my father sent me a letter after the dinner reunion held at St John Vianney Church. I asked him, "Did my father discuss with you what was going on between us and them. Can you tell me what you said to them?"

Father mentioned. "Neil, I told your parents that I would pray for you and them at mass."

I remarked. "Well, I'm not happy that my parents are spreading gossip that reflects poorly on my family. It's hurtful to hear negative feedback portraying us in a bad light."

Father pointed out. "Neil I'm sorry to hear that so I will pray for both of you at Mass. God bless your family."

Sometime later, I contacted Aunt Anna my closet relative in the family. She didn't drive, so I called her on the phone to arrange a visit. "Hi, Aunt Anna. It's Neil, how are you?"

She replied. "Oh, okay Neil, how are you, your wife and children?"

I said. "We're all good. How are you feeling?"

She uttered. "Well… you know, okay I guess."

I pointed out. "I know you've never seen our children, so we would like to visit you."

Her voice grew softer as she spoke. "Oh… well not right now, Neil, wait until things get better between you and your parents and then you come over. I'll call you."

I stated. "Did my parents tell you why we haven't seen them?"

Aunt Anna spoke. "No, your mother didn't explain any details."

I declared. "Well maybe one day you might be interested in my version of events?"

She remarked. "Oh…okay, well it's been good talking to you."

Aunt Anna's rejection of my attempt to visit with her hurt me deeply. As far back as I can remember, I always treated her with respect and never did anything to cause her to reject or discipline me.

Several weeks after my phone conversation with Aunt Anna, I received a card from her son Michael containing a gift for my children for the holidays. Michael and I were the same age. We grew up together in the Bronx, and were like brothers.

Dear Neil,

> *My parents don't seem too keen about you visiting them since you don't visit your own parents. My car hasn't been running since before the summer I may be getting married. I have so many in my family with all the nephews and their children, so, it's all I can afford.*
> *My best to you, Joann and the boys during this holiday season.*

Michael

Aunt Anna and Michael's rejection of my request to visit with them was troubling, since I had not spoken or corresponded with them for some time. During my entire life, I was on good terms with both of them. To be rejected by my closet aunt and cousin was shocking and hurtful. It's amazing how many people believe half a story. There is an old proverb: 'If you heard half a story you haven't heard any story at all.'

In the mid- 50s, I vividly recalled visiting Nana and rushing downstairs to visit Cousin Michael. We were the same age; we played together like brothers. Nana and Aunt Anna were sisters and shared a two- family house on St. Lawrence Ave. in the Bronx.

Michael and I ran toward the vacant lots next to the elevated subway. We rummaged through the debris in the open lots while the kids in the neighborhood shot small pieces of linoleum at us with carpet guns. We found cover behind discarded furniture until the kids stopped shooting at us. Michael looked at me. "We should make carpet guns to fight back at them." I agreed.

"It's easy, we'll make an 'L' shape where the short end is the handle and the long end is the barrel. We'll buy a giant rubber band and connect it with a nail." By stretching the rubber band and placing a small piece of linoleum between it, the gun propelled the linoleum more than a hundred feet. After we made the guns, Michael shot at me as I hid behind a fifty-five- gallon drum. We chased each other through the lots for hours until the rubber bands broke.

The Fourth of July rolled around, and Michael and I were lighting sparklers on his front porch. After we lit off all of the sparklers, Michael lit a Roman candle shooting it into the air. He handed one to me, and I lit it holding it up, but it didn't fire. Michael looks at me. "Hold it above your head and twirl it around in a circle." I followed his instructions and the candle shot a few fireballs into the air. All of a sudden, the candle backfired and a fireball hit me in the face. I threw the candle down on the ground. Running into the bathroom, I splashed cold water on my face when Aunt Anna walked in and said, "What happened?" "A Roman candle backfired in my face." Aunt Anna applied ointment to the burned area. Fortunately, the fireball did not cause any damage to my eyes. That was the day I learned that fireworks were unsafe and I never lit one again.

Michael and I walked along Westchester Ave. and peered into the pet shop window. While inside he turned to me and said, "Look at the pigeons."

I said. "Wow, they're clean with nice colors. What kind are they?"

He pointed out. "The red and white one is a red teeger- tiplet,"

I stared at them. "Wow, they're beautiful. They're not like the pigeons you see under the elevated subway."

Michael's eyes were thinking something up. "If we had a pigeon coop we could take care of them and fly them."

I said, "Let's build one."

He remarked. "Yeah, yeah!"

After we collected wood from the lots and produce store, we stored it in his back yard. "What size should we make the coop?" I asked.

"We'll make it small because we'll buy only a few of pigeons."

Each time I visited Michael we worked on the coop, roughly the size of two milk crates with an enclosed area surrounded with chicken wire.

On our way to the pet shop, we counted our money. "I have a dollar fifty," I offered.

"With my three dollars, that should be enough," he added.

That was enough money to buy four dark gray pigeons. We didn't own pets, so we raced home carrying the pigeons in a cardboard box. I opened the door and placed them -one by one- inside the coop. What a wonderful feeling to hold a warm feathered bird in my hands, unlike anything I'd experienced before. One of them pecked at a bowl of seeds while the others walked under the chicken wire familiarizing themselves in their new home. We studied the area, mapping out the best vantage point for them to fly.

The next day we stood next to the coop, and I looked at Michael. "If we release the pigeons, how do they know to come back to the coop?"

With a surprised look on his face, Michael said, "They're homing pigeons, they know."

"Okay."

We placed the pigeons on top of the coop. Michael gently brushed against the pigeons with the back of his hand and one by one they flew upward clearing the surrounding houses. How breathtaking to watch the pigeons take flight, not confined to a small space anymore. After a short time, they were out of sight.

As we stood in the narrow backyard, our visibility was blocked by the adjoining homes. Unless the pigeons circled directly above us, they were out of sight. We watched and waited over an hour from different vantage points hoping to spot them. The pigeons did not return.

The next day we checked the coop, still no pigeons. I said to Michael, "Where did the pigeons go?"

With a sad look on his face, he told me, "You know the guy a few houses over has a large pigeon coop on top of his house. I'll bet he picked them up in his flock."

I spoke nervously. "Let's go see him and find out."

He pointed out. "Our pigeons weren't marked. How can-we prove we owned them?"

I moaned. "Yeah, I guess you're right."

The pigeons taught us a good lesson - Know what –the- hell you're doing before you do it. That was the first and last time that Michael and I were involved with pigeons.

At the age of eight, I slept overnight on many occasions at Nana's house on the sofa bed, while my parents enjoyed Saturday evenings out together. Before bedtime, Nana and I watched the Perry Como and the Lawrence Welk shows together. She sat very close to the TV due to her poor eyesight. When I worked as an air marshal, I recognized Perry Como in the first-class lounge area on a flight to Rome. I walked over to him. "Pardon me, Mr. Como, My Nana never misses your TV Show. Could I have your autograph for her?"

He looked at me. "What is her name?"

I uttered. "It's Josephine."

He wrote. "Dear Josephine, with fond regards, Perry Como." When I returned home with the autograph and handed it to Nana, she was speechless.

On Saturdays, at age nine, I walked a half a mile to Nana's house on St. Lawrence Ave., where I dusted, cleaned and vacuumed for her. She helped me vacuum when I used the heavy shiny steel vacuum cleaner with an external large black bag. The high pitch winding sound of the vacuum motor was frightening when I turned it on, so I called it the 'zoo zoo.' As I swept the steps, Nana looked down at me. "Be sure you get all of the dirt; clean it good; don't do a lick and a promise!" After I finished cleaning, she handed me a quarter.

Nana always ironed my baseball uniform forming a crease down the center like a pair of pants. When I played with a neatly pressed uniform, I felt it improved my game.

In 1960 after Grandfather died, Nana moved into her own apartment in our apartment building in the Castle Hill Projects. She was a quiet person, an older version of Mom. Nana lost her vision in one eye and was slowly losing it in the other. Periodically, I knocked on her door. "Do you need any help with anything?"

"Oh, yes dear, come in. "You see the chair over there, can you move it over here and try to tighten up the leg?"

Little things, but they were important to her. Nana sat in the chair in front of the cluster of windows with the shades up. I gazed at her. "Nana, what are you doing?"

"I can't walk around outside, so I have to get sun. Your body needs the vitamins from the sun."

I said, "Wow, with all the shades up, it's warm in here even in the winter."

"Oh, yes dear, it's wonderful during the day."

A year or so after the rift I was at home when the phone rang. "Hello."

"Neil, this is your Nana."

I said. "Hi, how are you?"

She ordered me. "Neil, you have to make up with your mother!"

I was shocked at her request and told her. "I haven't done anything wrong to my mother or father."

She declared. "Neil, it doesn't matter. You make up with your mother!"

I pointed out. "I'm not going to apologize for something that I did not do. Did my parents tell you about their visit to my house and why they ran out of the house after fifteen minutes?"

She demanded. "It doesn't matter what they did. It doesn't matter. You make up with them!"

I advised. "They need to apologize to me!"

Her voice lowered. "If you don't make up with them, I can't speak to you anymore, goodbye."

While I talked with Nana, my wife sat in the kitchen. I said, "You heard the conversation?"

My wife said. "How can Nana expect you to apologize to your parents if she hasn't heard our side of the incident?"

I said. "I know.

It feels like I'm losing everybody. Nana is not only rejecting me, she's rejecting her innocent great-grandchildren, without cause, which is mentally abusive. This situation we're in is taking on a life of only my mother's version of events."

Nana passed away in 1983, and she maintained her silence and never communicating with me again. At her wake, I spoke with Uncle Frank, my mother's brother. We stood next to each other, a short distance away from Nana's casket. Uncle Frank looked at me. "I understand that there is a conflict between you and your parents?"

I said, "Yes, I've attempted to resolve the issue, but they have not been receptive."

Uncle Frank took a deep breath and looked me straight in the eye.

"Neil, I have an issue with my son and his wife that we're trying to work out. I will ask your mother to try to resolve the issue between both of you, but I don't think she will listen to me."

I said, "Currently, I have been unsuccessful in my efforts to resolve the situation, so anything that you can do will be appreciated."

He replied. "I don't think she will listen to me."

Uncle Frank knew his sister well enough to know that she had a vivid imagination.

Uncle Frank passed away a few years later.

A few weeks later the phone rang. "Hello."

"This is your mother. What's wrong with you and your wife? Nobody in the family wants to visit you!" She hung up the phone angered that her brother confronted her regarding her relationship with her son.

I called her back and she answered.

In a raised voice, she said, "I'm the mother, and that's all you have to know. You're supposed to obey me!"

I pointed out. "I'm a married man in my thirties, the father of two children and you're speaking to me like I'm a child."

She shouted. "You're defiant; you're just like when you were young! You've always been defiant. I can't talk to you. We'll cut you off!" She hung up the phone.

I realized that family situation is like a cancer that's metastasizing, and I'm searching for the remedy.

8

PAROCHIAL SCHOOL

In 1958, I sat in the sixth- grade class as the desks were separated by long narrow rows that blocked the closet doors in the back of the classroom. Sister Edgar walked in front of the class after writing seventy-four in the upper left corner of the blackboard. The Dominican sisters at St Helena's maintained order and delivered organized lessons regardless of class size. Our class was later reduced to sixty-five students. What a relief to retrieve our coats from the closets in the back of the classroom without moving the desks away from the doors.

Every day I sat on the edge of my seat while Sister Edgar taught the class. Sister was a short, thin woman maybe in her fifties, with a pale complexion and dark circles under her eyes. She maintained a permanent scowl, rarely smiling, even during her conversations with other sisters. Her quixotic movements and strong clear, confident voice was not indicative of a woman of small stature. Dressed in the black habit, Sister conveyed a somewhat frightening appearance. She taught as a strict disciplinarian, with complete control.

I maintained a good conduct record consisting of A's and B's throughout elementary school, except for a swat now and then across the head for talking while standing on line. Catholic education was the place where we heard and learned the one- liners that the sisters used to control behavior. If the class was unruly Sister shouted-out, "Empty barrels make the most noise or one rotten apple spoils the bunch." That usually ended the disruption. There were some positive one- liners that remained with me such as: 'Patience is a virtue' and 'seek and you shall find.'

Sister stood in front of the class while she taught the method used to diagram a sentence. She wrote a sentence and a diagram on the blackboard and called out my name to fill in the subject and the verb." Being shy and easily embarrassed, I wrote the subject and verb in the diagram. She looked at me. "Now, what is the indirect object?" Unable to provide an answer, I stared at the blackboard. Sister scowled at me. "Listen here sonny boy, what is the indirect object?" The blood rushed to my head, as I could see out of the corner of my eye that all eyes in the class were on me. Sister bounced the wooden pointer on top of my head a few times. I guess she thought it might help me think clearly. "Mr. Buonocore, what is the indirect object? " Staring at the blackboard, I felt awkward and afraid of giving the wrong answer. Then my mind went blank. Sister resumed bouncing the pointer on top of my head with greater force and in a raised voice. "What is the indirect object…Buo…no…core!" My face turned red as a beet, as I stood there unresponsive. Feeling humiliated and criticized, I ignored the pain on my head. Sister spoke, in a derogatory tone. "Sit down, Mr. Buonocore!" Any little mistake, a wrong answer or no answer received punishment. If I did nothing and never tried anything, I wouldn't get in trouble for making a mistake. That's when I shut up and didn't speak and ask questions in class. Through the remaining years of my education including college, I was reluctant to volunteer answering questions in class for fear of providing a wrong answer. Subconsciously, I felt that my reluctance was related to the punishment I received from Sister Edgar in the sixth grade. There is a definite relationship between shyness and classroom performance. Many years after college, I had no fear answering or asking questions in any situation.

After school, I walked into the apartment while Mom watched soap operas. I said, "Hi."

Without turning away from the TV screen, she nodded. "Hi." Quickly I walked into the bedroom, I lay on the bed dwelling about the humiliation I experienced earlier in class. I did not mention the incident in school to

Mom for fear of punishment, for not being smart enough to answer Sister's questions.

Months later, Sister sent me and four classmates to retrieve books from the stock room. We sprinted down the hall, and when we arrived at the stock room, the principal walked out. In an angry tone of voice, she ordered, "All of you face the wall!" She retrieved a twelve-inch wooden ruler from the stockroom and proceeded to strike each of us across the back of our calves. While she hit us, she yelled, "Don't you ever, let me ever, see you do that again. Now, take these boxes and get back to class!" A student in our group wore shorts and the back of his calves were beet red from sister's swats. I looked at his calves and realized that wearing long pants was an advantage. Group punishment is easier to handle because you're not alone. You can comfort each other.

We sat in the classroom awaiting Sister Edgar's return. Sister Henrietta, nicknamed the 'Hen,' hurriedly walked by in the hallway. The class in unison made a cackling sound like a bunch of chickens. The Hen, an agile large framed woman, stood six-feet tall. There was a disturbance in the hall. Moments later the Hen pulled Tommy Sullivan with ease into the classroom by his necktie and pushed him up against the wall. Tommy was a student from the other class. He was a heavyset guy, tall for his age, one of the toughest kids in the sixth grade. Sister removed him from the bathroom where she caught him smoking. He stood in the corner of the classroom with his shirt unbuttoned and his necktie hanging far below his collar. The Hen looked at him and in a disparaging voice uttered, "Mr. Sullivan, who do you think you are?"

Tommy was silent. Sister hauled off and proceeded to punch him in the stomach with numerous alternating left and right blows. She maintained the cadence of a boxer as if she had done this before. As we watched from behind, her elbows whisked past her back punching in a measured rhythm. While Sister punched Tommy, the class chanted. "Hit'em again, hit'em again, harder, harder. Hit'em again, hit'em again harder, harder!"

After Sister finished, Tommy dropped to the floor, exhausted from the blows. He sat up against the wall with his hair messed up and his shirt hanging outside his pants. Sister walked out of the classroom and briskly returned. She walked over to Tommy and raised him up from the floor by his ear. While she escorted Tommy to his class across the hall, she held his ear while his head was cocked to the side gritting his teeth from the pain.

Tommy had been pegged by the nuns as a troublemaker, and once you're pegged you become a target. Certain kids deserve punishment and Tommy was a strong personality who could handle punishment. Corporal punishment can cause weaker personalities to retreat inside themselves or flee to another place because you never know when you'll be punished.

After class, I stood on patrol underneath the elevated subway on Westchester Ave. The traffic light glowed red. I felt a sense of pride every day when I placed the white canvas patrol belt and silver badge over my shoulder. The crossing guard duty provided me with a sense of value, responsibility and confidence that the school trusted me to represent them. Sometimes when my friends walked by, they yelled and pointed to the 'Robert Hall Clothing' store behind me and speaking in unison; "Your mother robs it, and your father hauls it." We all laughed, no matter how many times we heard it.

Walking into the apartment after school one day Mom was cleaning the stove as my two-year old sister stood on a chair in front of the kitchen sink. She was wearing a white undershirt and shorts as she played with the pots and pans in the sink. When I looked at her, she reminded me of a female version of myself when I was her age that I remembered from family photos. We were nine years apart and I loved her. As I stood next to her she lifted up a steak knife by the handle from the sink. Unbeknownst to her, the blade pointed upward as she started to raise the knife toward her face. I immediately grabbed the blade to prevent it from striking her. The blade penetrated deeply across my index finger. Mom stared at me.

"Oh no, what did you do! Put your finger under cold water until it stops bleeding." Blood poured out and cold water didn't work. Mom wrapped a washcloth around the wound to stop the blood flow. Later on, she applied Band Aids to keep the skin together. I changed the Band Aid every day for a couple of weeks. By today's standards the wound would have required several stitches. Till this day, the scar is visible on my finger.

9

RUBANO

On my way to school, I met the twins Brian and Barry they were classmates. Brian said, "Hey Neil, why don't you join the Boy Scouts? It's great, you'd like it. We wear a uniform and do all sorts of fun things like knot tying, tug' o' war and all kinds of games."

I told him, "I'll have to ask my parents if I can join."

He said. "Okay, because there's a meeting coming up next week."

After dinner that evening dinner, I approached my father. "Can I join the Boy Scouts?"

He replied. "We'll see; how much does it cost to join?"

I remarked. "I'll find out."

The next month I enrolled in Boy Scout Troop 119, where some of the Scouts were classmates from school. Scouting provided a good foundation for my life. By adhering to the scout motto, oath and law, which I had memorized, made an impact on my daily life. It's engrained in me. I can repeat it till this day:

The Scout Motto.........Be Prepared

Scout Law......A scout is trustworthy, loyal, helpful, friendly, courteous, kind, obedient, cheerful, thrifty, brave, clean and reverent.

At the meetings, we learned knot tying, map and compass reading, first aid, signaling, rank advancement, uniform inspection and many things pertinent to daily life.

On a cold winter day, the troop traveled to the YMCA on 161st Street in the Bronx for indoor activities. We placed our winter coats in the wall lockers and ran upstairs to the indoor track that surrounded the basketball court below. When the court became available, we shot hoops until we were exhausted.

I returned to the locker area to retrieve my brown leather bomber jacket and discovered it missing. The jacket was a hand-me-down from my brother that I greatly cherished. Together with the Scoutmaster, we searched everywhere for about an hour and were unable to locate it. I felt naked walking around outside in the cold weather without a winter coat. While sitting in the car on the trip home I pondered how someone could steal a winter jacket. I learned a good lesson to be aware of your surroundings and the things that you cherish. On the other hand, maybe there was another person who was in need of a winter coat and couldn't afford it. When I arrived home, it pained me to tell my parents that my winter jacket had- been stolen. Our family was not in a position to afford additional costs. It bothered me to put a burden on my parents.

In the spring, somebody donated a knapsack and sleeping bag and my parents bought me a mess kit. I was enamored with the collapsible drinking cup opening and closing it incessantly, filling it with water and amazed that it never leaked.

We traveled to the Boy Scout Camp, located in Alpine, New Jersey, for a weekend campout. In a clearing, we set up pup tents that bordered the woods and rolled out our sleeping bags and equipment inside.

The troop leader assigned Joe, an Eagle Scout to our group. He guided us into the woods and provided instruction regarding edible plants for survival. Joe pointed to a sapling. "See this tree here; that's a sassafras tree. We can make sassafras tea. I'll dig up the root and wash it."

I thought Joe was crazy. We returned to camp carrying plants and firewood. Joe boiled the sassafras root in water, let it cool and handed a cup to me. "Try this tea, I just made it."

I sipped it and sipped it again. "Boy, this is really good, it tastes like root beer."

Joe stated. "Yeah, it's used to flavor root beer."

I remarked. "Really?"

After that lesson, I paid close attention to Joe's instructions.

At night, we made a campfire and collected small tree branches, which we whittled to points on the ends, to hold marshmallows. We roasted them over the fire, one after the other, until the supply ran out. At bedtime, we slept four guys in one tent. Sleeping directly on the damp ground without a ground cushion I tossed and turned all night. I was uncomfortable sleeping without a pillow. You never sleep as well as you do in your own bed. In the morning, I was-drawn to the aroma of bacon and eggs as the adults cooked on the fire.

After two years I quit the Scouts, achieving the rank of first- class, earning seven merit badges, a far cry from twenty-one needed to become an Eagle Scout.

Scouting helped me develop my skills, ethics and increase my self-confidence that influenced my adult life. The memories, skills and friends that I made while a Scout have remained with me throughout my entire life.

Years later, I enrolled my children in the Scouts, hoping that they might learn the same ethics, skills, and values that helped me develop into an adult.

As a Scout leader, I volunteered my services to try to give back what I had learned. Many years later, when my children were of age they joined the scouts. A most memorable activity for my sons was the 'Soap Box Derby' race. Every scout was- given a specification sheet listing the requirements for the unpowered wooden racer. Together with my children, we gathered the materials from the lumber supply yard and scoured the salvage yards for wheels and metal parts to provide the materials needed to build the racer. Six weeks later, we completed the racers. On the day of the race, all the parents and friends stood at the top of the only hill in the neighborhood anxiously waiting for the whistle. The race was close as the winner won only by a few feet. My sons did not win, but my son Victor won an award for 'Best Looking Racer.' He painted a bald eagle surrounded by red, white and blue on the front of the racer.

In order to earn money, I decided to work after school delivering newspapers. I bought a handlebar basket to carry the newspapers for my route. The route consisted of sixty-five customers and when I returned to the office with extra newspapers I asked the dispatcher, "I have extra papers. Did I miss any customers?"

He said, "During the week, you get a couple of extras, but on Sundays that's exact."

Training school for paper- boys does not exist. Little did I know that the Sunday newspaper was double the weight of the daily edition. When I stacked the newspapers in my basket it was more than I could handle so I tied them down as securely as possible. On a cold Sunday winter morning I turned the corner, and the wind blew me to the ground. The newspapers blew everywhere. Scurrying to collect and reorganize each section in the wind, I must have been there for more than an hour.

A few weeks later, I rushed to deliver the papers as a thunderstorm rolled in. Plastic was not available, so I covered the papers with the extra copies hoping the rain wouldn't soak through. Customers do not like wet newspapers. Collection day is payday and that's when you get all the complaints from the customers:

"My paper was delivered wet. I didn't get a delivery. Why was the paper delivered late?" Constructive criticism is a good thing, otherwise how else can you improve.

After I paid the newspaper bill, the balance including tips left me with eight dollars for the week. I saved my money, depositing it regularly in the bank.

At the beginning of the summer, I threw a Spaldeen against the building. Richie Rubano, a kid who lived across the street walked over to me. Richie was a heavyset fellow, not the athletic type. "Hey, how ya do'in?"

I said. "Hi, Rich. You wanna play handball?"

He replied. "Alright." We hit the ball against the building for a while. Bored after playing ball, Richie looked at me and said, "Hey, let's get some candy at the corner."

I moaned. "I don't have any money."

He uttered. "Come with me anyway."

I said. "Okay."

Inside the candy store, Richie walked in and asked the guy behind the counter, "Do you have any Baby Ruth's?"

The clerk said, "I'll look." When he bent below the counter, Richie grabbed candy bars from the shelf and stuffed them into his pockets. I walked outside, since I did not want to be- associated with his theft. He paid for one piece of candy and walked out with a pocket full of candy bars. As we walked on the sidewalk, Richie looked at me with a smile on his face laughing. "That's how you do it. You want some?"

I replied. "No thanks."

Richie laughed as he stuffed his face while we walked.

We crossed the street and walked along the fenced-in property owned by Al, the junkman. The house was in need of repair, and surrounded by old bed frames, appliances, tables, chairs, fifty-five-gallon drums, anything that Al collected, enclosed by a high fence.

Al was a short middle-aged man, unshaven, wearing torn pants and unlaced leather boots. When people placed their trash out for pick-up, Al could be seen slowly pushing an old baby carriage and collecting almost anything that people discarded. On his way home, when he walked near the candy store, the teenagers pointed to him laughing. "There goes Al the junkman; look at the junk he's bringing home now."

We walked on the sidewalk adjacent to Al the junkman's house, and Richie lit a pack of firecrackers throwing them onto Al's property. The junkyard dogs started to bark. Moments later, one of the dogs cleared the fence and chased us down the street. Richie yelled out, "Holy shit, the dog got out!" While I ran, the dog gained on me. I jumped onto the hood of a parked car.

Richie waddled down the street laughing. "He let the dogs out, ha, ha, ha!" As the dog was about to grab onto Richie's leg, he jumped onto the hood of a car. We waited until the dog returned to the property and headed home.

Standing in front of Richie's building on Powell Ave., he turned to me and said, "Hey, you want to see my pet alligator that I caught when I was in Florida?"

I asked. "Where do you keep it?"

He mentioned. "I keep it in my bathtub."

I said. "Okay."

We walked inside Richie's apartment, as his parents weren't home. While in the bathroom, I looked inside the bathtub where a one-foot long alligator sat. Richie lifted the alligator up so I could look at it closely. "You can pet him if you want, but he bites. You see, he bit me on my finger so I put a band aid on it."

I said, "What are you going to do with the alligator when he grows larger?"

He turned away. "I don't know, I guess when I get tired of him, I could always put him down the sewer."

I remarked. "Really?"

I stood in the living room. Richie said, "Hey, you wanna shoot my gun."

I said. "What do you mean? How can you shoot a gun in an apartment?"

Richie pointed out. "I have this piece of wood that I use for a target and hang it on the entrance door. When I shoot into the target, the bullets don't go through it."

Richie opened the hall closet and removed a twenty-two- caliber rifle.

He loaded it and fired at the target. I said, "Are you allowed to shoot a gun in an apartment?"

He replied. "Nobody complains and the target catches the bullets."

I feared guns. While Richie shot the gun, I asked, "What if a bullet missed the target and went through the door and hit someone in the hall?"

He said. "Na, that won't happen."

I uttered. "I don't want to shoot the gun."

Being afraid of guns, I walked into the kitchen, out of Richie's sight to get away from the noise. I turned around and walked toward the hallway. As I walked through the archway at that moment, I heard the gunfire. The bullet passed inches away from my face, as I was directly in line with target. My heart dropped to the floor, and a chill ran up and down my spine. I yelled at Richie, "You could have killed me!" Richie put his head down and remained silent. I raced toward the door and ran down the stairs shaking, as my heart was beating feverishly. Knowing that I had been inches away from death a moment earlier frightened the hell out of me. I ran across the street and raced into the apartment. Heading straight for the bedroom, I ignored Mom. Lying on the bed, my heart pounded like a drum. I stared at the ceiling, thinking about what occurred and relieved that I walked out alive. I felt guilty that I was somewhere that I shouldn't have been, with someone that I shouldn't be with, involved in something that I shouldn't be doing. The incident was never mentioned to my parents for fear of being- punished for being involved with a troublemaker. I learned a good lesson that day. Choose your friends wisely. The recurring thoughts of that bullet passing inches away from my head, have never left my mind.

10

HIGH SCHOOL

In the spring of 1960, I was getting ready to graduate St Helena's elementary school. My 8 th grade teacher Sister Venard called me up to her desk. "Mr. Buonocore, report to the principal's office."

I walked downstairs into the office as the secretary looked at me. "Are you Neil?"

I said. "Yes."

She said. "Have a seat inside."

Mrs. Lane, the school administrator, walked in. "Mr. Buonocore, why haven't you registered for St Helena's High School or any Catholic high school?"

I replied, "My parents can't afford the tuition."

She uttered. "That's a shame because you have the IQ to do well."

I shrugged. "I'll go to public high school."

She clenched her lips. "O...kay, well good luck in high school."

I replied. "Thank you."

I returned to class and sat at my desk when Paul leaned over and whispered, "Did you get in trouble?"

I said. "No, I told her I'm not going to Catholic high school."

He replied. "Why not?"

I pointed out. "My parents can't afford the tuition."

He said. "Oh."

Our family's expenses increased after my sister was born a few years earlier and we were in the process of moving into a larger apartment. I felt bad about not attending Catholic high school with friends that I had made over the last eight years. I'll miss the fun in class, and the tackle football games we played on the gravel parking lot, adjacent to the elevated subway behind Joe Cirillo's house. The game was so popular that half of the eighth- grade class participated. I enjoyed the friendships I made in school, never disappointed by any of them. I'll miss them deeply. It was a helpless feeling to lose the relationships I made over the years.

Mom yelled from the kitchen, "You should register for DeWitt Clinton High School, where your brother went." My brother graduated high school five years earlier, and now he was on active duty in the Navy.

I yelled back, "Why should I go there?"

Mom pointed out. "You can go there and play baseball."

I said. "I don't want to go there."

While thumbing through the color section of the *Sunday Daily News*, I noticed a four-page article describing Machine and Metal Trades Technical and Vocational high school. The article displayed photos of students building a house in the classroom. Dad sat in his chair reading the news section. I looked at him. "Dad, look at the pictures of these guys building a house in school. Look at this one where students operate metal cutting machines in a machine shop."

I handed Dad the newspaper as he leaned back in his chair. He looked at me. "Those are shop classes in a trade school to learn a skill. When you graduate, you have a skill to get a job."

My eyes were glued to the article, as I read it to Dad. "They have all sorts of classes like: carpentry, machine shop, refrigeration and air conditioning and design courses too. I uttered. I wanna go there."

My father's brows knit together. "You know the school is located in Manhattan?"

I asked. "How much do I have to pay to travel to school?"

Dad remarked. "Students travel for free with a transit pass."

I said. "That sounds good."

In the summer of 1960, we moved into a three-bedroom apartment on Seward Ave., in the newly built Castle Hill Projects in the Bronx.

The sprawling twelve and twenty story buildings were clustered around playgrounds and courtyards.

The New York City housing projects (today known as Section 8 housing) at that time, offered larger and safe affordable housing for low-income families. A few blocks from the East River, the fourteen high rise buildings were separated by manicured lawns, shrubbery and trees. The interior was finished with polished tile floors and high gloss tiled hallway walls. Moving to the projects provided my parents with their own bedroom, which ended their sleeping on a sofa bed in the living room. The view from our second- floor apartment spanned several acres of undeveloped low-lying land. Far less congestion than where we lived on Pugsley Ave. I think my mother liked the larger apartment and the open space view. The pristine development could have been a model for future city housing projects.

In an effort to make new friends every day I headed to the park on Randall Ave. With a full basketball court, a few half courts, a handball court and enough room for stickball and touch football, I played everything. That's where I met my friends, Guy, Larry, John, Frank and Mike. We had a lot in common since our parents were of similar socio-economic backgrounds. Nothing was handed to us; if you wanted something you needed to work for it.

Summer ended, and on the first day of school, I boarded the 6:30 a.m. bus on Castle Hill Ave. At Westchester Avenue, I switched to the elevated subway and transferred at Parchester to the Pelham Express. At the age of thirteen, public transportation was a frightening experience for me, having walked every day to elementary school for eight years. The New York City transit system was the busiest in the world. The train arrived at the Hunts Point station which was the first express stop as we stood shoulder to shoulder inside the subway car. The doors opened and the awaiting passengers forced their way into the crowded car, like a herd of cattle. The commuters consumed every square inch of space, as the temperature rose inside the car. When the train pulled away from the station, we stood against each other like sardines. The man standing next to me held, folded and read the New York Times newspaper, oblivious to the crowd. Traveling on the subway at a young age was something that I needed to adjust to amidst a crowd of adult men and women commuters.

The train arrived at 96th Street in Manhattan where I fought my way through the crowded car to get off. Walking down 96th Street on the perimeter of Harlem toward the East River Drive, I entered Machine and Metal Trades High School shop building. In awe, as I looked around the home room at metal cutting machines that I had never seen before. I asked a student, "What kind of machine is that?"

He said. "I don't know but I can't wait to use it."

Mr. Capricio, the homeroom teacher walked over to us. "Boys, that is a milling machine, that's a lathe, that's a shaper and that's a drill press. If you're registered for machine shop, you'll learn how to use all of the machines in this room."

I replied. "I can't wait."

I enrolled in the Technical Course where both academic, trade and design courses were taught in preparation for college. Machine and Metal Trades was one of two schools in New York City that prepared students for the six-hour New York State Regent's Examination in Design and Construction. Whoever thought that a trade school offered a program that provided an opportunity to apply to college?

At lunch period, I walked toward the cafeteria, from where loud voices echoed throughout the halls. When I entered the cafeteria, the voices became clearer. Hundreds of students sat eating lunch, while others waited in line at the food counter. Some students sneaked in front of one another in line, as they expressed their displeasure at the barely edible goulash and baked macaroni. The cafeteria seemed somewhat chaotic, unlike elementary school where we ate lunch quietly in the classroom at our desks. Not knowing anybody and feeling insecure like all eyes were on me,

I became alarmed. Just three months earlier, I was walking to elementary school in the Bronx, and now, I am traveling on a bus and subway to high school in Manhattan. As I looked around the majority of the students were older, some the size of adults. Being a shy and quiet person, I kept my mouth shut, minded my own business and never looked anyone in the eye.

I noticed a table where a few students sat wearing jackets and ties figuring they were Tech students, so I sat down. That's where I met Frank Coffaro, a neighbor from the projects. For the next four years, we traveled together to school. Seated at a table, we ate our bagged lunch and watched an occasional milk carton fly over the table.

While I looked around the cafeteria it hit me. A white kid, surrounded by black and Puerto Rican students, was a culture shock. White students made up about twenty percent of the enrollment. The transition from elementary to high school was overwhelming because while attending elementary school there was not one student of color. Machine and Metal Trades high school was located in Manhattan and was accessible to any student who lived within the five boroughs of New York City. I lived in the projects, a predominantly white, low-rent community. High School consisted of students from varied backgrounds. Most of the students were children of hard-working families of limited means. They wanted their children to become educated and perhaps work in a profession that was better than their own. Regardless of race, color, creed or religious denomination, we were all in the same boat, attending school to get an education.

One day crossing 96th Street, I headed toward the academic building, just in time for the general science class. When I approached the classroom, the teacher shouted. "Come in, gentlemen, and have a seat. We'll start shortly. My name is Mr. Nicodemo, and you are here to learn General Science." Nicodemo, a portly man in his forties, balding and had a pointed nose, wearing a dark suit and tie. He lectured in a high- pitched voice, with vibrant energy, that traveled throughout the room and down the hall.

Weeks later while seated in class Nicodemo lectured, and focused occasionally toward the back of the classroom. He interrupted the lecture and yelled out, "Misek, shut up." Nicodemo paced back and forth between the desk and the door. Moments later, he opened the desk drawer and removed a steel pipe, two inches diameter by approximately a foot long. I thought the pipe was part of the lecture. Nicodemo wound up like a pitcher and threw the pipe toward the back of the room. Misek ducks down. The pipe penetrated the slate blackboard behind him, leaving a triangular hole. Nicodemo put his head down, shaking it back and forth and calmly utters under his breath, "Misek, I told you to shut up." He continued to lecture as if nothing happened. Everyone in the class looked at each other in disbelief. After eight years in parochial school, I had never witnessed an act so violent. After the incident, Misek became a model student.

While I sat at the drafting table in the design class Mr. Rupp addressed the class. "Gentlemen, this is the freshman Introductory Design Course for Technical Students, where you will be taught drafting and design. Look around, gentlemen. By next year fifty percent of you will be gone, and by the beginning of your junior year we will whittle the class size down to fighting weight." Mr. Rupp's prediction that the drafting class enrollment would diminish was accurate. Four years later, I was one of nineteen students who graduated from the technical course.

Sometime later, there was a ruckus in the courtyard outside the academic building. Students lined up at the windows peering outside. A crowd surrounded a student who had his arms raised-up like a boxer. He circled around a man. While I looked out of the window, I asked a student. "Who are those people that are fighting?"

A student replied. "The man is Hartman, a shop teacher and the kid is Tate."

I asked. "Why are they fighting?"

He replied. "I don't' know?"

Tate danced around Hartman, as he threw jabs at his body. Hartman jabbed at Tate. The crowd increased in size as the noise echoed throughout the courtyard. The classroom windows were covered with students peering out at the fight. Then Hartman threw his body against Tate and restrained him. Moments later, several teachers arrived and broke up the fight. While walking to class, I always thought that public school offered more freedom and less punishment. That simply was not the case.

We sat in Physics class while Mr. Lipton held a book in his hand and wrote formulas on the blackboard. Domingo raised his hand during the lecture. "Can I go to the bathroom?"

Lipton turned around from the blackboard. "Put a rubber on it, Sonny." The class roared as Domingo looked down dejectedly. While Bracy talked with Rivera in the back of the room, Lipton yelled out to them, "Put a rubber on it, Sonnies." Lipton used the word 'rubber' to thwart disruptions in class. Students who paid attention in class avoided Lipton's comments. After all, who wants to be associated with a condom -- especially on your mouth?

During machine shop class, we sat on metal stools while Mr. Kupperman lectured at the blackboard regarding safety and rules of conduct in the shop. He was a man in his late fifties, average weight with sparsely curly hair, wearing black thick-framed glasses. Everyone paid attention and anxiously waited to operate the machines. We didn't care about the type of machine we'd operate, just anxious to use any one of them. Operating a metal cutting machine is more fun than listening to some boring lecture in English or history class. Kupperman maintained strict rules of conduct and safety. This was paramount to operating any machine shop equipment. We learned how to use all types of instruments to measure materials accurately to one thousandth of an inch. Having that knowledge, we produced all types of products by cutting, shaping and forming metals used in industry.

Safety lessons were mandatory before any equipment was used. When metal is cut, hot chips fly everywhere and can attach to your skin, causing burns. All jewelry needed to be -removed and any ties or loose clothing needed to be removed or tucked away.

Weeks later, Kupperman lectured at the blackboard and looked toward the back of the room and yelled, "Tate, shut up!" Several minutes later, Kupperman lifted up a metal stool above his shoulder, I ducked down. He hurled it about twenty feet toward the back of the room and yelled. "Tate, didn't I tell you to shut up!" We looked at each other in disbelief. Tate's eyes opened as wide as lemons as he squirmed into a corner like a scared rabbit.

At that time, the public education system used trade schools as a dumping ground for unruly or students that were unable to succeed in the traditional academic environment. There were some unruly students in the vocational program, but the students enrolled in the technical program were well behaved. Shop classes in trade schools helped your mind work in a different environment. Learning a trade is useful to earn income as opposed to boring classroom instruction. Trade schools prepare students for jobs in specific fields or as technicians in support roles in engineering and architecture where traditional schools do not. Historically trade schools have been underestimated for their value to society. Try to find a good plumber or carpenter today.

I was summoned to the guidance counselor's office one day, where Miss Hayward informed me that I needed to register for a language course in order to attend college. With a full schedule, I substituted my homeroom class and attended the 7 AM. Spanish class. It made for a long day ending classes at 3 PM.

Mr. Glantz taught Spanish. A man in his late forties, medium height, stocky build, with semi balding dark curly hair. Glantz was a polished educator, well-spoken but had an effeminate voice. He was a nice man and most of us believed he was gay. I wondered how he was assigned to teach in a trade school.

Glantz repeatedly corrected the Puerto Rican students regarding their usage of the Spanish language. He told the class, "Students, you are here to learn Castilian Spanish; forget the dialects, and slang, that you speak at home. Here you'll be tested on how well you master Castillion Spanish."

Glantz wore a dark suit and taught the class for the entire period as he stood in the corner of the room. I think he chose that position because it provided him with a clear view of the students to maintain order. Cruz talked with a classmate during the lecture. Glantz pointed at Cruz to stop talking. Cruz continued talking. Glantz waved his index finger at him and shook his head back and forth frowning. "Shouldn't do that." The class laughed. Cruz continued to talk. Glantz uttered, "Now settle down, settle down, perhaps you need a Japanese bath. That response always drew laughs from the students no matter how many times he said it.

During the spring of my freshman year, I worked part time after school as a messenger for the United Lawyers Service, located in lower Manhattan. At the end of the school day, I'd ride the downtown subway from 96th Street to Chambers Street near City Hall. At the office, I retrieved a leather portfolio and walked the route collecting legal documents from law firms throughout Manhattan. Upon completion of the route, I delivered the documents to the office for distribution.

During the summer, my parents spent a week on vacation in Long Beach about twenty-five miles from the Bronx. They rented rooms in a boarding house on New York Ave. Before the trip, I asked my father, "How can I work my job in Manhattan if we're on vacation in Long Beach?"

My father looked at me with a raised eyebrow. "Look, you take the Long Island Railroad to Manhattan and then transfer to the subway to get to work."

I looked at him. "The cost to commute from Long Beach to Manhattan for one week is thirteen dollars, and I only make fourteen."

My father pursed his lips. "If you want to keep your job, you'll need to suffer for a week." I wasn't happy about spending my entire salary to pay for travel, so I endured for one week. So much for a vacation.

One afternoon when I returned from school, Mom stood in the kitchen with a serious look on her face. "You have a letter in your room from, 'that girl' from Pennsylvania!" When I looked at the letter on my dresser, I noticed that it was opened. I sat on the bed and read the letter from Pat. A year earlier, I met her in Long Beach, and I had never corresponded with her. The letter was not an expression of love, but a friendly correspondence from her, expressing an interest in me. I guess she hoped that I'd write to her, but I did not. The content of the letter did not create a need for alarm on the part of my mother. Maybe she thought I might run-away from home and marry Pat. At the age of fifteen, my only plans were to play ball and finish high school. A one-time letter from a girl was not a big deal.

I returned to the kitchen looking at my mother. "Why did you open my letter?"

My mother put her head down and turned away not saying anything. I stared at her.

Angered at her I uttered. "This letter was not addressed to you, it was addressed to me!"

She did not respond. She ignored me as I returned to the bedroom and slammed the door. Mom was cold, and so cruel at times. She did not apologize for opening the letter. Her lack of respect for my privacy was troubling.

11

PART TIME JOBS

I walked into the kitchen while Mom washed the dishes. She turned to me. "You're going to get tested for allergies."

I remarked. "Why do I have to do that?"

Mom advised. "We have to know what you're allergic to because you sneeze and blow your nose in the spring and summer."

I pointed out. "My brother sneezes a lot in the summer. He sneezes repeatedly and I don't. Why isn't he getting tested?" I asked.

Mom uttered. "Never mind about your brother!"

I said. "When you and Dad smoke cigarettes, I sneeze, blow my nose and leave the room. Am I gonna get tested for cigarette smoke?"

Mom ignored me. "On Monday, after school, you take the train to Columbia Presbyterian Hospital on 168 Street in Manhattan for a three-thirty appointment."

I moaned. "Okay."

While I stood in line at Columbia Presbyterian Hospital, the nurse injected almost twenty different serums into my arm. They monitored the swelling to determine my body's reaction. The allergy test revealed that I was allergic to dust, ragweed and grass. During the next three years after school, I traveled to Columbia Hospital every two weeks to receive allergy shots. Allergic reactions were not noticeable to me prior to testing and I didn't notice any improvement after I received the injections, but I followed Mom's instructions.

At the end of my sophomore year, I responded to an ad for a sales job during the summer. Sales work was not a job for a shy, low self-esteemed person like me, but I thought that sales skills might be helpful.

At 9 a.m. I walked into the office of Family Publications located on Fordham Road in the Bronx. The office was empty except for a man seated at a desk. I looked at him. "Hi, I'm Neil; I'm here for the sales job."

He replied. "Hi, my name is John, I'm the manager. Have a seat in the other room there're two more guys coming."

John was in his thirties, short, thin build, with dark slicked back hair, wearing a gray shark- skin suit.

Minutes later John introduced me to Frankie and Johnny. "You guys are gonna work together. This is a copy of the pitch we use. You need you to study it, memorize it and when you're ready, I'll test you."

Later on, John walked over to me. "Okay, Neil, give me your pitch as if I was a customer."

"Hi, I'm Neil, one of the boys from the neighborhood..."

"Check three, as you hand the customer the card which contains the magazine selections,"

I looked at him. "What do we do after we give the customer the card?"

John said. "You get them to select the magazines they want and sign the card."

I asked. "What if they don't want to buy any magazines?"

He pointed out. "You tell them that they have several choices, and they only need to pay a small amount per week for a wide variety of the magazines of their choice."

After the pitch, the potential customer will be engaged to make a selection of at least three magazines of their choice. John explained, "It's important to keep potential customers focused on signing up for subscriptions." Once a customer agreed to a subscription the manager met with them and closed the deal.

The next morning at 9 a.m. we sat in the office as John introduced us to Pete, the route manager. A man in his late twenties, he was of average height, thin build and dark complexion. He wore a dark suit and tie, as he smoked a cigarette with an air of confidence. Pete dropped us off at a cluster of apartment buildings located on Mosholu Parkway in the Bronx.

We followed John's instructions. Starting at the top floor, I knocked on the door. The occupant responded. "Who is it?"

I replied. "Route check."

Most people that answered the door opened it out of curiosity. If the potential customer refused to open the door, we used the word 'Avon.' After the door was opened, I would smile at the customer saying: "Hi, I'm Neil Avon." Then I started my pitch. That approach always worked. After knocking on a few hundred doors, by the end of the day I was depressed. Some people are courteous, some don't answer and some will slam the door in your face. At the end of the day, I became more confident in dealing with people but no sales, no money.

I met Frankie after he finished the apartments across the street. "How'd you do?" I asked.

Frankie's eyes were downcast. "I couldn't sign up anybody." We sat together on the stoop outside the apartment building.

Pete rolled up driving a brand new red 1962 Ford Galaxie 500 XL convertible. He shouted, "Get in, boys!"

I said to him. "This is definitely the coolest car I have ever seen." Pete smiled, as his shirt collar was open, and his necktie was- lowered. He took a drag on a cigarette as if were a joint. This hot afternoon riding down the street with the top down in a red high-performance convertible, helped me forget about the day without a sale.

At the light, a car pulled alongside us revving the engine. Pete looked at us. "Guys, watch this." When the light turned green, Pete floored it. We raced along Mosholu Parkway, ahead of the hot rod as he hard braked at the red light. Pete looked over at the driver and in a put-on Latin accent yelled, "Hey meng, you got a cool car; it sound like a vaa....cuum cleaner."

We all laughed. When the light turned green, Pete gunned it, and my neck snapped back. We laughed all the way back to the office.

At the end of the second week, I signed up a few customers. Pete closed the deals. He convinced customers to purchase additional magazines, which increased my commission. One week I earned one hundred twenty-five dollars, which was fifty dollars more than my father's weekly salary. Commission is great when you have sales and terrible when you don't. It taught me to save for a rainy day.

After school, I couldn't wait to change into street clothes and run to the park to play basketball. We had good group of guys who played ball almost every day, and we remained friends over the years.

Some teenagers in the neighborhood were not interested in playing sports and preferred hanging out at the strip mall, gambling, or using drugs. The word was that the owner of the cab company floated loans to people who needed money. Gamblers are the loan shark's best customers. They believe that their next bet will bring them over the top. Charlie a neighborhood guy claimed he had a system for winning when gambling. Occasionally I'd ask him. "How are you doing with your gambling?" "Well, right now I'm a little ahead."

Six months earlier, when I asked him about his gambling he responded. "I'm a little behind."

I think most gamblers are in denial.

On the way to the park, Otto, a neighborhood kid walked over to me. "You want to play stickball for a dollar a game?"

"Okay." I'm not a gambler but I couldn't resist the chance to make easy money. We fast pitched against each other on the side of the strip mall.

A group of Otto's friends gathered around to watch us play stickball, as if he was some sort of leader. After I won two games, Otto quit. He paid me reluctantly and stared at me, "You ain't never been what I was." I didn't know what that meant, but I accepted his money and thanked him. That was the last time I was asked to play stickball for money.

The stickball game against Otto reminded me of the last time I played stickball in the old neighborhood. I walked toward the front door carrying my football equipment.

My mother stared at me. "You're not playing football anymore!"

I looked at her. "I have a game to go to."

She ordered. "You're not playing football; put those things back in your room!"

I moaned. "My friends are waiting for me."

Mom gritted her teeth. "You're being impudent, you're neurotic!"

I stood there shocked, as I watched my mother open the hall closet door and remove the black carpet sweeper handle that I used to play stickball. I ran down the hall towards the bedroom as Mom swatted me on the behind yelling.

"You're a street angel house devil; wait till your father gets home, just you wait!"

I sat on the bed in my room and waited a while. Then I opened the window lowering my football equipment to the ground. Walking towards the front door I turned to my mother. "I'm going to play basketball." My mother ignored me. I retrieved my football equipment outside and headed to the game where I played quarterback for our local team.

Several weeks later, the darkness covered the basketball court in the park as my friends and I headed our separate ways home. Walking on the pathway toward the apartment, Otto and Anthony confronted me. Anthony lived in the neighborhood, but he was not involved in playing sports. They stood in front of me. Otto glared at me. "Where ya… go'n?" I looked at them not responding. As I attempted to walk around Otto, Anthony grabbed me from behind. He restrained my arms. Fighting was something I avoided, but sometimes there is no choice. Otto punched me in the stomach. I tried to keep my stomach muscles flexed to reduce the pain. He applied pressure to the front of my body to keep me from getting away. Then Anthony jumped on my back and locked his arms around my neck, choking me. I had difficulty breathing. He increased the pressure around my neck as I carried him around. Wheezing loudly, I gasped for air. My legs became unstable since I was losing air. Seconds away from passing out my adrenalin kicked-in. With all my strength, I placed my arms on top of Anthony's shoulders and threw him over the four-foot chain link fence into the hedges. While I stood there, I wheezed and struggled to regain my breath. With anger on my face, I looked Otto in the eye. Now we were one on one. Otto slowly backed away. I don't know if he backed away because he feared me or frightened about my loud gasps for air. It appeared Otto sought retaliation for losing money to me when we played stickball. As I continued to walk home, I massaged my throat, slowly regaining my breath as my heart continued to beat like a drum. While I walked toward my apartment, the only thought was to regain my normal breathing. When I entered the apartment, I didn't say anything to my parents and headed straight for the bedroom. I lay on the bed, and thanked God that I survived the attack and barely avoided a crushed windpipe.

I have two uncles named Paul. Uncle Paul F. was the vice president of a small factory located in Mt Vernon just outside the Bronx. When he learned that I studied Mechanical Design and Construction in school he contacted me. "Neil, would you be interested in working at my shop on Saturdays?" I was surprised to hear from him. As a child, at times I overheard him refer to me as a ball buster. As an inquisitive child, I constantly looked- for things to do and sometimes it landed me in trouble. Looking back, I probably was a ball buster, but in a funny sort of way.

The factory contained manufacturing equipment including a lathe, milling machine, shaper and drill presses. I learned to use these machines in high school and hoped to show my talent to Uncle Paul.

On Saturday's I earned a dollar an hour hoping to gain work experience in the trade. The majority of the work in the factory consisted of organizing and clean-up. Uncle Paul said, "Hey, Neil, you can clean-up this area and sort out the fittings, and if you have any time left dump out those five gallon cans of screws and sort them out.""

I replied. "Okay."

The production machines did not operate on the weekends, so most of the time I worked alone. One afternoon, I heard a noise in the back of the factory. Behind the production machine stood a middle-aged man, medium height, dark wavy hair wearing a blue work shirt with a high neck white tee shirt. I asked him, "Who are you?"

He continued working. "I'm Joe the mechanic."

I said. "I didn't hear you come in."

He ignored me.

A few hours later Joe yelled over, "Hey, kid, hey kid, come here!"

I rushed over to him as he was dismantling the production machine. "What's going on?" I asked.

Joe looked at me. "Hey, kid, you got any fuel?"

I looked at him. "What?"

He said. "Do you have any fuel? "

I thought he needed a lubricating solvent.

I replied. "What kind of fuel?"

Joe gestured with his thumb in his mouth and his pinky finger pointing upward.

I said. "No, I don't have any."

I didn't feel that alcohol should be consumed when working on production machines that require close examination.

One day while working in the factory Harold, the owner called me into his office. "Neil, take my car to the hardware store and buy the items on this list."

"Okay. "His car was parked on the sidewalk, a few feet away from the front door. The black, 2-door 1964 Chevy Impala, with a red interior was less than a year old. Having never driven a car as cool as this, I started it up, put it in drive and headed toward the hardware store. When I braked at the stop sign, I heard a loud thump behind the front seat. I pulled over to the curb, opened the door and folded down the seat. I jumped back startled while a man laid on the floor. I didn't know if he was dead or alive. My heart pounded like a drum. Shocked as I looked at the guy, I nervously yelled, "Get the fuck out of the car!"

The guy slowly sat up in the seat not saying anything and climbed out. I yelled at him, "Stay the fuck away from my car! " Later on, I learned that he may have been homeless and needed a place to take a nap, choosing the boss' car. He scared the daylights out of me. Ever since that day, I check the back seat before entering any car.

On a hot summer day in August, Uncle Paul walked over to me in the back of the factory. "Neil, you see that melting pot, that contains liquid zinc?"

I said "Yeah."

He pointed out. "Using the ladle, pour the zinc into the molds on the floor to make the five pound ingots."

I replied. "Okay."

He mentioned. "When the zinc hardens, turn the mold over, let it cool and make as many ingots as you can."

I said. "Okay."

The molds sat on the floor as the heat waves emanated from the melting pot. The high-speed fans circulated the air around the shop, but the temperature near the melting pot seemed to be unaffected. I dipped the ladle into the eight hundred-degree molten zinc and poured it into each mold one by one. The sweat dripped down my forehead as my tee shirt became saturated with sweat. While filling the molds I became careless and splashed liquid zinc. A droplet the size of a quarter traveled into the air and landed on top of my hand searing into my skin. I yelled out and shook it off immediately. Rushing into the bathroom, I ran cold water on the burn for several minutes to try to reduce the pain which didn't help that much. While holding a wet towel on my hand, I walked into the office. The bookkeeper Mrs. Urz turned to me. "Neil, what happened?"

I uttered. "I dropped liquid zinc on my hand."

She said. "Oh, you poor dear, let me see if we have something for that."

I moaned. "I hope so."

She replied. "I'll put this ointment on it, but you should see a doctor when you get home."

I said. "Thanks a lot."

When I arrived home from work, we all sat at the dinner table while Mom served dinner. She looked down at me. "What's those Band Aids on your hand?"

I pointed out. "I dropped liquid zinc on it."

Mom looked away. "Oh."

The scarring from the burn slowly decreased to an oblong shape, remaining visible for more than forty years.

12

SPORTS

My commitment to organized sports started when I was ten years old. While visiting my grandfather, I found him sitting in the living room watching the Yankee game. He loved baseball. During the 1956 season, Mickey Mantle hit home runs from both sides of the plate for a record third time. My grandfather didn't talk much, but when he learned that I played baseball, it became the topic of discussion when I visited him. A thin man, six feet tall wearing amber colored wide-rimmed glasses, he worked as an electrician. Every morning at breakfast, he toasted ten to twelve slices of Duggan's whole wheat bread. He lined the slices up on the countertop like soldiers, smearing on butter and then washed them down with a half a pot of coffee. I think his metabolism and the activity at work burned up the calories during the day.

I stood next to Grandpa as he looked at me. "So, you're playing baseball now, Boy?" He always called me boy. I don't know why.

I replied, "I signed up late for the organized Little League team, so they put me in the clinic." The clinic was set-up for ball players that needed to improve their skills or registered late for the league.

He handed me two books. "I want you to have these baseball books. Read them; you might learn some things that can help you in baseball."

I said. "Really?"

He nodded his head. "You read them, Boy."

I agreed. "Okay."

The Little League field on Zerega Ave. in the Bronx was an empty lot set below the level of the street. The infield contained small craters and stones absent of grass while the outfield contained sparse patches of weeds.

While I fielded balls in the outfield, the coach directed me to the batter's box. He pitched balls to me while I hit one after another. When the baseball clinic ended, a man walked over to me. "My name is Charlie Monaco and I'm the manager of the ESKA Club." He stood tall, with olive skin, unshaven, muscular arms with hands the size of a baseball mitt. "Would you like to play for my team?"

I looked up at him smiling. "Sure."

He said. "Come here to practice on Tuesday at five o'clock."

I responded. "Okay."

On Tuesday, I arrived at the ballfield and shagged fly balls in the outfield. Later on, the manager directed me to the batter's box. Any pitch that was near the plate, I hit. Charlie yelled at John while he played first base. "Get in front of the ball; it won't hurt cha." Charlie stood behind home plate in the catcher's position and yelled to the pitcher, "Pitch to me as hard as you can." Charlie caught two or three pitches with his bare hands as an example for us not to be afraid of the ball. Charlie said, "You see, the ball won't hurt cha." After I finished batting Charlie said. "Neil, go to first base."

At the end of practice, Charlie walked over to me. "Neil, from now on your position is first base."

I eyed him with uncertainty. "I don't have a first baseman's mitt, this is a fielder's mitt."

He stared down at me. "I don't care what kind of glove you got, as long as you keep catching the ball."

Smiling at him, I said, "Okay."

At that moment Charlie benched John, the Coach's son and assigned me to play first base.

The next week, I dressed in a gray baseball uniform with yellow trim and a yellow cap with a large red colored E on the front. The uniform was a boost to my self-confidence and pride. As member of a team we relied on each other that built comradery.

Two seasons later, I saved up money from my newspaper route and bought a first baseman's glove at a local sporting goods store. After soaking the glove with Neatsfoot oil, I placed a ball inside and tied a string around it for a few days to break it in.

On my way to practice, I met Tommy Ponticelli at his house on Virgil Place. Tommy played shortstop and third base for our team. He was a good all-around ball player. Tommy said, "You got a new glove."

I replied. "Yeah, I just bought it."

He slipped it on his hand and punched it a few times. "Nice, you broke it in already."

I said. "Yeah," shaking my head.

Tommy nodded in agreement.

While walking to the ball field, we met Eddie Kranepool who was returning from baseball practice. Years later, Kranepool played professional baseball for the New York Mets from 1962 to 1979. Tommy introduced me to Eddie since he lived in the neighborhood. Eddie was older and had played first base on our team a few years earlier. Eddie was well-known in the baseball community for his consistent hitting ability; the newspapers had written frequently about his high level of performance.

Nodding his head toward me, Tommy said to Eddie, "He just bought a new first baseman's glove."

Eddie said. "Oh yeah, let's see it."

He slipped the glove onto his hand, and returned it to me as he clenched his lips and shrugged his shoulders. He looked at me with raised eyebrows. Eddie held up his first baseman's glove and declared. "This is my glove."

It was larger and higher quality than mine as he stood there with a smirk on his face.

Eddie commented. "Now, that's a first baseman's mitt."

I was humiliated by Eddie's arrogant display that his glove was better than mine.

The first time I noticed the glove in the sporting goods store, I knew I had to have it. After saving for almost a year I refused to let Kranepool's disparaging comment affect my baseball abilities.

We played softball during gym class on a fenced-in asphalt surface adjacent to the high school. Mr. Altman, the gym teacher approached me. "Neil, why don't you try out for the baseball team?"

Puzzled, I said, "I didn't see a baseball field nearby, where does the team play?"

He pointed out. "We use the ball fields in Central Park and travel to the home fields of our opponents."

I said. "Okay, I'll try out."

The next week I tried out for the high school baseball team and was assigned a starting position at first base as a sophomore.

A few weeks later we traveled to James Monroe High School located in the Bronx for an exhibition game. Ed Kranepool played first base for Monroe, and at that time, the major- league scouts paid closer attention to him.

Kranepool batted with a man on base. With two outs, he fell behind in the count. On the next pitch, he struck out. I laughed at him. He threw the bat down the first base line at me. I said to myself, that was not sportsman-like behavior. Razzing opponents in sports is accepted behavior including professional sports.

The next inning, I singled to right field. As I led off first base, Kranepool snarled at me. Eddie was known to have poor sportsmanlike qualities.

I received the mail today.

Below is a recreation of the letter sent to me.

Dear Neil,   *July 5, 1963*

You have been selected to try out for the Journal American All-Star team on July 15, 1962 at 9 AM at the Parade Grounds Baseball Park located in Brooklyn New York. The Hearst Sandlot Classic will host the United States All-Star team vs the New York All-Star team at Yankee Stadium on August 15, 1962.

One hundred selectees will tryout and twenty- five finalists will be chosen to create the New York All-Stars. The Journal American Ali-Stars will compete against the Unites States Al-Stars at Yankee Stadium on August 14, 1963.

Tommy Holmes
Manager, Hearst Sandlot Classic
Journal American All-Star Team

I sat on the edge of my bed as I read the letter in shock that I had been-selected for the tryout. When my father arrived home from work, I met him at the door. "Dad, can you drive me next week to the Parade Grounds in Brooklyn for a baseball tryout for the Journal American All-Star team."

With a surprised look on his face, he asked, "What's that?"

I informed him. "On Wednesday August 14, 1963, the Journal American All-Stars will play against the United States Stars in the Hearst Sandlot Classic at Yankee Stadium," I asserted with pride.

My father replied, "Okay, I'll drive you there."

If a miracle were to occur and I made the team, I'd be playing at Yankee Stadium on the same field the greatest baseball players of all time, like Babe Ruth and many others have played. It reminded me of the time a few years earlier, when Tommy and I traveled on the bus and subway to Yankee Stadium in the west Bronx. The only seats we could afford were the seventy-five cents bleacher seats, in right center field. We didn't care. Walking into Yankee Stadium where the echoing sound of thousands of fans sent a chill up and down my spine. Tommy and I sat on the bench seat with no back, as I stared at the dark green manicured lawn abutting the burnt orange clay soil. The panoramic view of thousands of grandstand seats reaching over a hundred feet in height capped off by the white façade was breathtaking. We sat on the edge of the bench glued to the presence of the Yankee ballplayers in person.

We hoped to see Mickey Mantle, as players fielded balls, wearing the legendary pinstriped New York Yankee uniforms. Mickey never arrived in center field until the game started. Just to be in his presence and watch the back of number seven, was a memorable experience.

The day of the try-outs, my father dropped me off at the Parade Grounds in Brooklyn where I checked-in at the field desk. They attached a number to my back.

It appeared unusual that the inclined bleachers were filled to capacity with all middle-aged men at nine o'clock in the morning. I asked a player at the registration desk, "Who are those men sitting in the stands?"

He replied. "Those guys are scouts for the major league baseball teams."

I said. "Are you kidding me?"

I knew I had to step up my game. The men in the bleachers were going to scrutinize every move I made on the field, and they had the power to decide my future based on my ability. I was shocked to learn that all of the fans seated in the bleachers are major league scouts.

The majority of the tryout players were proficient hitters and fielders, and larger in stature, unlike anyone that I had faced as a baseball player. As a one hundred fifty pound sixteen-year old, I had never competed with baseball players of such high caliber.

The coach directed me to first base. The coaches cycled us for a few innings through our positions and batting. I felt I had done well at first base scooping up three or four bad throws from the infielders. By the end of the first-round, fifty prospects were eliminated from the original one hundred players. I was shocked that I made the first cut.

At the next round of tryouts, I faced Joe DeLuise, a right-handed pitcher who was later signed by the majors. His fastball clocked-in the low ninety-mile an-hour range. I singled and the next time up I grounded out.

Batting against DeLuise reminded me of a game we played against George Washington High School, in upper Manhattan. We were down by two runs. The pitcher threw in the ninety-mile an hour range allowing no hits. With one man on base I swung at the first pitch, barely getting my bat around and hit the ball to the opposite field. The catcher stood up and yelled. "Ho....ly shit." The ball cleared the left field fence. We tied the score. At that time, I had figured that most pitchers generally threw a strike on the first pitch. I became a first pitch hitter and found that to be successful for me throughout my career.

The New York Journal American All-Star Baseball Team consisted of twenty-five of the top prospects from the five boroughs of New York. Several players received contracts from major league baseball teams. After competing at the tryout and watching the high caliber of ball players, I realized that I did not possess the ability to play professional baseball. I lacked the physical characteristics, the speed, dexterity and power required to play major league baseball. I loved the competition surrounded by players that performed at a higher-level than I had ever experienced before. It makes you better and improves your performance. For years after the tryout, I continued to play organized baseball.

The following week I received a letter listing the names of the players selected for the New York All Star team. I didn't make the team. I'll never forget the opportunity to have played on the same field with a group of highly skilled ball players in my career.

The effect that sports made on my life was not realized until years later. Being quiet and shy, I felt somewhat isolated in my family. Sports provided me with a strong sense of belonging and mutual respect. It helped me to cope with my limitations. When I played baseball, I experienced moments of glory scooping up a bad throw or batted out hits. As part of a baseball team the bonding and approval was a major factor in helping me cope with success and failure.

Years later, I worked a home remodeling project for a customer named Al Cucinello. He worked as a baseball scout for the New York Yankees. Al walked into the basement and looked at me. "Listen, I want you to make me a cedar closet where I can protect these Yankee uniforms."

I mentioned. "You know in 1963 I had a tryout for the New York Journal American All-Star team."

Al was not impressed. He relayed a common story during tryouts as a Yankee scout. Al said, "I've watched many baseball prospects over the years. One day my neighbor George approached me." He asked me. "Al, would it be possible for my son to try-out for the Yankees? He played varsity baseball, batting over .350. He's fast and he has a good arm. Can you take a look at him?"

He directed. "Have your son come down to Yankee stadium for tryouts in August."

When the tryout ended, George looked at me.

He asked, "Al, how did my son do?"

Al pointed out. "Tell your son to go to college."

Al looked at me. "Neil, I've seen hundreds and hundreds of ballplayers tryout for the Yankees and one thing we look for in a ball player is the ability to throw a ball a long distance, with top spin, so when the ball hits the ground, it's propelled forward."

I replied. "I never knew that. I wondered why I was never taught to throw a ball with top spin all the years I played baseball. No wonder I never made it to the major leagues ha ha ha." Al laughed.

13

SUMMER

On a warm summer day late in the morning, I sat in the Number 13 bus heading towards the subway. I transferred to the elevated subway to Pelham Bay and boarded the bus toward the Pelham Bay Golf Course. Looking for work as a caddy, I sat alone in the staging area. I stopped a park employee as he passed by. "Is this the caddy area?"

He pointed out. "Yeah, everybody already teed –off. You need to get here early in the morning, if you want to get work."

I said. "Okay, thanks."

While seated on the bench, a man approached me. "Hey kid, are you a caddy?"

I yelled. "Yeah."

He said. "My name is Lou, here's my bag."

Lou was in his thirties, short and stocky, with a round face. He reminded me of the actor Mickey Rooney, the five-foot three, bundle of dynamite. I put my hand through the strap of the oversized golf bag and placed it on my shoulder. Lou looked at me. "Kid, you can put the bag down, I'm waiting for the rest of my group."

I replied. "Okay."

Minutes later three guys walk over to me. "Hey kid, we need to put our stuff in Lou's bag." They loaded up his bag, to lighten up their load on their own bags.

Not knowing anything about caddying, I figured how hard could it be. At the first hole, Lou asked for a driver and we were on our way. The first hole was a par five and Lou managed a seven. Of the four golfers, Lou was the worst player and the guys picked on him.

At the eighth hole, Lou and John hit their balls into the rough. We located the balls a short distance away from each other. Lou turned to me. "Give me a nine iron." I handed it to him. He lined up the shot and swung.

John stood nearby and said, "Lou, that was a good shot, I didn't see the ball, but I think it's up on the green." I didn't see a ball in the air. I bent down where Lou had swung. The ground was soft, and I placed my hand into the hole and removed the ball. Lou had driven the ball underground. I held it up. "Here's the ball." Lou's jaw dropped.

John looked over laughing hysterically. "Lou, I … can't believe you did that, ha, ha, ha. You swung and buried the ball underground, ha, ha, ha. The kid, ha, ha, ha, the kid pulled it out, ha. ha, ha. I'm never gonna forget this as long as I live."

The other guys walked over, and now everybody's laughing. Lou was red faced and filled with rage. He ignored me and remained silent. At the next hole, Lou turned to me, now speaking angrily. "You should've left the ball there!"

I was red- faced and embarrassed by his comment. ignoring the shot and dropping the ball somewhere else, did not enter my mind.

Lou maintained his anger at me, as I followed him through the course. The guys in the group continued laughing all the way to the eighteenth hole. Relieved that we were finished, I carried Lou's bag to his car. Lou remained angry, and he was reluctant to give me a tip. John said to him, "Lou, you need to give the kid a tip. After all, he did carry your bag for eighteen holes." Caddies were not employed by the golf course, there was no salary. They only earned their money from the tips given to them by the players. As Lou stood there embarrassed, he reluctantly handed me five dollars. I thanked him. John glared at Lou and clenched his lips.

John walked over to me. "Hey kid, take this, take this." He handed me a few dollars and said. "Kid, you made my day, I'll will never forget this as long as I live." John wasn't alone I never forgot that day myself.

Weeks later on a warm August day, my friend John Clohessy and I shot hoops in the park on Randall Ave. as the heat waves rose from the asphalt court.

John asked me, "Do you have any money for carfare to the beach?"

I said. "I only have a quarter."

John suggested. "It's pretty hot, why don't we sneak into the Castle Hill Beach Club for a swim?"

I looked at him. "How do we get in?"

John uttered. "Let's walk down there, I'll show you."

We stood on the perimeter of the beach club, peering in through the six-foot chain link fence with three rows of barbed wire on top. The temperature increased as the sun stood almost directly above us. Many of the lounge chairs were occupied by sunbathers as some of them applied sunscreen lotion to each other. The security guard walked through the area. John said, "There's Blackie the security guard, he's on the lookout for people who are not members."

Blackie, a dark tanned Italian guy diligently worked security at the pool wearing a blue uniform and policeman style hat with a square badge. When living in the Bronx nicknames are commonplace.

I looked at John. "That woman on the lounge chair keeps waving at us, do you know her?"

John replied. "No, but I think she's motioning that the coast is clear for us to come in."

I replied. "Why would she do that?"

He said. "I don't know, let's go."

We scaled the fence, over the barbed wire and tumbled onto the grass. We split up and headed toward the outdoor lockers. While standing in the locker area I started to uncover my swim suit. I heard a ruckus nearby and looked up as I watched the entire row of wooden lockers being overturned. Seconds later, John ran over to me. "Come on, come on, let's get out of here!"

I said. "What happened?"

John said. "I just had a fight with Blackie."

We ran towards the entrance, through the gate, out the door and up the street.

I asked him. "What happened?"

John quickly explained, "Blackie asked me for my pass. Then he started to get physical with me, so I knocked him down."

I uttered. "John, you knocked over the entire row of lockers."

He described. "Well I hit him, and he fell against the lockers."

I said. "Does that mean we can't go back there I asked half-seriously."

He smiled. "Yeah."

At the age of fifteen John Clohessy maintained a powerful punch. One day John and I were horsing around with each other and he hit me. I had it coming. Thank God, he punched me in the arm because any other place would have caused an injury. His punch had the power of a jackhammer. I knew someday that John had the potential to become a successful boxer.

John was an easy going and loyal friend. He was protective of our group of friends. For years, we played basketball with the black and Puerto Rican kids in the neighborhood without any incidents. Except for this one time when playing basketball. Richie, a six foot five black guy, had words with John during a game in the park.

The next day, John and I sat inside the luncheonette at the strip mall. Richie walked in and looked at John. "Let's finish up from yesterday."

John walked outside and stood with his back to Richie. John yelled to Richie, "Are you ready?" Richie acknowledged him. John turned around with a clenched fist and hit Richie in the jaw, knocking him down to the ground. At six foot-five, he dropped to the ground like a log.

John Clohessy later became a professional boxer with twenty-two professional fights to his credit. He lost to Chuck Wepner in his hometown of Bayonne, New Jersey. Had the fight taken place in New York, in John's hometown the outcome may have been different. Wepner went on to fight

Mohammed Ali. John's brother Robert Clohessy is an actor who can be seen on the TV series "Blue Bloods."

Two years later John received financial assistance to play college football for Colorado College located in Denver, Colorado. John readied for the trip. A group of us gathered outside of the luncheonette while John described the landscape of Colorado Springs. "You've never seen anything like it; these giant colored rocks stick-up out of the ground like 50 to 100 feet in height. In the summer, you can see the snow on Pike's Peak Mountain, it's high up in the clouds."

Larry held his hands up to his chest motioning with his fingers. "Why don't the four of us drive to Colorado, drop John off at school and see the sights?"

I looked at everyone. "I like the sound of that."

Guy offered, "I'll use my car." We all nodded in agreement.

The following week, Larry, John and myself loaded Guy's 1962 Chevy Bel Air as we headed toward the George Washington Bridge. We entered route 80 heading westbound, relieved that we cleared the heavy New York City traffic. Traveling and exploring new areas of the country for the first time was refreshing for us. We all felt good about the trip, unaware of the importance of a vacation and its effect on our mental health.

We alternated driving about twelve to fourteen hours a day. We hoped to make the trip in two days.

Late in the afternoon I was driving west on interstate 80 in Elkhardt, Indiana. A police car pulled me over. The trooper walked up to the car as I rolled down my window. I stared at his gun belt, and with his hat on he was about 6- foot- 10". He looked down at me and said, "You were driving over the limit, license and registration."

I looked at him. "I'm sorry, officer, I guess I was."

He ordered. "Well, this is the way it works, son: You can pay the fine right here which is $23.25; or you can spend the night in jail and appear before the judge in the morning."

Larry exited the car and walked over to the officer. "I'm a police officer with NYPD, can you extend us some professional courtesy?"

The officer looked at Larry's ID and returned it to him. "Well, Larry, if you were driving, it'd be a different story, but you should've shut him down."

I looked at the police officer. "We'll pay the $23.25 and be on our way."

As we continued driving, Larry continued joking about the officer's comment to slow me down. In fact, each time I sat behind the wheel, Larry repeated the officer's comment verbatim. Any time we needed a laugh the officer's comment brought laughter even until this day. Humor was the driving force that seemed to kept us going.

Money was tight for us on the trip, so we registered in a hotel for two and four of us slept in the room. By the second day we traveled on route 80 and observed the Rocky Mountains for the first time, having never seen such a vast mountain range in our entire lives. We headed south on route 76 toward Denver and observed the snow-capped Pikes Peak in August as it stood at 14,000 feet. Our eyes were glued to the magnificence of the mountain while we traveled.

We entered Colorado Springs where the red rock sandstone formations with pink and white tones coordinated with the backdrop of Pikes Peak. The brilliant blue sky above the mountains was breath- taking to say the least.

We arrived at the college dorms where we unloaded John's suitcases. He was grateful. The four of us were raised in families of modest means and John was the first in our group to receive an athletic scholarship. We said our goodbyes and wished him success.

Mr. Altman, the baseball coach, walked into my design class. "Neil, I sent your batting average record to the *Daily News* for posting in the sports section for honorable mention in the New York City Baseball League."

I said. "Thanks, I'll look for it."

At the end of my junior year in high school, I finished the season with a .363 batting average.

In June 1963, at the end of my junior year, I had not applied to any colleges. I received a letter from Denison University, outlining the details of their offer. I couldn't believe that I was being recognized by people that I had never met. I walked into the kitchen. "Mom, look at this letter, I've been offered to play baseball for a college in Ohio."

Without looking at the letter, she turned away. "You're not going anywhere; I'm not having you out of this house, like when your brother was away in the Navy!"

I looked at her. "Why not, it's an offer to attend college and play baseball."

Raising her index finger in the air, she started speaking in a loud voice. "I told you, you're not going anywhere; you're going to finish high school and become a locksmith!"

I uttered. "A locksmith, I don't want to be a locksmith. I'm going to college!"

My high school curriculum provided me with artistic and creative training besides learning math, science and engineering drafting; the skills to work as a tool and die maker or in a support role in the engineering field, if I did not attend college. I walked into the bedroom and slammed the door shut in disgust. My mother dismissed the fact that my high school curriculum consisted of not only shop classes but valuable courses in: machine design, strength of materials, geometry, trigonometry, physics, chemistry, and at the end of the senior year, a rigorous six hour New York State Regents exam in mechanical design and construction. It consisted of courses that were more valuable and offered greater potential, than working as a locksmith. My mother already planned my career. but she forgot to inform me.

Years later at a social event, I was seated next to a man who received a Master's Degree, and was working as a teacher. When he asked me about my education I said, "I have a Ph.D. in Mechanical Design and Construction from Machine and Metal Trades High School."

With a surprised look on his face. "How, is that possible?

Looking at him with a straight face, I said. "You go there."

We laughed together. Believe it or not the courses I studied in high school provided me with knowledge that far surpassed what I learned in college.

A partial or full scholarship is a valuable commodity, especially when your family lacks the funds. After my mother disapproved of the college offer, I started to wonder if her decisions were an attempt to keep me from becoming successful. The probability of offers for a baseball scholarship was good, but I wasn't willing to get my hopes up to have them denied by her. I was depressed by my Mom's rejection of the offer to play baseball. I never approached my father about the letter, because my mother always convinces him to side with her. I realized that sports served to distract me from what was really going on in my home.

I decided to forgo varsity baseball as a senior and work a part-time job after school. Saving money to pay for college locally was my main concern.

Continuing to play baseball, I participated in the sandlot league for the Port Castle Baseball team and the CYO team playing double and triple headers on the weekend.

On a cold winter day after school, Larry and I walked into my apartment while Mom watched soap operas. A good time of the year to build-up our muscles in order to impress the girls at the beach the following summer. We lifted weights in my bedroom for about an hour and then Larry headed home. My mother walked into my bedroom. "Why did you bring him home with you?"

I told her, "We wanted to lift weights. Can't I bring my friends home without you saying anything? That's why I don't bring my friends home. You always criticize everything I do."

My mother's eyes opened wide as she clenched her teeth not answering me and walked out of the room. I slammed the door shut.

It occurred to me that the only time my mother spoke to me was out of necessity. The extent of our conversations consisted of: "Neil, it's time to eat." Or "Neil, be home at six o'clock." Or "Neil, take out the garbage." I never heard the words, "Neil, come over here and talk to me. Tell me about your day in school."

I couldn't understand what I did wrong to be treated that way? I knew I wasn't a bad kid, but I felt like an outsider. When my mother spoke on the telephone to her friends and relatives, she talked for hours. She talked with everybody but me. I might as well be a stranger, or invisible, for the attention she paid to me.

14

PRESSURE

More than three years had passed since the rift with my parents.

In March of 1983, I received a letter from my father's brother Paul B., who lives in Florida:

Dear Joann and Neil:

> *Thank for your letter and gifts for my grandchildren. It was nice of you to write to Helen and me.*
>
> *I'm taking this occasion to ask both of you to clarify a situation that has arisen three years ago between your family and my brother and Marion. Recently I was informed by my brother that he and Marion have not seen Victor and Christopher for over three years now. This appalling situation stunned me. Upon further questioning my brother and Marion, they emphatically denied ever giving either of you, provocation for assuming this position.*
>
> *Not only are they denied seeing the children, but Neil does not wish to talk to his parents, nor even want to know they exist, nor communicate with Richard or Merita.*
>
> *In your letter to me and Helen, you state, "We are sure you are very happy being close to your children and their families." How can you say this, when you prohibit your children from seeing their grandparents for the last three years. Why should my brother and Marion suffer?*
>
> *Both of you must have a very compelling reason to assume this abnormal attitude. I wish to know what the reason is, in*

order to put my mind at rest. You would have to have a very solid reason to base your decision on.

May I call your attention to the fact that if we did not have our parents, none of us would be born into this world. We owe our very existence to our parents, every human in this world. In China parents are highly respected, more so than in other nations. This respect to our parents, was preached by Christ himself as one of the Ten Commandments. Last Tuesday evening March 15, CBS News had a segment on the legal rights of grandparents to see their grandchildren when unduly denied. Also, a book written on this subject. There is a state law to provide for their rights. I am going to recommend to my brother and Marion to act legally for the inherent right they have to see Victor and Christopher, unless you have something concrete, as to why they should not.

May I hear from you soon.

Respectfully yours

Uncle Paul B.

Uncle Paul's recommendation that my father take legal action against us was frightening, since my father moonlighted transcribing court cases from the Surrogates Court. He sectioned off part of the bedroom where he made a sound-proof cubicle listening to tape recorded testimony and transcribed it, using a high–speed electric typewriter. Depending on the locale, Surrogate Courts conducted matters such as adoptions, guardianship and related family matters. Aware of my father's knowledge of court procedure and attorney litigation, I found it worrisome.

When I lived at home, my bedroom was adjacent to where my parents slept. At times, I heard my parents involved in lengthy discussions regarding some of the details of the cases Dad transcribed. These details were never discussed in my presence.

Shortly thereafter I was contacted by the school nurse at St Mary's parochial school where my children attended. I met with her in her office. While standing there she looked at me.

"Your son is very thin. Is he getting enough nourishment?

I looked at her. "My son has a good appetite. He eats everything and has no desire for additional food."

She looked at me. "Why is he so thin?

I replied. "Maybe he has a high metabolism and burns up the food. I hope you're not suggesting that we don't provide enough nourishment for him?"

She paused for a moment and looked at me with apprehension.

"Well, you know he is very thin."

I looked at her angrily. "Why don't we have the principal join us in the conversation?"

The principal walked in and after I explained the content of the discussion with the nurse he immediately ended the meeting. I didn't think too much about the issue. Months later my wife was at the school where she occasionally worked as a volunteer. She stood in the hall outside the office while a female staff member spoke loudly on the telephone. She heard, "Yes, Mrs. Buonocore, okay, Mrs. Buonocore, goodbye Mrs. Buonocore."

My wife heard her name mentioned and walked into the office. "I'm the only Mrs. Buonocore that has children attending school here!"

The woman's face turned red, she put her head down and was non-responsive. We learned that my parents were making inquiries at the school to gain information about our children without our consent. If my parents wanted to know about their grandchildren they could have called or visited with them but they chose not to do so. They wanted everything on their terms. Creating a cloud of suspicion on their son and his children is a manipulative action that created dissention. The nurse's inquiries concerning the food that we provided for my children for proper health were heading in the direction of labeling us as unfit parents. Those inquiries did not reflect favorably on us as a family and created mistrust by the school staff.

After the rift with my parents, over the years, there were several instances where cars parked near my home as the occupants watched our activity. There were occasions where my wife had been followed, which had not occurred prior to the estrangement from my parents. Shortly after the rift on several occasions, I noticed a maroon Toyota parked near our home. On one occasion the driver parked in front of our house as there were no cars parked on the street and walked across the street to my neighbor's house. After the driver left, I knocked on my neighbor's door. "Joe, If you don't mind me asking, who was that woman that came to your door earlier?"

He said. "She asked if I had seen any unusual behavior with your children."

I asked. "Did she give any more information than that?"

He replied. "No, she just said anything unusual."

I insisted. "Who is she working for?"

Joe said. "She didn't say."

I asked, "Did she have any identification or a business card?"

He replied. "No."

I suggested. "If she or anyone contacts you about my family I'd appreciate it if you would let me know?"

He said "Absolutely Neil"

I replied. "Thanks."

There were several occasions when the same car parked near the house for hours. One day I approached the driver. "Can I help you?"

The driver responded. "I'm waiting for someone.?"

I said. "Why don't you wait in a different area."

The driver immediately left the area. When I looked further into the driver's background, I learned that she was a private investigator. A private investigator is not required to disclose the name of their client since it is confidential. If the investigator is working directly for an attorney, their disclosure is protected by the attorney client privilege. These surveillances coincided with the pressures we experienced since the rift started with my parents.

Late one evening I heard an explosion in the front of the house. I looked outside as the smoke rose from the front of the driveway. I didn't know what to make of it, but the noise was greater than a cherry bomb. I walked closer to the road and noticed that my mailbox had been blown up. The metal mailbox was unrecognizable except for the base attached to the wooden post. It appeared that someone used a high powdered explosive possibly an M80. That was the only explosion I heard that evening. I didn't know what to make of the explosion so I contacted the police department as the Postal Service suggested. I removed the damaged mailbox and post and opened up a post office box at the local post office for mail delivery.

If my parents pursued a 'grandparent's rights' case against us, Uncle John my mother's brother and his wife were the only family members that might support our position. The only drawback was that they spent most of the year in Florida and I was unsure if their support would be available to help us if we entered litigation.

We arrived at Uncle John's house as he and Aunt Terry packed their camper van. They were 'Snowbirds' who spent most of the year in Florida and traveling throughout the country. As a child and after I was married, our families spent the holidays together at each other's home. Whenever Uncle John visited, he examined my hair and smiled at me. "Hey, Gagootz."

I always laughed. At times, he called me 'gagootz. I didn't know the meaning of the word, but it sounded funny. Translated in his Sicilian dialect 'gagootz' is defined as 'head like a cucumber or a squash'. Uncle John looked at me. "You need a trim, sit down." In his earlier profession, he worked as a barber. While he cut my hair, he smiled and occasionally uttered 'gagootz'. We'd laugh together. It never took much effort for me to laugh. Even at a young age, I was easily amused. Uncle John was a quiet man who avoided conflict at all cost. He was devoted to his mother, who now lived with my parents. His wife, Terry was a more confident and outspoken person and disliked by my mother.

We sat at the kitchen table.

I said. "I'm ashamed of my parents' behavior. They have not disclosed to the family their behavior at my house which created the estrangement between us."

Aunt Terry told me. "Your mother wants to shame you and break your spirit. Early on when the dispute started with your parents

I asked your mother. "What's going on with Neil?"

She responded in a surprised tone of voice. "Oh, …I don't know, …we don't see them…we don't know what's going on with them."

I looked at her. "You have just reinforced my feelings all along. As it stands right now, I feel that I have lost them through detachment. They have mistaken my quietness for weakness. We have been removed from the Christmas card list because we are not receiving cards from the immediate and extended family anymore. I don't know anyone in the family that I have disrespected or have given just cause to stop sending Christmas cards and ending their contact with us. It appears that the negative gossip about us has spread throughout the family. I read somewhere that gossip is like taking a down feathered pillow, slicing it open and emptying the contents into the wind, waiting a moment and try to recover all of the feathers and stuff them back into the pillow. You can never get the feathers back. Once a story leaves your mouth you never know where it ends up."

They both looked at me not saying anything.

I pointed out. "After the incident with my parents on the second day of January and for a number of months thereafter we've been receiving numerous hang up calls. All the calls we received were made during the day within a two- hour time frame."

Uncle John looked at me. "I can tell you that we have seen your mother on a few occasions, using the pay phone located outside of the post office two blocks from her house."

I informed him, "There's no reason for her to use a pay phone in close proximity to where she lives, she has a phone in her home. She doesn't want a record of the calls made from her house."

Uncle John clenched his lips.

I mentioned. "My parents' actions are causing me to live in fear of rejection and isolation from any family member or relative. It has been almost four years and I have not heard one word from my brother or sister since this impasse started. It appears that there is no one in the extended family that has attempted to contact us. My parents have betrayed my trust and have damaged their parental and grandparent relationship."

Aunt Terry looked down for a moment, and then she made direct eye contact with me. "Neil, I'm not going to get into it, but we don't get along with your parents, so it's easier for us to be away from here during the holidays and most of the year. Being retired, we spend most of our time in Florida avoiding any situations that cause us unpleasantness."

I said, "When you're away, we don't have anyone to share the holidays with and enjoy each other's company and they know that."

She said. "Neil, you know what is best for you and your family, and that's how you handle your situation. Right now, you cannot travel like us and get away from here because you're working. Maybe you should consider moving?"

I finally said, "Well, considering what's been happening, I need to do something to change this unhealthy situation."

15

LAWYER

After we received the letter from Uncle Paul B. from Florida, the private investigator tactics, hang-up calls and my parents actions the threat of litigation between my parents and my family became more prevalent. I knew we needed advice and direction so we decided to contact an attorney.

On July 7, 1983, we traveled to Mineola where we sat in our attorney's office Mr, Yellon. He asked, "How can I help you?"

"A few years ago, my parents felt we dishonored them by sharing Thanksgiving with the in-laws. During the holidays, my father threatened to have my children taken away from us. Subsequently, my father's brother wrote a letter to us, recommending that he pursue legal action against us. My father transcribes court cases for the Surrogates Court in New York City and is familiar with the attorneys that work in the court. The Thanksgiving incident created a rift in the family, which has remained until this day. After almost four years of no contact with my parents, we are receiving annoying phone calls, letters of condemnation, investigatory tactics and family abandonment. My grandparents do not want to speak with me, unless I apologize to my parents, and my sister and brother have been silent for more than three years."

The attorney looked at me. "Where were your children at the time of this incident? "

I said. "They were seated on the steps inside the house a short distance away."

He ordered. "I want you to bring your children to a clinical psychologist to find out if they were traumatized by the incident."

I replied. "Okay."

The attorney clasped his hands together in front of his chest. "I'm going to call your parents right now." He punched in the numbers. Hello, Mrs. Buonocore, I am the attorney for your son and his wife. Do you plan to pursue legal action against them?"

Mr. Yellon spoke briefly with my mother and when the conversation was over he looked at us and said, "Your mother expressed her rights pertaining to her grandchildren and did not confirm or deny her legal intentions." Mr Yellon's conversation with my mother was not reassuring to me.

I looked at him. "What do we do now?"

He replied. "Right now, you wait and see if your parent's want to proceed against you in court."

The respect and love between my parents and I had diminished, so I felt a third party should handle the situation. Weeks later, I contacted my parents arranging a therapy session, hoping to reduce their anger and come to some sort of common ground. Below is a list of the therapy sessions that my parents and I attended:

We met at Dr Grossman's office located in Wantagh.

First Session	August 29, 1983
Second Session	September 1, 1983
Third Session	September 6, 1983
Fourth Session	September 20, 1983

At the first session, I said to the therapist, "My parents feel that I should abide by the commandment, 'Honor thy father and mother.'"

The therapist replied, "Your son is an adult and he has his life, so you need to respect and honor each other."

What was going through my mind at that moment was the commandant, 'Thou shalt not kill', because I felt as though my heart had been ripped out and I was dying a slow death from the family abandonment.

During the four therapy sessions, my father was almost silent as my mother did almost all of the talking. My parents did not apologize for their threat to have my children taken away. At that point, I realized that a private conversation with my father would be futile, since my mother was controlling the situation. They stood their ground and they were not conceding to any wrongdoing, never expressing any emotion. My parents resisted the therapy as outside interference from reality that would challenge their understanding of their world.

The therapy sessions reinforced my feelings all along that my parents were not attending the sessions to resolve our issues, but I felt I had to try. They used the therapy sessions as a fact- finding mission. After the fourth session, when my parents departed, I looked at the therapist. "I don't see any emotion, kindness, affection or love in them."

He responded. "The trust bond has been broken between you and your parents, and that's making it difficult."

That was when I knew the relationship was probably over.

During the early part of the estrangement, my parents called me requesting to visit their grandchildren. I agreed to the visit, and my parents arrived at my home meeting the children in the den. I asked my wife to remain upstairs during their visit since my mother did not like her. When my parents arrived, they did not embrace or show any affection toward their grandchildren. They remained in the den wearing their coats and half-heartedly attempted to play and talk with them. Grandparents are supposed to be warm and generous to their grandchildren, and have a very close and loving relationship. They generally try to provide the things that they did not give their own children when growing up. They didn't even bring a gift of some sort for them. My parents did not express any love or affection for their grandchildren during the time they were there. Their visit lasted about twenty minutes, and they left. From the beginning, it appeared they intended to keep their visit short. The visit did not come from the heart but an attempt to create a scenario to perpetuate the 'soap opera drama.'

The rift was a game changer for us and altered our lifestyle. We wanted to have more children, but now we were dealing with a family situation where our moral support base was gone. Essentially the entire immediate family had abandoned us, and that was emotionally abusive for us and our children. Normally the grandparent's role is to support their adult children in raising their grandchildren, and to love their grandchildren unconditionally.

After four years of coping with the estrangement from the immediate family, I realized that I was suppressing the family abandonment and I didn't know how to counteract the loss. I needed to develop methods to reduce my stress. My wife maintained an upbeat positive attitude toward the children and me to keep up our spirits. I don't know how she was able to maintain a cheerful persona. We worried that there was a possibility that my children may suffer, because of the loss of the love and affection from their immediate and extended family.

Whenever I thought about the rift and hit bottom, no matter where I was, I'd drive to a church and pray to God for guidance, protection and help my family through this ordeal. Later on, I realized that you don't have to be in God's house to pray, so I prayed everywhere. Maybe those prayers were answered and the strength was being directed through my wife.

To raise our spirits, I'd rent comedies or comedy club videos, so that we all laughed together. Humor is important; it's the best medicine, so I made sure that as a family we watched the videos at least once or twice a week.

Having a good sense of humor was an important factor that generally helped me to cope with the family estrangement. When I was depressed, I'd play Rock and Roll, 'doo- wop' lyrics from the 50's. The lyrics from that music was uplifting, positive and for the time being helped me forget about the abandonment.

I remained tight-lipped about my parents' threats, and due to the early rejection by members of the immediate and extended family, our attorney suggested, we keep quiet. When I realized how inflexible my parent's attitudes were, I stopped hoping for some miraculous change. My wife and I were on our own, since there was no one that we could rely on to provide emotional, let alone financial support if a lawsuit was to ensue.

If my parents pursued a grandparent's rights case, our financial situation was insufficient to cover the expenses. We were living from paycheck to paycheck. In preparation for future litigation I needed to make money. I decided to moonlight working home improvement projects. In order to get the ball rolling, I placed an ad in the newspaper and spread the word among coworkers and neighbors. The response was favorable. The downside was that I worked the projects after hours, mostly on weekends. My full- time job involved a fifty to sixty-hour work week, so maintaining the house and moonlighting projects left little time for me to spend with my family. Sometimes I didn't know if I was coming or going. The reduced quality time I spent with my wife and children bothered me. I didn't know what else to do. The anxiety was handled as best as possible, feeling like I was in survival mode. My wife concentrated keeping our children busy with sports and activities. We concealed from the children, that we were-being shunned, harassed and intimidated, but as they grew older, they knew that something was wrong. What was missing was the grandparents, aunts, uncles and cousins, the holiday and birthday celebrations. I knew that I would be unable to replace those family members and that always haunted me.

The first moonlighting project I worked was significant. Unbeknownst to me, this was the start of my second career. The project was located in Sayville where the paint had peeled off the third level of a house that had been painted six months earlier. The house was built in the 1800s. The homeowner hired me to redo the third level by removing the peeling paint from the wood shingles. When I placed the old forty-foot wooden extension ladder against the house, it started to bend, as I climbed up. When I reached the top of the ladder, I was five feet below where I needed to be, in order to complete the job. I met with Mr. Skelly the homeowner and explained to him that the ladder was not long enough to reach the taller areas of the house. He sighed. "Who am I going to get to paint the house now the Fire Department?"

"Let me figure something out," I offered.

The next day when I arrived at the jobsite and attached scrapers, sanders and rollers to an extension pole, to make-up for the additional height that was needed. While I stood on the round ladder rungs, I did not feel secure. Looking down at the ground, chills ran up and down my spine. While working I prayed to God to let me safely finish the job, and I would never attempt a risky project ever again. Desperation can cause you to take risks. I said to myself, "What am I doing here," wondering if the work was worth the risk?" A fall from the top of the ladder at that height could be deadly. I stopped looking down and hurried to finish. Upon completion of the project I learned a good lesson- choose your projects carefully.

As time went on I became more selective and chose projects with a lowered physical risk. At first, I selected any small project where money could be made quickly, anticipating my parents' next step. The bathroom projects required plumbing and electrical work, and I performed that work without a license in desperation to earn money.

The remodeling work was demanding and kept me away from spending time with my wife and children. I didn't realize that I was setting the groundwork for my second career. The work was somewhat therapeutic and helped me cope with the estrangement, diverting my mind from the loss of my immediate family and extended family.

Years later, I worked for a building contractor and learned all aspects of the building trade. In 1996 when I retired from the government, I started a second career, forming a home renovation company, having established a following of customers from my moonlighting days.

16

TEENAGER

In 1963, I watched American Bandstand where teenagers danced the lindy to the latest rock and roll songs. I hadn't learned the lindy, and I didn't know anyone that could teach me. I didn't know if my mother knew the lindy, but I was embarrassed to ask her. Sports and work consumed most of my time and learning the lindy was not at the top of my list.

On Friday evenings, together with my friends we dressed up with a coat, tie and plenty of cologne hoping to have fun at the Church dance. Most of us never learned to dance the lindy. We waited for the slow music to find a partner. If you danced too close to your partner, Father Whelan walked up to you and frowned at us. "Leave room for your guardian angel."

Guy and I stood at the edge of the dance floor, when his cousin Tommy walked over and grabbed my necktie. "Is this that new French material, gar… b'age?" We all laughed. Tommy, a stocky five-foot eight, danced with plenty of rhythm. When the fast songs played, many girls danced together, some with boys. Tommy cut-in and danced with two or three girls at the same time. He'd dance around each of them, making them feel as though they were part of him and they loved it. We gathered around Tommy clapping and chanting. "Go Tommy go, go Tommy go." While Tommy danced, he'd unbutton his shirt, loosen his necktie, laughing and smiling. While we cheered, he cranked it up another notch loving the attention. When the music stopped, Tommy walked over as the sweat dripped down his face.

I smiled at him. "Tommy you're something else."

He laughed.

On a warm spring night Guy, John, Larry and I stood outside the luncheonette at the strip mall. That was our hangout, a place of activity where we socialized. After all, it's not where you are; it's who you're with. In the beginning the strip mall was a safe place for us to congregate, but years later the heroin junkies started using it to hang- out and we had to deal with their presence.

A brown 1952 Dodge four-door sedan pulled up to the curb and stopped. The window rolled down, and Mike McCleland looked over at us. "Hey guys, want a ride?"

Without hesitating, we jumped into the car. Mike was under age, and he didn't have a driver's license. I sat in the front seat and said to him, "Mike, where'd you get the car?"

He replied. "It's my pops, I borrowed his keys." Mike proceeded through the parking lot and onto the road. The car was not equipped with power steering, so he had difficulty making turns. Each time he turned widely at a corner, we burst out laughing. We traveled along Olmstead Avenue as Mike steered toward the curb. He stopped under a tree where the lighting was poor. I opened the front door. Moments later Mike decides to back up the car not realizing the closeness to the tree and damages the door hinges. He looks at me frowning. "Oh… shit." I tried unsuccessfully to get the door to close.

I turned to Mike. "I can't fix this. What are you going to do?"

"Let's get out of here." was all he could say.

I asked. "What are you going to tell your father?"

Mike swallowed. "I'll park it, and hope he don't notice it."

I held the door closed during the ride back to the projects. After that night, we didn't see Mike for a month. We learned that his father punished him by not permitting to meet with his friends.

In the spring of 1964, Frank Coffaro and I sat on the Pelham Express subway on our way to school. We traveled to school together every day for four years. Frank asked, "Hey, can you come with me after school tomorrow to look at some used cars in the north Bronx?"

I said. "Sure."

Frank worked at the neighborhood deli in the projects and had been saving his money to buy a car. Most of the time we were strapped for cash and after playing basketball, we had a big appetite. When Frank was working at the deli, he'd make a sandwich for us and sneak it out without the owner's knowledge. Frank hated to see his friends starve.

After school, Frank and I entered the subway at 96th Street and after two transfers, we exited in the Williamsbridge section in the north Bronx an hour later. We walked several blocks and decided to grab a slice at a local pizza joint. Frank and I must have looked out of place since we wore jackets and ties and carried wide vinyl attaché cases for our books and drafting equipment. After we finished eating, we walked towards the exit. An older guy with dark slicked back hair, wearing a black leather jacket and a gold chain around his neck stepped in front of me. "You got a quarter?"

I glanced at him. "No."

He waited a moment and then spoke snidely. "I asked you for a quarter?"

I replied. "I don't have a quarter. "

I sensed anger in his voice that he'd hit me. Instantly, I flexed my stomach. At that moment, he launched an uppercut into my stomach. I stared at him for a few seconds gritting my teeth displaying anger from the pain. The guy backed away from me realizing that his punch was ineffective. I walked toward the door. When I reached outside, I let out a sigh of relief.

Frank looked at me. "Are you alright?"

I said. "I'll be okay, I flexed my stomach a second before he hit me to absorb the impact.

I asked. "You saw what he did?"

Frank said. "Neil, the guy didn't know what to do when you didn't do anything."

I remarked. "He took his best shot and it didn't work. I guess he had second thoughts."

Thank God, he didn't continue to hit me. Even if I had a quarter, I wouldn't give it to him. I never thought twice why the bully chose me instead of Frank until later on in life. Most people look at me as an easy mark. I surmised that a familiar looking face and a slender build makes a person more approachable by strangers.

Later on, in my teenage years, I noticed that my sense of humor fully developed along with my friends. My father maintained a sense of humor, and I think I inherited some of it from him. Today, that type of humor is referred to as 'Affiliative Humor' combined with a 'Self Enhancing Humor'. It's a good natural attitude toward life, laughing at yourself and the idiosyncrasies of life in a constructive non-detrimental manner. Trying to find humor in everyday situations when you may say the wrong thing or do something stupid and you become the target. Humor was used to deflect stress, and I didn't realize it until later on in life. When we played sports or just hung out, looking for something to do or just blowing off steam, together with my friends, we joked around with each other. Whenever we gathered and developed a sarcastic banter, such as lighthearted name calling, well-timed zingers were the norm. We referred to it as 'sounding on each other.' Unknowingly just to keep our sanity, some of us found humor in a word, a phrase essentially in the phonetics, which is the way words are pronounced.

I remember one time when Tommy and I were seated in the movie theater, joking with two girls who sat nearby. Eventually we sat next to them. The girl seated next to me was named Candy. By the end of the movie I was caressing her. The word traveled in our circle of friends that Neil met Candy girl at the movies. For months and years thereafter, now and then, when we stood in a group the guys sang 'Candy Girl' by the Four Seasons. We all laughed.

Good friends are people you can mess with without offending, and they could do the same to you, but very protective of each other. I'm rarely rude to people I don't know. I'm only rude to people I like. It's actually ironic. By insulting we're showing affection in an unusual way. When you're truly comfortable around someone, you won't feel the need to walk on eggshells, with regard to their feelings. By playing at each other's faults means we're paying attention to each other. We never poke fun at personal matters that we know will offend our friends. True friends understand there's a line and won't cross it. Whenever we met as group in front of the luncheonette, in a car driving or just out somewhere, we never discussed any personal problems or issues that we had at home. When we were together, we were happy just to be around each other, enjoying each other's company and talking about this or that and poking fun at each other.

Being able to laugh at yourself and your friends you learn not to take everything seriously, which is a valuable thing your guy friends can teach you.

Having a good sense of humor was an important factor for me, but I did not fully understand how important humor is to survival. It can lower your stress hormones and makes you feel healthier and better able to handle emotional stress, making us happier. Below is a list of some of the benefits of humor:

It lowers your blood pressure.

It boosts the immune system.

Improves your cardiac health

Triggers the release of endorphins.

It produces a general sense of well- being.

While living at home, I did not have long conversations with my parents or siblings. I was not a conversationalist at home, but more conversant with my friends. My parents didn't promote conversation. They rarely had open conversations with me about any subject. It seemed like everything was a secret. Sometimes I felt like a step child.

While eating dinner at the table, Mom and Dad spoke with each other in Italian. Whenever they did not want me to know the content of their discussion they spoke Italian. They discussed the pimples on my face. As a teenager, I was embarrassed by my acne. I didn't know what caused the pimples, and I didn't know how to get rid of them. Humiliated as I listened to my parents discuss my skin condition for several minutes, they offered no solution. My parents talked about the fact that the number of pimples on my face had increased, but they did not offer a remedy for me to eliminate them. After eating dinner in record time, I stood up from the table and looked at my parents. "You know, I've studied a foreign language for the last two years. I know exactly what you've said to each other and I don't like it!" My parents lowered their heads. They were silent and never defended the content of what they had said to each other in Italian.

Teenage years are difficult enough. A solution or a suggestion by my parents to improve my complexion may have increased my self-confidence and helped me avoid embarrassment outside the home. Maybe they were right not to provide a solution for my pimples, causing me to deal with the embarrassment and humiliation making me a stronger person. After the incident, my parents never spoke Italian in my presence.

I thought my life as a teenager was normal with respect to my friends. A feeling of mistrust for my parents started to creep up. My mother spoke frequently on the phone and sometimes I'd hear her talk about me, since my room was adjacent to her bedroom. "Oh, you know how he is, he's very shy." When my mother talked on the phone or out in public she was quite a conversationalist, but when it came to talking to me she was a closed book. She made me feel like an outsider.

My brother had been discharged from the Navy and slept in the bedroom where my father worked transcribing. Working a full-time job on the midnight shift, my brother attended college full time during the day. He was never home. The nine-year age difference between my sister and me did not provide any common interests and very little interaction. With a wide difference in age, there was a distance between us.

For the life of me, I never understood why my mother never developed a relationship with me. Before I was married, she blamed me for not having a relationship with her. She commented, "You don't talk to me; your brother talks to us. What is wrong with you?"

I walked away saying to myself. "Why does she always lay guilt on me?" She never hugged or complimented me or displayed any emotion toward me as far back as I can remember. There was never a solution for a better bond between my parents. I spoke a bit more with my father, since we had common interests such as fishing, cars and sports.

While Dad worked, Mom was more available, but we rarely spoke to each other. For many years, I always felt that she talked more about me than to me.

17

CROWN DIE CASTING

While in high school on Saturday's, I worked at the Crown Die Casting factory where Uncle Paul F. was the vice president. Under the direction of Mark, the shop foreman I worked as his assistant. While we were in the process of repairing a production machine, Mark turns to me with an annoyed look on his face. "Neil, whatever you do, when you get out of school, don't work here." I guess he trusted me not to repeat it to my uncle.

I looked at him. "Why'd you say that?"

He pointed out. "They hired me to work here Monday to Friday for a salary, but I've worked every Saturday for the past few months for no additional money. My trade is a tool and die maker, but I'm not using those skills working here. This job is geared for a repairman. I have a shop at home in my basement, where in the evening and weekends, I fabricate dies, jigs and molds for customers in the manufacturing business."

I put my head down and clenched my lips, simply saying, "I understand."

Mark knew that I was not utilizing the skills I learned in trade school working in the factory.

After completing four years of education in machine shop and mechanical design, I was never given the opportunity to utilize those working in the factory. On many occasions, I sat at a table and dumped a five gallon can filled with nuts, screws and fittings and sorted them out. This menial type of work was a humbling experience, far beneath my capabilities, but I needed a job and I grinned and bared it to earn money.

On the way home from work I sat alone in the middle subway car at the last stop on Dyre Ave. in the Bronx. A man entered the car. He appeared to be in his early twenties, medium height wearing a black trench coat and short brim black hat. He walked over and stood directly in front of me with his hands in his pockets. He stared down at me gritting his teeth, not saying anything. I felt uncomfortable. The right side of his overcoat protruded toward me. Thinking he had a weapon or something in his pocket I stood up and pushed him back toward the opposite side of the car where he fell against the seat. Running out of the car, I ran away never looking back. My heart pounded like a drum while I continued to run toward the engineer's car or in search of anyone. When I entered the engine car, I looked down at a woman seated near the door. "I had to get away from that guy in the other car. I don't know what's wrong with him." The woman put her head down, clenched her lips and shook her head. Her response was not comforting. I sat down waiting for the engineer or the conductor to arrive. You never know what kind of people you'll meet when traveling on the public transportation system. At any time, you could be sitting in a bus or subway with people that have problems from mental illness, criminals, drug peddlers, homeless people and God knows what. When traveling,it's important to stay alert and awake.

About six months later, I walked into the office at the factory. I told Uncle Paul, "I'm not able to continue to work here because my baseball schedule has changed to Saturday doubleheaders."

He replied, "Neil, I'm sorry to lose you, I hope you'll be happy whatever you do."

I said. "Well, I appreciate the opportunity to have worked here; it's been five years."

He said, "Has it been that long?"

I uttered. "Yeah, it has."

I was indeed thankful to have earned money working part time at the factory. After working there for five years, I was never able to utilize the skills I had learned during the four years of design and machine shop training. College was the place to go if I wanted a career.

I wanted to go to college but I didn't want to put my parents in debt; it wouldn't be right, and they couldn't afford it. While working part- time I saved my money and was prepared to cover the cost of college tuition for the first semester.

In September 1964, I attended classes at Bronx Community College, majoring in Mechanical Engineering Technology. When the first semester ended, I was placed on academic probation after receiving a 1.53 index. College classes shocked me, and I wondered if I had made the right choice. I thought that the part time job and sports activities may have affected my grades.

During high school, my grades were above average, so I needed to adjust to the college style of education. A predominant academic or parochial style high school education would have taught me better language skills. Some of my friends attended parochial high school where they studied Latin and read about Plato and Socrates. I learned how to use a lathe and design machine parts, which I found to be much more interesting and more beneficial later in life.

The following semester I reduced my credit load, which added an additional year of college, graduating community college with 81.5 credits. By reducing my credit load, it allowed me to spread out the cost of college. Reflecting on three years of community college, I can honestly say that my decision to attend a trade school was the right choice. In high school, I received a valuable education that I used during my life, as opposed to the education I received attending three years of college. By today's standards my high school education would be equivalent to earning a Ph.D. Had I attended a Catholic high school, I always wondered about the direction a strictly academic education would have taken me?

During the summer break, my friend Guy and I worked as seasonal caretakers in the housing projects where we lived. Every day we reported to the garden shop, and selected the equipment needed to cut, edge the grass and trim the hedges and shrubs.

At the end of the day, we stood in line in the office, waiting to punch out. There was a commotion among the employees. I looked at Moe. "What's goin' here?"

He replied. "It's payday, man, everybody's happy."

Guy and I returned to the garden shop to retrieve some personal items. As we walked through the building, we heard a ruckus in the basement. We opened the door and walked in as the noise increased. A group of housing employees gathered in the boiler room. Walking closer we noticed they were shooting dice. We never witnessed or played dice before, so we moved closer and watched intently. The players rolled the dice on the concrete floor, and when the dice hit the concrete wall, they spun incessantly. After a few rolls, I became fascinated by the high number of dice rotations before they stopped. I'm not a gambler but as I watched the shooters, it appeared that they may have an even chance of winning. In casino craps the dice are thrown onto a table covered with felt and when they hit the honeycomb covered walls and immediately stop. Call it a feeling, call it whatever you want, I'd rather put my money down shooting dice against a concrete floor and wall.

Payday for Housing employees was every other Thursday, so many employees cashed their checks. With a good amount of cash in their pockets, some guys felt lucky and mustered-up a dice game. Calvin, a short black man in his early forties, spoke with a deep voice. He wore a short brim straw hat with a colored band. He held several bills in his hand and then crapped out. Artie picked up the dice. A man in his thirties, pocked mark face, long nose and brown slicked back hair. As a long cigarette dangled from his lips, he spoke like he had marbles in his mouth.

He said. "Don't worry bout a fuck'n ting ear. I'm fork'n hot, let's see a fork'n seven over ear, ears fork'n forty."

He rolled the dice, and crapped out. He threw his head back as he slapped it and closed his eyes yelling. "Fork'n bastards!"

Coriano, was the next shooter. A stocky Puerto Rican guy in his late thirties, with close cropped black hair and an unblemished sunburned face. He shakes the dice in his hand and rolls a seven.

He uttered. "Yeah, dats it, ladies."

The next roll Coriano throws down his entire paycheck in cash and looks at everybody.

He declared. "Shoot thee hole fuck'in sheck."

He waited for the players to fade his bet. Coriano shakes the dice in his hand and on the first roll he hits a five. He rolls a few more times as the sweat dripped down his worried face. The next roll he craps out and turns to Calvin as if nothing had happened.

He said. "Hey, man, loan me twenty."

Guy and I looked at each other, shocked that Coriano lost his entire paycheck on a dice roll. We learned a good lesson- gambling is not for us.

18

MILK ROUTE

After quitting my part time job at Uncle Paul's factory, I needed to find a job to cover the cost of college and expenses.

I searched the classified ads and found a job opening at Chesterfield Milk Company located in Yonkers, just outside of the Bronx. I walked into the office and looked at a man seated at a desk. "Hi, I'm here for the job that was advertised in the newspaper."

The man walked over to me and shook my hand. "Hi, I'm Bob Aulicino. I run the routes in the Bronx."

I looked at him. "Hi, I'm Neil."

Bob stood six-foot tall, heavyset, with dark hair and spoke with a strong confident voice. "The job involves collecting payments from milk customers on Friday evening and Saturday morning which takes about three hours. I'm paying twenty dollars for Friday collections and fifteen dollars for Saturday collections."

I told him. "I'll take it." At that time, the minimum wage was a $1.15per hour.

Bob said, "Come in on Friday, I'll pay you $20 to go with my guy, and he can break you in on what you need to do."

I replied. . "Okay."

On Friday at 5 p.m. I arrived at the office and met Tipps, a short slender black man in his early twenties, with large lips and a friendly smile, who spoke with a high-pitched voice. He looked at me, "My name is Tinashe but everybody calls me Tipps."

I said. "Okay."

Later we met in the south Bronx on Bryant Ave and 180th Street, where we parked our cars. As we walked the route, I noticed the customers were of limited means and some unsavory characters in the neighborhood. Halfway through the route, I asked Tipps, "Is this neighborhood safe?"

He said. "Well, I ain't never had any problems."

The following week I collected the route on my own. I returned to the office, where Tipps tapped out his cash collection on the adding machine. Tipps handed Bob the tape along with the cash he collected. Bob said to him, "You have fifty-six quarts credit?"

"Yeah, well customers say they didn't receive all the milk they ordered."

Bob said, "Look, if a customer got shorted, they're supposed to call the office and report it. Any future deliveries after we set the bottles, we knock on the door, so the customer is notified of the delivery. But fifty-six fuck'n quarts credit, are you kidding me!"

With a raised eyebrow and clenching his lips, Tipps looked away.

A few weeks later, I was sitting in the office tapping-out while Bob yelled at Tipps, "Forty -one fuck'n quarts credit!"

Tipps skimmed money at least ten to fifteen dollars at a time and Bob knew it, but he couldn't prove it. All Bob could do was to yell at him, hoping that he'd be more realistic when adjusting the bills for credit. Customers received credit on the spot when they paid their bill. When I collected, the credits averaged between ten and fifteen quarts which was reasonable.

A few weeks later I returned from the route when Bob approached me. "How do you like the collecting so far?"

I eyed at him with concern. "Is this route safe?"

He said. "Look, let me say this, if you get held up, just give them all the money and tell them you'll give them a fifteen-minute head start before you call the police."

I answered. "Okay."

That response was not comforting for me. I guess the salary overshadowed my judgment.

Six months later, on a Friday evening, I approached the end of the route. I entered the five-story building on Honeywell Ave. The entrance hall contained an elevator in the middle adjoined by stairs with apartments on both sides. After collecting a customer on the first floor, I placed the money into my pocket. Not interested in walking up four flights of stairs to collect the next customer, I headed for the elevator. When I noticed that the elevator was available and it had never been available, so my antenna went up. Quickly I scanned the area and hesitated a moment feeling that someone stood adjacent to the elevator wall, on the stair landing a few feet away. Out of the corner of my eye, I noticed a heavyset man quietly standing against the wall of mailboxes. The hair on the back of my neck stood up. I turned around and raced toward the front door. A man jumped off the steps running toward me as the heavyset guy closed in. I was not a fast runner, but fear can do strange things to you. One guy was inches away from me, just about to grab me. I swung the front door open with all my strength and knocked him down, while the other guy was a short distance away. When I reached the courtyard outside another guy waited for me. Running up to him we faced off. By a stroke of luck, I dodged him and ran up the street into the building. Three white guys shot dice in the hallway. My heart beat like a drum, while I breathed heavily, managing to say, "I'm a milkman, three black guys across the street tried to rob me." In one motion, one guy scooped up the money and the dice, while the other two guys ran down the street after the would-be robbers.

I ran to a pay phone and called the office. "Bob, three guys just tried to rob me. I'm not collecting anymore."

Bob said. "Just come back to the office."

I arrived at the office and Bob greeted me in a lowered voice. "How you do'in?"

I replied. "I'm all shaken up."

He uttered. "Sit down and relax. Did they get the money?"

I said. "No."

With a surprised look on his face, he asked, "They didn't?"

Bob counted the cash which totaled $363.00. "Holy shit, you had some night."

I looked at him. "You know, Bob, it's almost like these guys knew that I was at the end of the route and they wanted to cash in. Had I entered the elevator it would have been all over for me - a knife in the stomach, a bullet in the head. I get the chills just thinking about it."

Bob replied. "What did these guys look like?"

I replied. "One guy was skinny; one guy was short and the other guy was heavyset black guys. I don't know if I can do this anymore."

While at home I lay on my bed staring into space thinking about what had saved my life during the attempted robbery. Running the event through my head, I felt as though there was an invisible shield surrounding me, because not one of those guys laid a finger on me. The only thing that came to mind was that a guardian angel had protected me, providing with 'street smarts,' a situational awareness. There isn't a playbook to survive in a hallway being outnumbered three to one and untouched. Assessing the environment, I was in, who's in it, and what're the available angles, helped me survive. I trusted my own judgment but put myself at risk.

A few days later Bob called me on the phone. "Neil, I have something in the works. I don't want to lose you. I'll call you next week." Two weeks later Bob called me on the phone. "Neil, come to work on Friday. I have a New York City Detective that will accompany you on the route."

I said. "Okay".

I arrived at the office on Friday. Bob introduced me to Pete, an NYPD detective. A man in his early thirties, medium weight, clean cut, sandy colored hair, wearing a tan trench coat. Pete and I met up the beginning of the route and he shadowed me while I collected.

Halfway through the route, Pete turned to me. "Neil, I wouldn't collect this route without a gun."

I hesitated and looked down. "I need the money and I don't know if it's worth it either?" He shook his head.

As we approached the end of the route I looked at Pete. "This is the building where they tried to rob me," I explained to him the circumstances surrounding the attempted robbery.

Pete said. "Neil, you're a very lucky guy to have survived."

I put my head down and shook my head in agreement. Pete accompanied me for the next four Friday collections without incident.

Bob called me at home. "Neil, do you have a friend that could walk the route with you?"

I replied. "My friend Vinny can do it."

He said. "Have Vinny go with you when you collect and when you return to the office I'll pay him fifteen dollars."

I told him "Okay."

Friday at five-thirty in the evening, Vinny and I proceeded to collect the route without incident. We arrived at the attempted robbery building on Honeywell Ave. We walked into the building where two guys stood in the hallway. I looked at Vinny. "Let's get the hell out of here; those are the same guys that tried to rob me." We ran down the street and returned to the office. Bob sat at his desk. I told him, "The guys who tried to rob me last time waited for us when we entered the building on Honeywell Avenue."

Bob said, "What did they look like?"

I pointed out. "One of them was a skinny black guy about 5' 8, in his early twenties."

Bob replied. "You're describing a guy that I fired."

I remarked. "I can't do this work anymore," I blurted, "it's not worth it!"

Bob sat down with a worried look on his face. "Okay, okay."

The next week, he called me on the phone. "If you want, you can work with Harold delivering milk, this way you can get away from collecting."

I answered. "Okay."

On Monday at three in the morning, I parked on an empty street across from the diner on Tremont Ave. I noticed the milk truck parked in front of the diner without a driver. I walked inside. Harold, a medium built light skin black man handed me a cup of coffee. "Let's go to work."

On a warm summer night in August, we arrived at the first stop on St. Ann's Ave. "Neil, this is the list of the apartments. Fill up the carriers with what you need and be sure to pick up all of the empties."

I loaded eighteen quarts into two carriers and walked into a six-story building without an elevator. I didn't know that a six-story apartment building existed with only two apartments on each floor. Of course, the milk needed to be delivered to the two customers that lived on the sixth floor. After delivering milk to the second building the sweat poured down my face as I returned to the truck.

Upon completion of that portion of the route, we traveled about a mile to Bryant Ave., where Harold double-parked in front of the building. I loaded twenty-four quarts into two carriers. On my way back, I noticed a guy running out of the truck carrying bottles of milk. I yelled at him, "Hey, what are you doing?" The guy ran down the street. I placed the carriers on the ground and removed a full quart of milk and launched it like a football toward the thief and yelled, "Hey, you forgot one!" He turned to look back as the airborne bottle that nearly missed him and dropped the bottles he held onto the sidewalk. The pool of milk covered the sidewalk from the building to the street.

Harold returned to the truck and said. "What's goin' on?"

I pointed out. "A guy just robbed milk, so I threw a bottle at him and he dropped the bottles he had stolen!"

He said. "These sons of bitches, always looking for something for free."

Six months later, Bob called me. "Listen, I have a smaller route you can collect in another area if you want to try it?" I agreed to collect the smaller route located on Southern Blvd. bordering the Cross-Bronx Expressway.

I collected the route for a few months without incident. One Friday evening I collected a customer on the third floor and walked downstairs. At the stair landing between floors, I was met by a six-foot tall black man wearing an overcoat. He held a gun as he breathed heavily. He looked at me. "Get against the wall." He pushed the gun into my back as I wet my pants.

He ordered. "Give me all the money!"

My legs started shaking. I fumbled nervously inside of my pockets to collect all of the money.

I replied. "Look, you can have all the money, just leave me alone and I'll give you a fifteen-minute head start." He was silent. "Do you want the change?"

He responded. "Yeah, give me all the change too!"

I said. "Please leave me alone, and I'll give you a fifteen-minute head start.

He glared at me. "Get up there!"

He ordered, pointing with the gun to the next floor, turned around and ran down the stairs. I sat on the steps for a few minutes and waited for him to exit the building. Then I knocked on the previous customer's door and asked him to call the police. The police responded and interviewed me and I provided the details of the robbery.

At the office, I told Bob, "I can't do this work anymore; my luck's run-out."

Bob said. "Neil, I don't know what to say to you, or what I can do for you?"

Looking down I said, "Just pay me and I'll be gone."

Two months later Bob's brother, John, called me on the phone. "Neil, I have a route on the Grand Concourse, would you be interested in collecting for me?"

In a stern voice I said. "John, if I had a machine gun I wouldn't collect any of your routes, goodbye!"

I sat in the bedroom doing homework when my mother yelled to me, "There's a detective on the phone that wants to talk to you!"

It didn't make sense for me to tell my parents about the robbery since I had quit. "Hello. Neil, this is Detective Schmender from the Forty-Sixth Precinct. Can you come down to the precinct to look through some photos to identify the person that robbed you?"

I said. "Well, I'm in college, and right now I don't know if I would have the time to do that."

He said. "Well take down my number, and give me a call when you can do it."

I replied. "Okay."

After I hung up the phone, my mother walked into the bedroom frowning at me. "Why is a detective calling you?"

I replied. "He wanted some information about a robbery."

She said. "Oh."

My mother's response reinforced my decision not to inform my parents about the robbery. She never pursued any interest in my life.

19

PROJECTS DECLINE

One afternoon during the summer, I walked by a vacant lot on Olmstead Ave. across the street from the projects. A cluster of Granite boulders stood high above the street. It seemed unusual that in a low- lying swampy area, a granite cluster protruded there. The area was used as a hang- out for kids in the neighborhood. As I walked by, Moe a neighborhood kid, ran around the boulders yelling at his friends. "Here they come - Vietnams!" Moe ran-up to the top of the boulders and with his arms stretched out, he jumped off yelling, "Here I come - Superman!" He hit the ground. Moe was scratched up and disoriented while his friends assisted him. Unsure of Moe's condition, due to his injuries or the repeated use of inhalants and drugs, he was never the same person after that accident.

Several months later while I walked through the neighborhood Frankie, a heroin addict approached me. "Hey man you got a dollar?"

I replied. "No, I don't have a dollar."

He uttered. "Come on, man, what about fifty cents?"

I said. "Frankie, I don't have any money."

Frankie held his hands up to his chest and pointed toward me. "Look, man, I'll give you this shirt I'm wearing; it's an Italian fuck'n knit shirt that costs fifty fuck'n dollars. You can have it for five dollars."

I remarked. "Frankie, I told you, I don't have any money."

I continued to walk home.

Periodically Frankie and other junkies used the hallway near the luncheonette where we hung out. The junkies tried to mingle with us but they would ease on into the hallway where they would sniffle, itch and nod - off.

My friends and I did our best not to get involved with Frankie and others like him. We remained in our group and the junkies huddled together. Most of the time, the junkies were high. If anyone showed up that they knew, they'd walk out in a stupor or stand in one spot, with a runny nose or scratching their face, garbling their words or not saying anything. They were harmless but depressing to watch. I didn't understand why people would inject their body with a substance that was not prescribed by a doctor. A heroin addict could be one shot away from death. Junkies place their life in the hands of a supplier who may be another junkie, or some dirt bag unconcerned about their buyer's well-being, adhering to no standards of medical safety, focused only on profit and their next fix.

After observing junkies in the projects, I realized it doesn't take long if you don't stay away from them, you could wind up like them. There was an uneasiness when a junkie approached me thinking that they'd poke me with a needle and somehow, I'd become hooked on drugs.

Watching the junkies, I, subconsciously, gained an incentive to strive for a better life. It taught me a great lesson because when I looked at them, I felt a little fearful and wondered about the dark part of their life. Their helplessness made me sad. They had nothing to live for, but the next fix. They may have never experienced the better part of life, love, children family and/or achieving self–worth. The more I watched the junkies congregate, the more I needed to find a way out of the neighborhood. My friends and I never discussed the junkies and their condition. I felt that the circumstances in the neighborhood were just part of life and it was something I had to deal with. We avoided close association with the junkies but we were polite to them. There was a fine line between my friends and the junkies. Playing sports, attending school, studying, working and locating other surroundings as much as possible helped my friends and me maintain our sanity and kept us away from using drugs.

After having lived eight years in the newly built Castle Hill Projects, I realized that the neighborhood was deteriorating. The New York City

Housing Authority cleaned the interior of the apartment buildings and maintained the grounds. When the median income was lowered in the projects, it brought in a lower class of tenants with many problems. We lived on the second floor, and I used the stairway daily to enter and exit the building as the urine smell permeated the air. As a result of the lowered standards, at times, tenants threw bags of kitchen trash out of the windows onto the lawn. Most of the residents ignored the black plastic bags pretending it was outdoor debris that was collected by the maintenance workers, but that was not the case. Residents throwing trash out of apartment windows when garbage receptacles were available on every floor in every building is something I never forgot. Some low socio-economic people, can transfer a host of issues into an area from psychological problems, to drug issues which eventually leads to crime. The twelve- story building that we lived in contained twelve apartments on every floor. During the time I lived there, my next-door neighbors were the only people I knew. I couldn't tell you who lived in the other ten apartments because they were rarely seen.

Housing projects isolate and concentrate the lower class, dependent on welfare, suffering from high unemployment rates, teenage pregnancy, single parenthood and a climate of serious crimes. Working families are not home during the day and busy in the evening. Some families turn a blind eye and ignore the deteriorating conditions because they have no other place to go. Others are unaware of the neighborhood's incremental deterioration. The projects are the only choice for families of limited means. I observed the progression of the Castle Hill Projects from the time we moved there as follows: When a frog is placed in a pot of hot water, it will jump out. If the frog is placed in a pot of cold water on the stove where it doesn't perceive danger, it will remain in the pot. As the heat is slowly increased, the frog eventually dies. Incrementalism creeps up on you until it's too late to do anything.

The housing project was an affordable place for my parents to live. It was not a place where I might grow my spirit, intellect and emotions. At nineteen, I worked part time earning enough money to pay for my college tuition, automobile insurance, maintenance, clothing and spending money.

College and work consumed most of my time, not permitting much time for enjoyment. Families that raised respectable girls in the projects were very protective of them, and they did not want them hanging out on street corners. The chance of meeting a girl who was raised with good values was limited. At that time, some of my friends enlisted in the service, as our country was heavily invested in the Vietnam War.

While I lay on the bed in my room and stared into space, I thanked God for having survived two robberies. I was thankful, that my parents provided a place for me to live, a roof over my head and food to eat. Mom was always at home since she didn't drive, and relied on Dad to drive her everywhere.

My mother knew I didn't trust her. I don't know what caused her to feel that way. Outside the home, I was never involved in any trouble. My friends were good and honest people, raised by hard working parents. As my responsibilities and independence increased, the distance between my mother and me escalated.

Dad worked two jobs and he relied on Mom to run the family. As long as there were no issues, I had minimal contact with him. After my brother was married, he moved to Queens; my sister was nine years younger. I don't know if the wide age difference between my brother and sister was planned by my parents or just happenstance. The relationship between my brother and sister was not close due to our wide age difference. We did not have much in common. I never recalled sitting down and having any long conversations with my brother or sister while living at home. When I was home, they were not home and vice versa. It's like we were raised independently of each other.

Rarely, if ever, did I call my brother or sister unless there was an urgent matter. I was not a talkative person with them, and I guess that followed me during my adult years.

20

NEIGHBORHOOD

When the weekend rolled around, within my group of friends we always planned to have fun. The unspoken word in the neighborhood was get out; get away to somewhere, anywhere. After ten p.m. on a weekend night, you did not want to be seen hanging out in front of the luncheonette like a bunch of losers. I always felt that there was an urgency to get out of the neighborhood as the night progressed, or become ensnared in the perils that existed there. Nobody stood on the corner and yelled get the hell out of here. The unspoken word can be more powerful than the spoken word.

1965 was the time when authority and politeness were questioned and the break of all boundaries of right and wrong were accepted. It was the start of the era of 'sex, drugs and rock and roll.' Psychedelic, mind-expanding drugs were becoming popular. Drugs became very accessible and popular among recording artists and the population.

Our group of friends did not use drugs; we drank alcohol and very few of us were having sex. Eighteen was the legal drinking age at that time. A big night for us was to buy a quart of Schaefer beer at the deli, walk down to the lots and chug it down.

The weekend was our time for enjoyment, we looked for an outlet, a good-time to meet girls and enjoy their company. We stood in front of the luncheonette, deciding where to go for our weekend for entertainment. At this time, nobody in our group was dating, so we were anxious to herd–up on Friday night in search of fun. If one of us was able to borrow his parents' car, we'd pile in and drive anywhere, just to get out of the neighborhood. Larry said, "You know, the Riviera Lounge in Yonkers is good place to go on Fridays. I heard that place jumps. They have good entertainment." We all agreed to meet at the luncheonette at eight thirty on Friday evening.

In need of transportation, I asked my father. "Can I use your car tonight to go out?"

He replied. "Where are you going and what time are you coming home?"

I mentioned. "We're going to Yonkers."

He ordered. "Alright, but make sure when you bring it back, you put gas in it!"

I said. "Okay."

My father was reluctant to let me use his car, since the insurance liability cost was high due to my inexperience as a driver. He often reminded me. "If you want to use the car, you need to get your own insurance."

I replied. "Okay."

On Friday evening at eight-thirty, I rolled up to the strip mall driving Dad's black 1950 Buick four-door sedan. Larry, Guy and Mike hopped in. At the Riviera Lounge, we waited in line at the door, while they checked ID's. The line increased due to the scheduled live entertainment; we paid the five-dollar cover charge. Inside, the dimly lit spotlights shined on the bright red curtains and red carpet. A few couples danced on a small dance floor while we walked- up to the mirrored bar and bought a drink. Guy said, "This looks like a good place; there's a lot of good looking girls here."

I said. "I'll say." As we stood in a huddle, we scanned the area and started to line up girls for a dance. Unlike other clubs, every other woman was attractive, well-dressed, right down to the hair makeup and jewelry.

Larry said, "You see that blonde with the wavy hair and the tight skirt? I'm going to ask her to dance."

Mike walked over. "I just got turned down to dance."

Guy and I asked girls to dance and were- turned down. Larry looked at us. "The girls here are stuck up."

I remarked. "It's almost like they know what they want and we don't measure up." Being turned down to dance was a blow to our egos.

Guy griped, "I'll bet a lot of these girls are from the rich areas in Westchester County."

Larry uttered. "Yeah, I think you're right. Maybe this place is out of our league."

I said, "After the show let's head over to the Inwood Lounge?"

Guy replied. "Sounds good to me. Let's get up close for the show."

The band played, as the crowd increased on the dance floor around the stage. At ten o'clock, they introduced the 'Ronettes,' one of the top female vocal recording groups at that time. No more than five feet away, we watched three young good looking female vocalists shaking their bodies and harmonizing to the voice of the lead singer Ronnie, as they sang their hit song, "Be My Baby." The trip was worth it just to see the Ronettes perform up close. They were followed by Larry Chance and the Earls. When they sang their hit song, "I Believe," no matter how many times I heard it, chills ran up and down my spine. The song was mesmerizing. Critical of live performances, I listened intently to see how close the live performance matched the record. Years later when I learned about lip syncing, it discouraged me from attending live performances. It's like you're getting cheated. You may as well listen to the record.

Weeks later, on a Friday evening, I met Guy and John in front of the luncheonette. We headed out to Community Gardens located in Queens. We didn't have much money, so a dance club without a cover charge was worth the trip. We parked the car near the train station a short distance from the Gardens. To avoid the cost of drinks, we cracked open a half pint of scotch. We shared it, as we chugged it down providing a good buzz to get us through the night.

The Gardens packed people in on Friday nights, listening to the live music of 'Ricky and the Vasels.' We stood on the side of the dance floor while many people danced. The 'Vasels' returned from a break and played

'Good Lovin.' Everybody danced. I watched two girls dance and cut in as her partner danced well. That's when I met Diane. She worked in the office for Columbia Pictures in Manhattan. I dated her for almost a year.

My relationship with Diane was a steady Friday or Saturday night date. I liked her as a person. On a few occasions while studying in my bedroom, I heard the phone ring. Mom yelled from the kitchen, "It's for you, pick up."

I answered the phone on the extension in the bedroom. While I spoke to Diane on the phone, Mom listened in on the extension in the kitchen. I yelled to her. "Hang up the phone!" After a few incidents of Mom's inquisitiveness, I started calling Diane from a pay phone. My relationship with her was congenial, but I was not in love with her and didn't have sex with her. I looked forward to getting away from the projects on the weekend, and she provided an outlet for me. Maybe I was selfish, but I was considerate and respectful to her.

Mom may have thought that my relationship with Diane was serious since I had been seeing her for almost a year. She never expressed any interest in Diane or asked me about my relationship with her. One day Mom walked into my bedroom. She didn't like Diane.

She said. "Why don't you go out with Donna or Barbara; they're... nice... girls."

I replied. "Ma, I don't like those girls, I'll pick the girls I want to go out with."

She ignored me and walked away. My mother always tried to set me up with her-friends' daughters, placing her in the selection and control process.

On one occasion, I was unable to use my father's car for a date with Diane. Out of desperation, I traveled two hours each way on the bus to Diane's house in Richmond Hill, Queens. At one thirty in the morning, on the trip back home, I sat alone in the back of the Q44 bus. At the next stop, a man in his forties, stocky build, wearing a tan trench coat and hat entered the bus. He carried two brown paper shopping bags and sat down next to me. I thought he sat there to speak with me, which has occurred before on public transportation. The guy sat there ignoring me. I thought that was odd, and I felt uncomfortable. Immediately, he rubbed his hand back and forth on his thigh while focusing straight ahead. Seconds later, he lifted his hand up from his leg and grabbed my thigh. I jumped up from the seat. Leaning against the window, I kicked him over onto the shopping bags.

I yelled at him. "You bastard, keep your hands to yourself!"

I rushed to the front of the bus, as my heart pounded like a drum.

I told the driver, "That guy just grabbed my leg. I don't know what's wrong with him!"

The driver remained focused on the road. "Just sit here, Kid, until you get off."

While I sat there, the molester exited the bus through the rear door at the next stop. That was the last time I traveled to Queens using public transportation.

My father sat at the kitchen table reading the newspaper. I told him, "Dad, I found a car for sale. Can you drive me to look at it?"

He answered. "Where is it located?"

I said. "It's in Brooklyn."

Dad replied. "Okay."

We exited at Rockaway Parkway and rolled up to the attached brick house that bordered the Belt Parkway. The 1956, faded green 2 door Chevy sedan,sat in the driveway. I didn't know anything about cars. I looked at my father. "What do think?"

Dad pointed out. "It has some rusted areas, but let's see how it drives." The owner started it up. "The engine sounds good; can we drive it?"

He said. "Go ahead."

My father sat behind the wheel and listened for any noises as we traveled through the neighborhood.

Dad said. "If you can live with the rust, it seems alright."

I loved it.

I looked at the owner. "How much are you asking for it?"

He answered. "I'm asking a hundred, but I'll take seventy-five."

I replied. "I'll take it."

Two days later, I sat behind the wheel driving my Chevy, to the Bronx. I felt proud to be the owner of a 1956, two- door Chevy, standard shift, V8. I thought the Chevy was the coolest body style. The gas tank filler was concealed in the drop- down tail light; it was hard to find unless you knew where to look for it.

As long as the weather was good, I worked on my car in the parking lot in the projects. Mechanically, the car was okay, but the body contained areas where the rust created large holes. Without any knowledge of body work, I bought a can of auto body filler, read the instructions and proceeded to get started.

The top portion above the headlights was completely rusted- out. After I sanded the body above the headlights, the hole was large enough to fit my hand in it. I sanded the rusted metal by hand to remove the rust. After rolling- up newspapers, I stuffed them underneath the hole to prevent the body filler from dropping down and oozing out. I didn't know what else to do. Later on, I learned that welding new metal is the proper method of repair, but I was unable to afford a professional repair.

While I worked on the car, Cousin Babe, a housing policeman assigned to the projects made his rounds. Babe was my mother's cousin, and his beat was the projects. He walked over to me, "Neil, what are you doing?"

I pointed out. "I'm trying to fix the rusted-out areas above the headlights."

He looked at the rust. "You'll never fix that."

I continued working and didn't say anything. I knew the repair was a challenge and Babe's comment was an incentive for me to get it done. After all, I owned the car, free and clear, rust and all.

The body repair wasn't perfect, but most people wouldn't know the difference. When the body work was completed, I brought the car to Earl Scheib for a $19.95 paint job. Later on, I sprayed the rugs green with upholstery paint and installed leopard terrycloth seat covers. The car was heaven to me. Now with my own transportation, I had my ticket to get out of the projects at any time.

I attended high school in Manhattan and worked since I was nine years old, never realizing that I developed life's most valuable lessons. The lessons I learned were not taught in school or from books; they were learned through different life experiences. You'll know when people are trying to get over on you, and that's called 'street smarts.'

Intelligence that you gain outside of school through experience increases your situational awareness. You assess the environment you are in, who is in it and what the available angles are. Life experience or 'street smarts, 'provides the knowledge to know when people are trying to get over on you and to trust your own judgment about people and what matters. It means you have learned to take what has happened to you, good and bad, think about it and learn to improve from it. You have put yourself at risk and survived, or thrived, or have scars. You have been tested and have a bank of experience to depend on when you're tested again. How much can you know about yourself if you have never been in a difficult position?

Life experience is tactical knowledge you gain through involvement, whereas book smarts, relates to what you learn in school. Someone with tactical knowledges is generally intelligent, has good common sense, and knows how to handle unfortunate situations letting their intuition drive their behavior and is comfortable navigating through unfamiliar situations. Life is about making mistakes, and failing at something and not making the same mistake again, thus improving.

21

JOANN

As a practicing Catholic, I regularly attended Sunday mass at St. Vianney Church in my neighborhood. Sometimes during the week, I'd go to church and pray thanking God for keeping me safe, and asking Him for His help to find someone that I could love and she would love me. The lyrics from the song "Dear Lord" by the Continentals could not have said my prayers any better. The song is about a man praying to God to send him a girl from heaven to love.

On Saturday afternoon, I entered the church confessional. "Bless me, Father for I have sinned. It has been three weeks since my last confession, I...................."

Upon completion of my confession, the priest said, "Okay, Neil, say five Our Father's and five Hail Mary's." Shocked and embarrassed that the priest knew my identity, I didn't know what to do. My understanding of confession was a place you could go anonymously and you're a stranger to the priest. Feeling uncomfortable confessing my sins to someone that knew me, I never returned to confession.

In January 1967, I graduated Bronx Community College with an Associate's Degree in Mechanical Engineering Technology. I learned that Grumman Aircraft Corporation, located in Bethpage, was hiring, so I applied there for a job. Grumman, the largest employer on Long Island, employed more than 36,000 employees.

Grumman Aircraft, later named Grumman Aerospace Corporation, was a leading producer of military and civilian aircraft. They developed the F-14 Tomcat that was prominent in the film 'Top Gun.' They also produced many aircraft used in World War II.

As the chief contractor for the Apollo Lunar Module, Grumman hired me in the spring, where I worked in the Engineering Department on the program that landed men on the moon.

Every morning I traveled with the car pool consisting of four Grumman employees who lived in the Bronx to Plant 35 in Bethpage, Long Island. The office building was the size of two football fields. At this location, hundreds of desks and drafting tables were filled with engineers, designers and support personnel. Having never worked a full- time job with regular hours, in a clean, comfortable environment was a dream come true.

One morning on my way to the coffee shop during a break, I noticed a dark-haired, attractive woman, well- dressed, medium height, long, dark brown hair. I started to take notice of her and discovered that she worked on the same floor.

Later in the day, I approached the file counter where the clerk had finished talking with the woman I noticed earlier. I looked at the file clerk. "Anny, who is that woman you were speaking with?"

She said. "Oh, that's Joann, she's engaged to a friend of mine."

I replied. I raised an eyebrow. "Oh, really?"

Weeks later, after the shift ended, I missed the carpool. While walking through the parking lot, a car rolled up next to me. Anny, sat in the passenger seat and to my surprise, Joann sat behind the wheel. Anny asked me, "Where's your car?"

I explained. "The carpool left without me and I need to get home."

Joann replied. "Where do you live?"

I said. "I live in the Bronx. Maybe you can drop me at the Bethpage train station down the road?"

She asked. "How long will it take you to get home by train?"

I remarked. "I'm not sure, probably a good amount of time."

Joann motioned to me. "Get in, we'll drive you." My jaw dropped.

I uttered. "Are you sure? It's twenty-five miles from here."

She said. "That's okay."

Joann and I talked during the entire trip to the Bronx, while Anny sat between us as our chaperone. I was captivated by her warm and unpretentious personality. After a while, we didn't know Anny sat there.

The next day I met Joann in the hallway at work. "Hi, thanks again for driving me to the Bronx yesterday."

She replied. "Oh, that's okay."

I pointed out. "I'd like to repay you for driving me to the Bronx, but I heard that you're dating someone.

She replied. "I am not dating anyone."

I remarked. "Anny said you're engaged."

She stated. "I'm not engaged or dating anyone."

I said. "Okay, well would you like to have dinner with me dinner on Friday?"

She replied. "Okay."

I met Joann at her home where she introduced me to her parents. Her mother was a short slightly overweight woman in her late forties. Her father stood tall, heavyset large framed man who spoke in a boisterous tone, like a drill sergeant. As a skinny, soft spoken, quiet type person, it didn't appear that her father was impressed with me.

After dating Joann for a few months, I realized that my life began when I met her. She had a radiant smile, a voice of confidence, a calmness and she'd light–up a room without saying anything. Most of all, she was selfless, caring and empathetic. Those qualities I had never experienced in anyone. Early on we realized we had a lot in common since both our families were of similar socio-economic backgrounds. As children, we both worked when we young, learning about life and helping the family. While dating, we found that we enjoyed each other's company, even if it was just a ride in the car to nowhere. Joann was a happy person who looked on the bright side of things. She avoided drama and was grateful for what she had and did not spend time wanting what other people possess. No matter where we were or what we did, being together was all that mattered.

Months later my parents stood outside of my bedroom in the hall.

I said "I want to let you know, that I am proposing to a woman that I've been dating."

My mother's jaw dropped. "Who is she?"

I answered. "I met her at work.

She's a technical aide at Grumman and she lives on Long Island. She's very nice and I love her."

My father spoke in a condescending voice, with a frown on his face. "Is she Italian?"

I answered. "She's half Italian."

My mother frowned. "We don't even know her!"

I pointed out. "Well, I'm in love with her, we have a lot in common, and she loves me. I'd like to introduce her to our family."

My mother pursed her lips. "What do we know about her?"

I stated. "You can ask her all the questions you want when she comes here to meet the family."

I was expecting my parents to be happy for me where marriage would relieve them of their responsibility, leaving them to care only for my sister. My mother's reaction to the engagement was not positive, since she was not involved in the selection process.

I met Joann at her home, and we traveled together to the Bronx to meet my family. She wore a dark blue dress with a matching scarf she had made herself. It made me proud. She learned to make clothing from her mother who custom made wedding dresses and clothing for customers in her basement. When business was slow, her mother fabricated blouse collars for a local clothing manufacturer. As a child, Joann worked with her mother. She'd fold, cut and press the collars, bundling them in stacks of fifty. There were instances where she worked at times until two o'clock in the morning, in order to meet the deadline for the morning pick-up by a local clothing manufacturer. After school while her mother worked making clothing in the basement, Joann cooked, cleaned the house, washed and pressed clothes and watched over her younger brothers and sister. These responsibilities at times, prevented her from completing homework and achieving better grades in school. But on the other hand, those responsibilities taught her about life, caring, and love, placing others above herself. She was intelligent with good common sense and knew how to handle unfortunate situations. I thought Joann's qualities would be pleasing to my parents as their future daughter-in-law.

We walked into the apartment. "Joann, this is my mother and father."

Joann replied. "Nice to meet both of you."

My father said. "Let me take your coat."

Mom wore her everyday housedress, nothing special. I felt a little embarrassed, since she did make some of her own clothing. Many of the clothes Mom made were bright colors, too vibrant for my taste, but that's what she liked. "Come, sit down and eat." The table consisted of a small bowl of condiments and cold cuts, hardly indicative of what my mother was capable of making. I enjoyed eating Mom's eggplant parmigiana, lasagna, and famous cheesecake, but nothing special was served that day.

The introduction of my fiancé to my family went as I expected. Everybody was polite and uneventful. It was probably the most conversation we ever had. As a happy person, I wondered how Joann would get along with my family. She avoided drama instead of getting caught up in other people's relationships or stress. Being happy, she chose to focus on things that she had more control over. She felt that paying attention to her own life and letting other people live theirs was a simple way to maximize happiness. While driving home, Joann looked at me. "Do you think they liked me?"

I uttered. "I like you; they have no choice; we're getting married."

A few days later, my mother stood in the doorway of my bedroom.

She said. "What ever happened to Diane? We… liked… her? We were close to her."

I gave her a puzzled look. "Diane and I were not compatible. She liked to be indoors, and I liked the outdoors. How close could you have been to her, since you only met her twice?"

My mother was silent and walked away after recommending the woman she approved of, the person of her choice, as my partner.

Prior to our marriage, in a telephone conversation with my wife, my mother cautioned her about my state of mind. She tried to end the engagement when she called her. "You know, when Neil was a child, he fell on his head, and it may have affected the way he thinks; he hasn't been the same since then."

My wife didn't know what to say to her, and the next time we met, she looked at me. "Your mother called me on the phone and dramatically explained to me that you fell on your head when you were a child and you're not well."

I said. "I fell from the top of the slide in the park and hit my head on the pavement at the age of five. Maybe that event would not have occurred if my mother was attending to me, instead of sitting on a bench on the other side of the park. That is not surprising that my mother implied that I was disturbed. I knew her tactics probably better than anyone, since I grew up under her control and dealt with her methods from childhood until I married." Joann was silent. I continued. "The fall on the head' incident was used by my mother to try to stop our marriage and used by her whenever she didn't get her way." Shortly after I married, my mother confronted me.

She uttered. "You couldn't wait to leave home to get married!"

I declared. "Yeah, I needed to get away from you and your control; it's unhealthy!"

Joann and I headed to Dr. Wycoff's office to obtain a blood test prior to our marriage. He was a retired army doctor who practiced in her neighborhood. Needles were nothing new to me, after receiving a few allergy shots every two weeks for three years. While in the doctor's office, he stuck me with a dull needle. I felt lightheaded. In need of fresh air, I stood up and walked into the waiting room full of patients, and passed out on the floor.

Dr. Wycoff stood over me looking down. "Get up! Get up you God dam chicken!"

As I lay there in a semi-conscious state, he waved his hand at me.

He said. "Ah, you nothing but a chicken."

He returned to the examination room. No one in the waiting room assisted me. Everyone stared at me wondering what occurred. After all, when the doctor calls you a chicken, he must be right.

22

HONEYMOON

A year later, Joann and I were married. We approached the island of St Thomas, Virgin Islands as I looked out of the window at the scenic mountain landscape and pristine beaches below. A chill ran up and down my spine as the Pan Am 727 Jet descended abruptly for a landing.

We checked into the Pineapple Beach Hotel, on the bay in the northern part of St Thomas. Anxious to see the sights, we immediately rented a 'Mini Moke' - a small lightweight utility vehicle with a canvas top, a perfect vehicle to travel around the island. We toured the beaches and up the mountain roads admiring the vegetation, the palms, the mango and papaya trees. The scenic view of the dark green vegetation against the turquoise water and the white sandy beaches was unlike anything we had ever seen before.

As we climbed the mountain the narrow road curved and followed the contour of the land, remnants of the volcanos. We approached the top of the fifteen-hundred-foot mountain admiring the cliffs and the water below. I heard a rumbling noise and looked up as a large boulder, about three feet in diameter rolled down from the mountain above and smashed into the road, just missing us. The boulder struck the road and rolled off the cliff. I stopped the Mini Moke and turned to my wife.

I remarked. "That boulder just missed us!"

Wide-eyed she said, "Oh my God!"

I walked back to where the boulder hit the road as the indentation was ever-present. The mountain above the road stood at a sharp angle, too steep to climb. There was no guard rail on the road as the cliff descended sharply, almost two hundred feet. I was unable to determine if erosion or someone caused the boulder to fall, nearly missing us.

My wife said to me. "If that boulder had hit us, we'd be at the bottom of the cliff. "Do you think that someone purposely did this?"

I remarked. "I don't know. Thank God it missed us."

Somewhat shaken–up we turned around and headed back to the hotel.

After three days in St Thomas, we traveled to the island of St Croix, where we settled-in at the Buccaneer Hotel. The next day we boarded a catamaran and sailed to Buck Island National Park Reef for an underwater tour.

Before we entered the water, the boat captain announced to us, "Sometimes there's a large barracuda near the reef named 'Charlie' and he's friendly. Charlie has inhabited the reef for many years, and there is no cause for alarm."

A group of a dozen passengers entered the water with snorkeling equipment, as a crew member guided us through the marked underwater trail. We snorkeled for about an hour and watched the brilliant blue tang, surgeon fish, doctor fish, parrot fish, yellow striped French grunts, as their primary and secondary colors flashed through the water. While on the bottom, I held out my hand as the fish schooled-up, drawn to me like a magnet. I was fascinated watching the fish swim in the crystal-clear water through the shades of the rigid multi-colored Elkhorn coral that rises up from the bottom as if were plant life. Staring at the schools of fish, I was mesmerized, watching them swimming over the coral reefs. It's like God had put them there for us to watch.

Later on, I surfaced and noticed that everyone was in the boat. They yelled to me. "Come on back, come into the boat!"

I looked underwater and noticed Charlie, the barracuda as he stared at me less than fifteen feet away. He remained near the surface, in a broadside position, and he appeared to be about six feet-long, much larger than I expected. Charlie remained still as we focused on each other. With my eye on him, I slowly swam toward the boat. When I arrived at the boat, they quickly hoisted me in. The Captain remained silent, with a look of concern on his face.

I looked at him. "All of the passengers boarded except me?"

He looked down. "Well, we had everybody get out of the water because Charlie was moving closer."

I pointed out. "You told us not to be concerned about Charlie, he's friendly."

He said. "Well he hasn't attacked anyone."

I mentioned. "You mean he hasn't attacked anyone yet?"

He clenched his lips, not saying anything as we headed back to shore.

In the spring of 1970, I daydreamed at my desk, peering out at hundreds of engineers. Some were seated at desks talking with each other, while others worked at their drafting boards. The environment in Grumman had become more relaxed after the first successful moon landing, which remains an historic event. As co-workers, Richie and I worked together for three years and decided to visit the Lunar Module (LM) in Plant 5. In order to preserve the LM's history, we dressed in clean room suits and snapped photographs of each other getting in and out of the space vehicle. Richie attempted to snap a picture of me inside of the LM, but security prevented him from doing so, since the interior remained classified.

Sitting at my desk I said to Richie, "I don't think I'm cut out for the engineering field; it doesn't hold my interest. I'm starting to look elsewhere."

He asked. "What kind of work do you want to do?"

I replied. "I think I'd like to work in law enforcement, but what type, I don't know."

I had a strong impulse that day, to find a career in law enforcement.

My friend Guy and I grew up together in the projects. He worked as a Secret Service Agent for the Treasury Department and suggested that I sit for the Treasury Enforcement Agents Exam. I followed his advice and sat for the exam.

Six months later on the last Friday in October at 10 a.m., the Section Chief notified us to report to the conference room at 2 p.m. Roger, the group leader commented, "Why would they have a meeting this late in the day?"

Richie locked eyes and said. "It's a layoff meeting."

Roger said. "The group supervisor told me that my position was safe."

Richie laughed. "It's a layoff meeting."

Richie and I emptied the contents of our desk into boxes while Roger watched us.

He mentioned. "Why are you guys packing? Do you think they're going to terminate both of you?"

I said. "You better start packing; remember the section chief wants to see all of us."

Roger shrugged it off.

At 2 p.m. the three of us marched downstairs. We entered the conference room as the Section Chief awaited us. "Gentlemen, I am sorry to inform you that you are being terminated as of today. Sign these papers and you'll be eligible for unemployment benefits."

Richie and I had discussed the possibility of a termination for months having noticed many areas of the company were downsizing, and now, we were part of the 13,000 employees who were laid off. The Lunar Module Program ended and we were terminated due to a reduction in force. Roger was devastated as he looked at us. "I can't understand this; Larry told me that my job was safe."

I felt bad for Roger. "I guess you can't trust what people say, only what they do."

When I walked into the apartment carrying a box, my wife looked at me. "What happened?"

I replied. "Take a wild guess."

She said. "You got laid off?"

My wife's employment ended a week earlier as I joined her in the ranks of the unemployed.

Immediately, I sent out resumes, knocked on doors, and pounded the pavement for weeks. Not one defense contractor or non- defense employer made an offer. Two lessons were learned after the layoff. If you're unable to find work, you may need to lower your salary requirements for security and work in a civil service position or relocate.

Focusing on law enforcement positions, every week I purchased *The Chief* newspaper. This publication provided a current listing of available positions for the city, state and federal government. *The Chief* was the best source of civil service job information. Weeks earlier, I sat for the Treasury Enforcement Agent's Exam and the Federal Service Entrance Exam, which increased my access to positions within the federal government.

23

TRAINING

In October 1970, Richie called me on the phone. "Neil, the Federal Government's hiring Sky Marshals through a 'walk' in' exam."

I said. "I didn't see it listed in the Chief."

He replied. "I read it in the Daily News."

I stated. "Well, I think I'll sit for it. Are you interested in taking the exam?"

He advised. "I'll take it at a later date."

Richie didn't take the exam and later moved to Virginia maintaining a career in the aviation industry.

The Sky Marshal Program responded to the wave of aircraft hijackings that occurred in 1970. Two American carriers, Trans World Airlines (TWA) and Pan American (Pan Am), airlines were hijacked, along with a Swiss Air, El Al and BOAC aircraft by the PFLP (Popular Front for the Liberation of Palestine). The PFLP was a secular Palestinian Marxist Leninist revolutionary socialist organization. The PFLP had offloaded the hostages and then blew up the aircraft in the desert of Jordan. President Nixon responded to the PFLP, and ordered the U.S. Customs Service to rapidly recruit and train more than 2,000 new employees both in-flight and ground security. These employees flew two months and worked one month of ground duty at selected airports. While in flight, the Sky Marshals were working undercover and when assigned to ground duty they wore uniforms providing pre-flight security for high-risk flights.

After passing the Sky Marshal exam, I reported to Manhattan for an interview on a Saturday morning. A Government agency conducting interviews on the weekend was unheard of at that time. They needed manpower and they needed it quickly. After the interview, I received a three-hour psychological exam and a physical.

A week later, I received a phone call from the U.S. Customs Service informing me that I was hired for the Sky Marshal position. My wife was not thrilled about it, but she was thankful that I was back to earning a paycheck.

When I was terminated from Grumman Aerospace, I needed a job that provided security and stability, which led me to a law enforcement career.

On December 4, 1970, I reported for orientation at the U.S. Customs House located in lower Manhattan. Customs provided a GTR (government travel request), hotel reservations, training requirements, and a brief orientation of the position. At the Customs office in Manhattan, we were sworn into the Treasury Department.

Three days later I arrived at LaGuardia Airport and handed the GTR to the ticket agent. She looked at me. "You know you're about the twentieth marshal to come through here today.

I said. "Really?

She spoke. "You fellows look so young."

I replied. "Actually, we're all different ages."

Fifty minutes later, the plane landed in Washington D.C. and within the hour I settled into my room at the Pick Lee Hotel.

On Monday morning December 7, 1970, I walked to the Treasury Department Training Center, at 1310 L Street, in Washington D.C. At that location, the Treasury Air Security Officers School (TASOS) consisted of four weeks of training. The class consisted of sixty-five candidates taught by special agents from all agencies within the Treasury Department. A four-week crash course consisting of: basic law enforcement procedures, search and seizure, constitutional law, arrest techniques, modus operandi of air pirates, psychology of skyjackers, firearms training focusing on accurately discharging a weapon inside an aircraft and the containment of an explosive aboard an aircraft in flight.

During the second week of training, we sat in the bus outside the training center, waiting to be transported to the pistol range. The school coordinator walked on board holding a clipboard. "The following trainees will exit the bus and immediately report to the office."

After reading the names of twenty trainees, we looked at each other bewildered.

John looked at me. "You don't think they would terminate all these guys at once?"

I replied. "I hope not."

The next day while seated in class we looked at twenty empty seats. Fear ran through everybody's mind wondering who would be the next candidate to be sent home today, tomorrow or next week? While the instructor taught the class, most of us were preoccupied staring at twenty vacant seats. John raised his hand. "I think all of us are concerned about the absence of the twenty trainees. Have they been terminated?"

The instructor replied. "The answer to your question is yes."

A trainee spoke from the back of the class.

He said. "As candidates, we sit here concerned about our future."

The instructor replied. "Look, the government wants employees of the highest character. If we discover anything negative in your background, you will be terminated."

The instructor lectured for a while then he stopped and made sure the class had his full attention.

He advised. "Look, occasionally a trainee has been summoned to the office while class is in session. Those trainees have been terminated. The Marshal program tested, interviewed, hired and trained officers in record time. Normally the federal hiring process takes up to six- months. We're expediting the process from months to weeks. Since the government needs manpower and they need it quickly, we hired employees based on the information they submitted on their signed application. The background investigation is used to validate their information and we're playing catch-up. If we discover anything negative in your background, you will be terminated."

We learned months later that the government had hired marshals who committed crimes from violent felonies to misdemeanors. The hiring process needed to be expedited to get marshals flying on board aircraft in record time.

We arrived at the outdoor firearms range. Firearms instruction was conducted by the uniformed division of the Secret Service. The range officer stood in front of the class. "We will teach everyone in this class to qualify on the firing range, even if you never fired a pistol before, or you're a big city boy, we will help you to qualify." The range officer's words were exactly what I needed to hear having no experience handling weapons.

Handgun qualification consisted of single action firing which required the weapon to be cocked before firing each shot. Standing behind the shooting table, I cocked the four-inch Smith and Wesson revolver and scored poorly after the ten second round of fire. Qualification on the bullseye target was a total score of 210 out of 300.

I stood on the range on the fourth day of qualification unable to qualify. What came to mind was an important lesson my grandfather had instilled in me at a young age. "Boy, you need to start using your right hand now, because if you ever need to use it for something you'll be as good as you are with your left hand." I took his advice and learned to use my right hand over the years. On the next round of fire, I switched the gun to my right hand. My control improved slightly and the sight alignment was a hair sharper. Afterwards, I mentioned the sharper vision to the range officer.

He explained at me. "Your vision in one eye could be slightly better than the other eye and that's why your score improved."

I said, "I don't know how that was possible."

I pointed out. "When I was a child during a snowstorm, I threw snowballs at the cars that passed from the stoop in front of our apartment building. The large snowflakes made for good packing. I heard a loud pop on the brick wall next to me. Across the street, Johnny Caniano, who lived in the building, packed another snowball. He stood six-foot tall and had a lanky build, pockmarked face, and black slicked back hair DA style. He always wore a black motorcycle jacket. Johnny was five years older than me and pitched for a local baseball team. I hid behind the stone railing on the front stoop and threw a snowball back at Johnny. A moment later, I was hit in the eye and thrown back onto the snow. The snowball felt like soft packed ice as I lay on my back. I never saw it coming. The impact had the speed of a fast-ball. My eye felt as if it was forced into my head as I saw stars and unable to see. The pain radiated in the top of my head. Crying, I ran upstairs and rushed into the apartment. " "Mom looked at me. "What happened?"

Crying loudly, I blurted out. "Johnny hit me in my eye with an ice ball!"

She said. "Lie down on the sofa."

I continued to cry. "I can't see, I can't see!"

My mother placed a warm cloth on my eye. After a while, I fell asleep. Later on, when I awakened, my vision was blurred. Through the night, I tossed and turned, worrying about my vision. The next day when I awoke, my vision improved, but not a hundred percent. The following day when my vision returned I was so relieved.

I looked at the range officer. "Remember the saying, 'hit him in the head to knock some sense into him.' Is it possible to hit someone in the eye to improve their vision?"

He laughed.

By the end of the fourth day of qualification, I noticed an improvement in my score. The trainee shooting adjacent to me failed to qualify on a completed round of fire and in disgust, he slammed the gun down onto the shooter's table. The range officer immediately removed him from his firing position, escorted him off the range and sent him home. A short-tempered personality is not welcomed in law enforcement. In desperation to increase their score, two trainees punctured their targets with a pen. After the training officers discovered the pen holes in the target, the trainees were sent home. Anyone who did not qualify by the fifth day was sent home. Requalification and make-up scoring was not part of the Sky Marshal program. On the last day of qualification, I scored 246 out of a possible 300. Had I not switched my shooting hand, I would not be working as a marshal.

After the basic firearms qualification, we trained inside a commercial aircraft mock-up, firing in a seated and standing positions. Firing a weapon on board a commercial aircraft requires many hours of training. There are many factors involved unlike any deadly force situations. Unaware of it at the time, the marshals had the highest firearms qualification of all U.S. Federal law enforcement officers and agents.

The interior of a Boeing 707 aircraft, contains 180 seats. This type of aircraft is confining and presents challenges for the marshal, if there were to be a weapon discharge. Aside from the safety of the passengers, the locations of the fuel tanks, fuel lines, electrical and hydraulic systems and windows are major considerations before discharging a weapon. We were informed by the instructors that if a window is blown out in flight, there is a ninety percent chance that the person seated next to the window will be sucked out of the aircraft, even if they are wearing the seatbelt. A person seated in the second seat, has a fifty percent chance of being sucked out. Discharging a weapon on board an in-flight commercial aircraft is something that requires a great deal of skill, quickly and safely, or no action at all. If we encountered an explosive we were provided the necessary procedures for its disposal. Everyone was taken aback and hoped that, a situation of that nature would never occur.

I passed the final exam. Thirty-five candidates graduated from the original class of sixty-five. At the swearing-in ceremony, we were issued a set of credentials, a badge from the office of U.S. Customs and a signed

Oath of Office from the Justice Department empowering us as Special Deputy U.S. Marshals. That's how the title 'Sky Marshal' originated. We were the only federal law enforcement officers in the country that maintained dual authority. Every officer was provided with a four-inch, thirty-eight caliber Smith and Wesson revolver and low velocity hollow point ammunition. The low velocity bullet flattens out and tumbles, remaining in the body, so as not to cause damage to another passenger or the aircraft.

24

SKY MARSHAL

The article written below contains a very accurate description of a Sky Marshal.

In April 14, 1974, *The Long Island Press* published this article:

'SKY MARSHALS HARD TO SPOT'

Would Be Hijacker Will Find Out Swiftly, Violently

Los Angeles—He could take the seat next to you in the jetliner, perhaps a young man with long sideburns who thumbs through a sports magazine, between glances at other boarding passengers.

Or he might be a Negro carrying a briefcase or a middle-aged man in a business suit or an Oriental chatting with the stewardess.

He could be any one of these-or two or three of them. On the other hand, none of them may be a Sky Marshal.

Instead it may be the long-haired hippie, striding aft to the coach section.

IT'S IMPOSSIBLE to single out these men who ride shotgun on many airline flights, to thwart hijackers. They could be any of the adult male passengers aboard, except the aged.

And when you think you spotted a marshal you can't be sure. For the men carrying a snub nosed .38 is an actor who has been taught to disguise his role with easy talk and a well-rehearsed cover story.

Nor can he be pinpointed by any cabin action against an offensive drunk, some oafish passenger who insults a stewardess. He'll never reveal himself unless there's an attempt at air piracy.

When he does make his move, it should be over in seconds, with the hijacker disarmed or dead on the cabin floor.

Nor will his partner-or partners-on the plane attempt to help him unless absolutely necessary, just in case there are other members of a hijacking team aboard not yet committed to overt action.

Who are these men that fly the skies today with the same mission as the shotgun guards on the stagecoach of old?

How are they trained? What's their routine/ How do they feel about their jobs? What are the problems, the dangers, the advantages of being a sky marshal?

PRESIDENT NIXON ordered armed guard protection for high-risk U.S. flights last September after a series of para military hijackings in the Middle East.

Although ground detection devices were coming into use, he decided that sky marshals were the only immediate answer to air piracy.

The initial cadre was composed of agents, security experts and military police from the Department of Justice, Treasury, Transportation and Defense.

The cadre was made up of Secret Service, FBI, Customs and Internal Revenue Agents and security men from the Federal Aviation Administration, the Army, Navy, Marines and Air Force on a temporary basis, 90-day service to get the program underway.

"Because time was critical, and these men were experienced in police work and weaponry, little more than a week's training was required at Fort Dix, New Jersey," explained J.R. Adsen, Chief of Investigations and security for FAA's western region.

"The majority of them have extended their service voluntarily to bridge us into the second phase now starting, wherein all new Sky Marshals will be customs agents assigned to FAA after a full month's training at Ft. Belvoir, Virginia.

These men must pass security checks, meet rigorous physical and psychological standards and qualify in all standards of the training program, *including marksmanship, with high scores in some 1000 rounds of shooting, And that's a lot of rounds!*

Adsen noted that much of the shooting is done in transport mockups that pose the same safety restrictions as flight cabin interiors, with seating arrangements and silhouette passengers.

"MARSHALS ARE TRAINED to shoot with either hand-or both, and the special ammunition they use is so designed that the .38 slug not penetrate a hijacker's body and endanger another person.

"This is due not so much to slower velocity, but to the hollow-point of the slug that flattens out and tumbles the projectile on impact with the flesh.

"Nor will the slug will penetrate the skin of an airliner," Adsen added.

"The Sky Marshal's job is no pie in the sky assignment," he emphasized.

"It's nerve-wrecking in that a man must always be on the alert, always watching, always judging; yet he should appear to be only an average passenger."

Two military marshals that had been flying out of Los Angeles International Airport since Oct 28, detailed for the Los Angeles Times this modern—day assignment of riding shotgun at 30,000 feet.

"PROBABLY THE toughest part of the job," they agreed with Adsen, "is watching people and their movements and listening to any telltale bits of conversation without ever appearing interested."

"It's a job that's all mental," they said, "all care and caution not to burn your cover while you keep an eye on everything and hold yourself ready hour after hour for a split- second decision-and violent action-if required."

"You can't preplan what you will do, except in the most general way, because if the threat hits, you'll have to cope with it as it develops. You never know what the situation will be; you'll have to determine almost instantly what you can and can't do in a given set of circumstances."

"The safety of the airplane, its passengers and crew, is always the first consideration," the two men said, "but it's surprising how much the marshal has going for him in protecting the flight."

"Gunplay may not be necessary," they pointed out, "for Sky Marshals are

trained in judo techniques and given the opportunity, can disarm a gunman before he knows what happened to him."

"We have a little bag of special tricks," Ferris and Davis said," and they can be most unpleasant for a hijacker. It's true we can't move until he moves, but then our advantage is that we know who he is, but he doesn't know us."

On Monday morning, January 3, 1971, I reported to the International Arrivals Building, at John F Kennedy International Airport (JFK), Queens, New York. Seated in a room with twenty-five fellow officers the Chief Air Security Coordinator Mr. Donahue provided a short briefing and called out twelve names. I was assigned to fly for TWA. The remainder of the marshals were assigned to fly for Pan Am.

At Hangar 12, we received orientation from a TWA instructor regarding the rules, regulations and general company policy. After the lecture, I spoke with Jeff, a coworker.

He said. "I got the impression that TWA feels that the government is forcing security on them."

I replied. "I'm with you on that, I didn't hear words like, welcome. we're happy you're here, we need you, etc."

He said, "Did they forget that one of their aircraft was blown up in the desert a few months earlier?"

I mentioned. "I wonder how we'll be accepted by the cabin crew?"

He moaned. "Yeah, that remains to be seen."

The second part of the orientation was provided by a guest speaker Captain Williams. Late in the year in 1969, he piloted the hijacked TWA flight 85. The hijacking was initiated by ex-marine Raffaele Minichiello, who boarded flight 85 from Los Angeles to San Francisco. At gunpoint, he diverted the aircraft to Denver where he released all passengers. He ordered Captain Williams to fly him to New York where the aircraft refueled. In New York, the FBI attempted to overpower him, but he fired a shot through the fuselage. The aircraft was permitted to takeoff and subsequently landed in Rome. No one was hurt, but after the incident,

Captain Williams was given a managerial position on the ground because they felt he would be more valuable to the company. The hijacking covered 6,900 miles, the longest in history. Minichiello was arrested by the Italian authorities, where he was acquitted on all charges except for weapons possession and sentenced to eighteen months in prison. The Sky Marshal Program was initiated the following year.

25

FLYING

In January 1971, I traveled to JFK Airport for the first flight as an air marshal. TWA was given the names of the marshals as they handled the monthly scheduling. Inside the TWA hangar, I met with partners Clayton and John. Clayton was an ex Mississippi Deputy Sheriff, and John previously worked as a port steward for Pan American Airlines.

The captain entered the briefing room in full uniform and introduced himself. He said. "I'm Captain Exum." A tall, trim gray-haired man in his late fifties, speaking in a strong, calm voice. At that time, 747 pilots were the top of the heap, flying the newly built state of the art aircraft. For the most part, commercial pilots started their careers flying in the military. Having flown commercial aircraft for most of their career, with numerous hours of training, 747 pilots worked their way up the ranks, logging many years of experience.

The captain was the overseeing authority on board the aircraft. He has the final decision regarding any actions that the marshals may take where a decision is required. Immediate action by us is a judgment call and we take full responsibility for that action. A shoot-out at thirty thousand feet is a situation that we would want to avoid. It is the last resort. During training, many scenarios were presented and ingrained in us by the instructors. The most important factor imbedded in our mind was to always use good judgment. But if the situation required that I fire my weapon, I would strive to get the bullet into the full body mass of the hijacker. A wild shot could be catastrophic and that type of action must be avoided at all cost.

A few months earlier, terrorists hijacked five aircraft, flew them to the desert and blew them up holding the passengers as prisoners. That is a situation that we'd strive to prevent at all costs. As marshals, that scenario was constantly running through our minds while we were in - flight. A terrorist group that attempts to hijack an aircraft that's manned with armed guards needs to first locate and neutralize the marshals.

The captain provided us the signals, used in the event of a hijacking.

Clayton looked at the captain. "Are there any crew members in civilian clothes, who might have access to the cockpit or anyone authorized to carry firearms?"

The captain replied. "Once the passengers are aboard, if there is anybody on-board the aircraft that you should know about, I'll have the crew inform you."

After the briefing, we boarded the crew bus and arrived at the TWA terminal where we split up. At the counter, I provided the ticket agent with a TWA issued credit card, specifying the flight number and requested an economy class ticket to London.

Since marshals were armed, when I entered the boarding area I cleared security with my weapon using the code word we were given. Upon entering the 747 aircraft, I was in awe as I peered out over hundreds of seats, in an unconfined space, unlike the smaller aircraft at that time. The 747 required three marshals, two in first-class and one in economy. I sat in the rear section of economy class, where I was unable to observe with clarity the first-class passengers more than two hundred feet away. We taxied down the runway in the 230- foot-long jumbo jet nicknamed after 'Fat Albert', the cartoon character.

Moments later we were airborne, and I looked out of the window over the water above south Queens. The aircraft started to turn, roll and reduce power. We were not gaining altitude. The aircraft remained in a rolled position. The more I focused on the land below, the more it appeared we not gaining altitude. The objects below were not decreasing in size. My heart beat like a drum. We remained at a constant altitude, not indicative of a takeoff. My stomach turned, and I felt sick saying to myself," *my first flight and we're going down."* A short time later, the seatbelt sign turned off. I took a deep breath. The passenger count was low, somewhere around twenty-five percent capacity. Walking into the rear galley I looked at the stewardess as she prepared drinks on the cart. "Why did the pilot decrease the power and turn sharply during takeoff?"

She shrugged. "When we take-off from that particular runway, the pilot needs to reduce power due to the 'noise abatement program' for the residents who live in Howard Beach, Queens. The engine power is not increased until we've cleared the area."

I uttered. "I thought we were going down."

She said. "Well, if you've never experienced that type of maneuver I could see why."

I remarked. "What a relief, thanks."

During the second month of flying, I sat in the first-class section on our way to Madrid Spain. When the seatbelt sign turned off, I headed to the upstairs lounge. My partner remained in his seat. Reading a book, I sat alone while the stewardess placed a small bowl of jumbo shrimp with cocktail sauce on the table in front of me. I ate one shrimp, then another and before I knew it, I consumed nearly all of them. Minutes later the captain exited the cockpit, walked over and nodded to me. He was a distinguished looking gentleman in his late fifties. He reached down and ate the remaining shrimp. With a stern look on his face he said, "Boy, do you want to ride home with me?"

My face turned red. I looked at him not saying anything, wondering why he was angered.

He said. "Next time, don't eat my shrimp!"

I answered. "I'm sorry. I thought the shrimp were for the passengers."

He rolled his eyes in disgust and returned to the cockpit.

Later on, a group of people gathered around in the lounge laughing and joking as they ordered drinks. A passenger checked me out. "Hey, would you like a drink?"

I said, "Sure. I'll have a scotch and soda."

I ordered a drink in order to maintain my cover. to blend in with the passengers. At times, passengers play the game, 'guess the marshal.' On rare occurrences such as this, marshals were permitted to have a drink.

The guy gazed at me. "So what kind of work do you do?"

I used my cover story. "I work for Grumman Aerospace in the engineering department."

He shook his head up and down.

That was usually the extent of the conversation with people flying in first class. After two years of flying, I can count on one hand the number of first- class passengers who have engaged in much conversation during international flights. For some reason economy passengers are much more talkative.

The following month, I traveled to JFK Airport scheduled to fly to Tel Aviv, Israel. My partner and I boarded the smaller 707 aircraft which required two marshals. The captain announced that our non-stop flying time to Tel Aviv would be twelve hours. The single aisle 707 was filled to capacity with 180 passengers as I sat in the rear of the economy section. After reaching cruising altitude, the seatbelt sign was turned off. Everyone in my section lit up a cigarette. The cabin area became engulfed in smoke, as the exhaust system barely worked. My nasal system became irritated. I stood up and walked toward the rear galley and looked at the stewardess. "I can't stand the smoke in here what's going on?"

She said, "This is a tour group of Canadian Jews. I never worked a flight where the entire cabin area was filled with heavy smoke."

I mentioned. "What's the odds, that every member of a tour group were smokers? Do you think the trip was financed by a tobacco company?"

She grinned. "Anything's possible."

While seated in the aircraft for a few hours, I felt as though the moisture slowly withdrew from my body, as my throat was constantly dry. I craved liquids. Little did I know that while flying in an aircraft the humidity level is one hundred fifty percent less than normal air-conditioned space? Water extraction from the body is unavoidable. The longer you fly, the more dehydrated you become. Dehydration places stress on the body causing fatigue, and that is the enemy of the marshal.

Sometimes I wear sunglasses and put my head back to appear as if I'm sleeping, just to blend in. As a marshal if your constant focus is on the passengers and crew your effectiveness is short-lived. It's important not to draw attention to yourself and maintain your cover.

One of the most difficult things to do, is to sit in a comfortable seat for twelve hours and remain awake. While walking, I noticed a stewardess asleep in a jump-seat. I thought she might be ill, but I learned later that crew members are permitted rest time on flights that exceed 9.5 hours according to their union contract. Marshals can't sleep and can't drink alcohol; it's torture. I fought to remain alert as my eyelids felt like bricks. The lights in the cabin were turned off. After, losing count of the number of cups of coffee, I walked into the rest room and splashed cold water on my face. Two meals had already been served. Walking into the galley I pulled the curtain. I looked at the stewardess. "Do you have anything to eat, I'm hungry?"

She answered. "We'll be serving breakfast in a few hours."

I advised. "I can't wait that long. Do you have a snack or something, I'm starving?"

She replied. "I can give a meal now."

I said. "Another meal, that would be great, thanks."

Nobody ever considered what it takes for a marshal to remain alert for twelve consecutive hours. I learned several tactics that I used to remain alert on future flights: eating, drinking, writing, thinking, reading, watching, walking, standing, talking, and stretching.

My partner and I arrived at Lod airport in Tel Aviv Israel late in the evening and stored our weapons in the security room overnight. At the hotel, we checked in and entered the high-rise building that bordered the

Mediterranean Sea. The view of the stars from the hotel window as they glittered with clarity, combined with the moon's reflection on the sea was unlike anything that I had seen before. Anxious to admire the view in the morning, we ate dinner and turned in for the night.

The next day we departed Tel Aviv returning to New York. The flight was uneventful, but we learned about the massacre that occurred at Lod Airport. Three members of the Japanese Red Army in conjunction with a Palestinian Terrorist Organization assassinated 26 passengers and injured 78 in the baggage claim area. A day earlier we cleared through that same baggage claim area during the same time-frame. Thank God, we just missed that horrific event.

After a few months of flying, many of the marshals were surprised by the treatment we received from the stewardesses. My partner Jeff complained to a stewardess that if she smiled more, it might help business. He explained that when passengers are not nearby, it would be nice to talk with us for a minute or two it breaks up the monotony. The stewardess walked over to my seat as she was highly insulted by Jeff's comments. "Your partner thinks stewardesses should walk around with smiles on our faces."

I said, "He's right. Don't you realize that besides being good for business, it sets the mood for us? It's a morale booster. You would be amazed what it does for us. Being seated on a plane for eight to ten hours is boring. A smile now and then can really help. If you treat the passengers better than you treat us, we stick out like a sore thumb."

She lapsed thoughtful. "I guess you're right."

I mentioned. "You think if you're nice to us, we'll get the wrong impression, perhaps a come on. Quite a few of us are married, just like some of you, and we're just hard-working guys trying to make a living. We miss our wives and so a little conversation or a smile never hurt anyone."

Not to make any excuses for the stewardesses, but at that time many of them received college degrees from some of the best colleges in the country. After all, many stewardesses were looking for relationships with someone above the GS -5 level government marshal earning six thousand dollars a year. I heard the marshals who flew for Pan Am Airlines had more positive experiences.

26

FIUMICINO AIRPORT

Several months later, I sat in the boarding area at Fiumicino Airport in Rome. Four Middle Eastern men were seated nearby. What caught my eye was the fact that they maintained carry-on luggage, which was uncommon for international passengers.

My partner and I sat separately in the first-class section which was procedure. The steward and the Director of Customer Service stood in front of me with concerned looks on their faces. "The captain was unable to make the briefing because he received an intelligence report that there are three Arab suspects on board that will attempt to hijack the flight."

I locked eyes with him. "Do you have a description of the suspects?"

He replied. "No, that's all we have."

I wrote a note and said. "Give this note to the marshal in the economy section."

The note informed him, that we received information from the captain that there are three suspects on board that will attempt to hijack the flight. There is no description of the suspects at this time.

Trying to assess the situation before takeoff, I observed a group of Middle Eastern men sitting in the economy section. There was no way of knowing if these passengers were connected with the captain's information, but it certainly added a measure of credibility. The first-class section was at half capacity. Behind the curtain in the galley, I met with my partner, Jeff. We changed our seats, sitting as close as possible to the economy section. We instructed the stewardesses to close the upstairs lounge and the curtains that separated the first-class section from economy class. All stewardesses assigned to the economy class were told to avoid using the first-class section. Closing the upstairs lounge provided us with the advantage of covering both aisles because normally one marshal was assigned to the upstairs lounge. While I sat in my seat, I noticed fear on the faces of the crew as they performed their duties. A stewardess, who worked in the economy section stood at my seat and spoke nervously. "Do you know what these suspects look like?"

I replied. "What we know, is that they are Middle Eastern men, dark complexion, average height, late thirties."

She did a double take. "That description fits about forty men in my section."

I said. "Yes, we're aware of that. All I can tell you is, try to relax and don't worry about it; that's why we're here. These guys are not looking for you; they are looking for us."

You can't blame the crew for being scared. After all, who wants to be held as a hostage and watch their aircraft blown up in the desert?

The optimum time for a hijacking is within the first hour after takeoff, when the aircraft contains the most fuel. We trained for this situation and now we sit and wait. My stomach was in knots, while seated in first- class, my heart raced. I had no appetite and continued to drink coffee and club soda. Holding a book open in front of me, I was not reading, as my eyes remained focused on the aisle, watching and waiting.

Shortly after takeoff the seatbelt sign turned off. A short time later I heard the rattling of the curtain in the track as it opened up behind me. A Middle Eastern man stood there. A man in his thirties, he was 5' 8" stocky build with a mustache wearing a dark suit. I turned and looked at him smiling and uttered, "Hi ya!" He did not respond. He stood there, with a blank look on his face. I focused on his eyes as they quickly scanned the first-class section from side to side. Waiting and waiting I did not take my eyes off him. It felt like forever, but only seconds had passed. The seat on my left was vacant as I held my hand gun underneath a newspaper. A moment later, he turned around and returned to his seat. I breathed a sigh of relief. Moments later, I handed the stewardess a note to deliver to the marshal in the economy section, notifying him to keep an eye on the subject and see if he makes contact with anyone else.

Shortly thereafter, an unruly drunk caused a ruckus in economy class. The stewardess passed a note to the marshal to assist her. As marshals, our primary purpose is to prevent the aircraft from being hijacked. Stewardesses have been handling drunks since the beginning of commercial aviation. Drunks are more common onboard aircraft because the barometric pressure is lower than on earth. The cabin pressure diminishes the body's ability to absorb oxygen, producing light-headedness. Consequently, it's easier to get drunk flying in an aircraft than it is on the ground. If the marshal becomes involved with a drunk, he has blown his cover. The incident may have been a diversion by the hijackers to identify the marshal. Alert or no alert we never handle drunks.

Time dragged on as we remained on full alert. I continued drinking coffee still unable to eat, but I became more confident that we were in the clear. Nearing the fifth-hour, we were beyond the half-way mark. After flying nine hours we landed safely in New York. In retrospect, we felt that the information was a 'dry run' for a future hijacking: or the hijackers didn't feel confident enough to hijack the flight. We will never know if there were hijackers on board that day. We strongly believed that our flight was a failed hijacking, or an intelligence-gathering mission for a future hijacking. I earned my pay that day with more gray hairs.

After a few months, our flying hours were increased to as much as one hundred sixty hours per month. Flight hours for airline employees were limited to eighty hours per month according to their union contract due to fatigue and health issues. Aside from traveling and living out of a suitcase an air marshal is not a glamourous position as one would think. The flight hours were sometimes twice the allowable hours that were permitted by the airline personnel. Flying through six to nine time zones every day for a week is not glamourous. The effects of flying are commonly referred to as 'jet lag.' Flight travel disrupts the body's circadian rhythm. This disruption profoundly affects body temperature, heart rate, blood pressure, hormones and state of mind.

Marshals were at the mercy of the government to schedule us for the good of the service. Years later, a lawsuit was filed on behalf of the marshal's for back pay, and we received a settlement. The settlement amounts varied from a few hundred to a couple of thousand.

While working as an air marshal, I felt guilty that I was traveling around the world, while my wife and family were not part of my experience. While traveling I learned about life, getting out of my environment learning to talk to people, understanding a different way of life and different cultures, developing confidence and open mindedness. The lay-overs were short in most countries and only permitted time for rest and dinner. In order to take advantage of the travel to Europe there were times that I gave-up my rest and utilized the sightseeing services in major cities because I knew that I would never have this opportunity again.

During the early part of the marshal program many employees were terminated for a number of reasons. Terminations resulted when employees listed erroneous information or failed to list pertinent information on their employment applications. The first year of employment as a government employee is a probationary period, and at that point, the employee is technically considered an applicant. Terminating a probationary employee does not require a high degree of misconduct. The government wants employees who have good character.

Employees that violated the alcohol consumption regulation were also terminated. In an effort to terminate some bad apples, customs agents scheduled a month of turn-around flights with employees of questionable character. A turnaround flight was flying to a destination and returning home the next day. Since the layover was less than twenty-four hours, if they consumed alcohol on their layover, they violated the alcohol consumption regulation. Marshals were prohibited from consuming alcohol within twenty- four hours of reporting for duty. Customs agents observed the marshals on their layover in foreign countries. After the month ended there was a mass termination of marshals, weeding out a number of bad employees.

Not knowing the full context of the mass terminations created a firestorm among the ranks. Many officers were concerned that the termination process was somewhat devious, and employees were dismissed for minor infractions that could have been remedied by disciplinary action. Initially I was annoyed at this method of terminations but later I became in favor of it and here's why:

A few months later my partner Kevin and I laid-over in Los Angeles after our return flight to New York was cancelled. We finished dinner, and I retired to the room for the night. Kevin remained drinking in the restaurant since we were off duty the next day.

There was a knock on the door. I awakened and opened the door. Kevin stood there.

I asked him. "Why didn't you use your key?"

He eyed me as he swayed from side to side. "I couldn't find it."

Kevin walked in and turned on the light in the room.

I sat up in bed and looked at him. "What are you doing, I'm trying to sleep."

He glanced at me. "Don't fucking bother me!"

He swung his arm around and knocked the table lamp onto the floor.

I yelled at him. "What are you doing!"

Kevin drew his weapon and pointed it at me. "Don't fucking move you cock sucker!"

I immediately rolled off the bed, out of his sight, hiding behind the mattress on the floor concerned about his next move.

Kevin ordered. "And don't fucking come out of there!"

Shortly thereafter, he placed his gun on the table and walked into the bathroom. I stood up, emptied his gun and collected the extra ammunition.

Walking into the bathroom, I confronted him. "I'll give you your gun back tomorrow. I'm not your partner anymore; don't apologize to me, stay away from me!"

Kevin remained silent, as he put his head down. When we arrived in New York, I said, "I'm having you removed as my partner." Kevin was silent.

While Kevin was drunk, he could have pulled the trigger and killed me. How did I survive that incident, I'll never-know? I thought that Kevin was a friend, but he was just another co-worker with a drinking problem, I needed to get as far away from him as possible. I didn't want him to lose his job, but maybe he should have. When we arrived in New York, I again confronted him. "If I were you, I would resign." A short time later, Kevin resigned. Maybe he realized he had drinking problem?

27

GROUND DUTY

When the marshals were assigned to ground duty, we worked in the international terminals at JFK Airport, covering the out-bound flights. While assigned to the Pan Am terminal, we walked into the boarding area and entered the jet-way. All flights to Puerto Rico were considered 'High Risk Flights' due to their proximity to Cuba. At that time, many of the hijacked domestic flights were flown to Cuba. Hijackers believed that when they arrived in Cuba, Castro would welcome them as revolutionary heroes. That was not the case. Hijackers were interrogated for weeks by the Cuban authorities and then sent to live in squalid conditions for the rest of their life

While passengers boarded the outbound flights, one officer manned the magnetometer (metal detector) while four officers stood at a long table searching carry-on luggage. Three other officers and I were assigned to conduct pat-downs of boarding passengers. On high-risk flights, all male passengers were physically searched. Discretion dominated our search criteria. An elderly person in a wheelchair or physically disabled persons, and/or a child, were all green- lighted. The Israeli Airline, El Al, maintained the best security record in the airline industry, whereby all passengers were physically searched, and many of their high security techniques that prevent hijackings were employed.

A passenger wearing a black suit and shaggy short hair approached me for a pat down search. When I wrapped my hands around the passenger's thigh area, the leg felt soft. Realizing I just searched a woman, I immediately stopped. "Okay, you're done."

She looked at me and smiled. "Thank you." I think she was pleased with the search. I didn't know what to make of it. I guess I avoided a lawsuit.

A short black man in his fifties wearing a checkered sport coat and a straw hat walked through the magnetometer, not setting it off. I searched him and felt an object in his crotch. We moved to a secure area. I told him, "Drop your pants." When he dropped his pants, I discovered a loaded small caliber silver-plated automatic weapon secreted in a homemade holster sewn into his jockey shorts. That was the first and last time in my career that I discovered a 'crotch-holster'.

Weeks later, I stood in the jet-way as passengers cleared the baggage inspection. I selected a man for a pat-down. He wore a brown tailored three-piece suit with a short-brimmed hat, as he held the hand of a young child wearing a matching suit. He moved closer to me. When I patted him down and felt an object in the small of his back, I asked him, "What's on your back?"

He smiled as he looked at me. "That's for my back, I got a bad back."

I said, "Come with me."

John and I escorted him into an empty jet-way. Staring at him, I didn't know what to make of it, thinking he might be carrying some type of explosive.

I ordered him. "Take off your jacket and face the wall."

I pulled out his shirt and lifted up his undershirt. A clear plastic bag, the size of a large envelope was taped to his back with medical tape. When I removed the package from his body, he grunted from the pain. I asked him, "How does this white powder help your back?"

He stood there silently as his jaw dropped and his eyes grew to the size of lemons. John held the package.

I ordered him. "You're under arrest!"

We handcuffed him and escorted him to the office. The package tested positive for cocaine, weighing three-quarters of a pound. The majority of the outbound narcotics seizures were for possession of personal use, but this quantity of cocaine placed it in the drug dealer category. Searching the passenger further revealed a savings bank book from Puerto Rico with a $25,000 balance and a gold omega watch. We notified the duty agent.

After the arrest, the word traveled through the ranks because this narcotics seizure was far above the norm of personal use. Fellow officers peeked into the office giving thumb- up, acknowledging with a head shake or positive comments.

Al and Frank worked the same flight searching carry-on luggage. Al, an older officer, walked over to me. "Neil, make sure you tell the duty agent that Frank and I pointed out this guy for you to search."

I asked. "What are you saying?"

Al replied. "Mention to the duty agent that we pointed out this guy to you."

I told him. "Al, I was assigned to pat down male passengers and you didn't alert me to give this passenger a strip search."

Al turned away and walked out of the office. I know I appear to be a pushover, but his request was not genuine.

The subject was selected, searched and arrested without Al's involvement. Unsure of Al's attachment to my arrest, I surmised he wanted to be part of it. The furthest thing from my mind is to exclude information from fellow officers that lead to an arrest. Some coworkers used methods to ingratiate themselves to move up the ladder. Al was one of them.

Marshals were hired from all walks of life:

Mike McConnel a retired Air Force Colonel, owned a restaurant. Fred Zederbaum was an editor for the New York Times. Keith Balcom was a furloughed Pan Am pilot. Vinny owned a Bait and Tackle shop, John Moore worked for General Motors. Tom was a retired NYPD Detective, Lenny was a recent college graduate who majored in history. Bobby graduated Law School.

John, the Customs duty agent walked into the office and looked at me. "I ran this guy's criminal history and NCIC. He's got a record as long as your arm. Good work. Give me the details and I'll contact the U.S. Attorney."

A few months later I spoke with the duty captain Angelo Gorasi at headquarters as he leaned back in his chair. "I'd like to be placed on the list for permanent ground duty. I noticed in the terminals there are officers that consistently work ground duty."

He eyeballed me. "There is no permanent ground duty, and you were hired to work air security."

I said, "I understand. Can I submit a memo in case you need ground duty volunteers?"

He rolled his eyes with discontent. "Go right ahead."

The Marshal Program had been in operation almost two years without a successful hijacking in flight that was staffed with armed guards. However, in the latter part of 1972, a passenger hijacked an American Airlines 747 aircraft to Cuba. According to the marshals on board, the stewardess escorted the hijacker very quietly into the upstairs lounge, without alerting the marshals. The stewardess notified the captain that the hijacker held her at gunpoint. The marshals were alerted and devised a plan to change clothes with the steward and overtake the hijacker in the upstairs lounge. The captain disapproved the plan and decided to fly to Cuba. After the hijacking, we learned that the hijacker did not have a gun, only a hard object that he forced into the stewardess' back that felt like a gun.

I spoke to the marshals that worked the hijacked flight and they were confident their plan would have succeeded. The decision by the captain that day to fly to Cuba, may have sealed the fate of the Air Marshal Program; or did the airlines need an excuse to end the program because they were losing revenue from the seats occupied by non-paying marshals; or was it the Master Agreement between the Department of Treasury and the Department of Transportation calling for a two-year crash program? Publicity regarding the hijacking remained minimal for security reasons. Shortly thereafter, the Air Marshal Program ended. The appearance that marshals covered flights needed to be maintained. Many years after the marshals no longer provided air security, most passengers believed that the flights were staffed with armed guards.

The Air Marshal program prevented hijackings and over the two years that it existed, there were thousands of weapons and narcotics seized. There's no way of knowing how many hijackings were prevented. Even with the numbers in our favor, the program ended. The Air Marshal Program resulted in: 3,828 arrests, 48 were made aboard aircraft, 21 in response to an announced threat, and 27 for other causes involving safety of the aircraft such as assaults on crew members. The arrests for illegal narcotics, and people with weapons who attempted to circumvent ground screening were part of that total number. In addition, air marshals seized or detained over 66,481 potential lethal weapons from passengers during pre-departure screening.

After September 11, 2001, the government used law enforcement agents from Customs, DEA, FBI and wherever they could get manpower to fly as marshals. Under the Transportation Security Administration (TSA), the Federal Air Marshals were trained, and replaced the agents on loan from other the agencies, with a force totaling 4,000 employees.

28

PATROL DIVISION

In January 1973, the Air Security Program ended, and the marshals were absorbed within various divisions in the government. The majority of us were converted to Customs Patrol Officers. Others were converted to special agents, inspectors, import specialists, and the remainder accepted positions within other federal agencies.

The U.S. border consisted of thousands of miles of land and water, contiguous with Mexico and Canada not to mention thousands of miles of open waters on the east, west and Gulf coast. Manpower was distributed around the country to build up the border force, thus narrowing the gaps where smuggling occurs. The Patrol Division provided law enforcement where the other divisions of Customs were unable to do so. We filled the gaps along the borders.

The previous week, I worked as a marshal undercover at thirty thousand feet, protecting the lives of airline passengers and crew. Today I stood as a guard at the entrance door to the Customs arrivals area at JFK Airport. It was a shock to my ego, since my assignment did not make use of my training and experience. I could handle it, since I worked menial jobs while growing up, but envious, watching coworkers in plainclothes apprehend smugglers.

Captain Driscoll supervised the plainclothes officers assigned to the arrival terminals. He could help you, or he could hurt you by your assignment. As much as I wanted to work in plainclothes, I refused to kiss up to him. While growing up I was raised that if you wanted something, you needed to work for it. Kissing up to the boss was not a skill I possessed. I stayed away from Driscoll - out of sight, out of mind and did my job.

Joe Serrao, an ex- marshal walked over to me. "Neil, you've been jamming the door for a long time."

I nodded. "It's almost a year now."

He pointed out. "I thought you would have received some recognition from the arrests you made on ground duty."

I said. "You would think so."

Joe looked at me. "Can't anybody put a good word in for you?"

I crossed my arms. "When you work for the government, there are many coworkers and only one or two friends if any."

Joe replied. "Ain't that the truth."

Months later, Driscoll called me into the office "Hey, Kid, on Sunday you're assigned to work plainclothes on the 3 to 11 shift."

My jaw dropped. "This Sunday, like in three days?"

He said, "That's right, kid."

I replied. "Okay, thanks, Captain."

I figured that Joe may have put in a good word for me to the captain. On Sunday, I walked into the office located in the International Arrivals Building (IAB) at 2:45 pm and signed in on the clipboard. I looked at Driscoll "Hey, Captain."

He looked up. "Hey, Kid."

In the passenger arrivals area hundreds of people scurried around retrieving their luggage, while others with worried looks on their faces lined up at the baggage belts for their customs inspection. The sky-caps leaned on their carts in front of the baggage belts, anxiously waiting for customers.

Freddy Conklin, an experienced plainclothes officer, walked over to me. "There's the Sabena flight from Brussels; we can look for diamond smugglers." Freddy stopped a Hasidic Jew who cleared the baggage inspection. The passenger was in his late twenties wearing a black overcoat and hat with curled sideburns hanging down his face. We identified ourselves as customs officers. Freddy looked at the guy. "Let's see your passport and customs declaration."

After questioning him, Freddy returned the passenger's documents releasing him. Not satisfied with the passenger's answers, I removed the passport and declaration from his hands.

I asked. "What kind of work do you do?"

He replied. "I work for my father in business."

I said. "Did anybody give you anything to bring back with you?"

He spoke. "Nothing special."

Examination of his passport revealed several trips to Belgium in a short period of time which is sometimes a red flag.

I said. "Take your bags and come with us."

We escorted him to a private room. While inside the room, I looked at the passenger. "Remove your overcoat and place the contents of your pockets on the table."

During the pat down search, I felt a hard object on top of my index finger in his crotch area.

Staring at him, I ordered, "Drop your pants. What's in your crotch?"

He turned away.

I said, "Pull the girdle down!"

An object hit the floor.

I replied. "What's that?"

He looked at me as his eyes opened as wide as lemons. "Diamonds, you got me!"

I asked. "Is that what's not so special?"

He remained silent.

The package, was half the length of an Italian sausage, and wrapped using layers of condoms, tied at the top with thread. In the office, I sliced the package open with a knife as the diamonds spread out covering half the sheet of paper below it. We counted fifty large white diamonds, and there were over two thousand 30-point diamonds ranging in colors of blue, yellow, red, and green. The intense color and fire as they glittered was amazing. I placed the subject under arrest for smuggling. The appraisal of the diamonds, was valued at $114,000. By today's standards the value of this seizure would be equivalent to 1.4 million dollars.

After working as a plainclothes officer for thirty minutes, I was elated. The diamond seizure created a firestorm in the plainclothes unit. Officers who worked in plainclothes for many years were unable to recall a diamond seizure of that magnitude at JFK airport. After the diamond seizure, secondary examinations of diamond dealers hit an all-time high for about six months. I focused away from the diamond dealers and into other smuggling areas, considering my chances of apprehending other types of smugglers would be better. Shortly thereafter I arrested an arriving passenger from Colombia in possession of two kilos of cocaine secreted in his underwear below his waist. Months later at a Customs awards ceremony, I received a Special Act award for the diamond, and cocaine seizure.

Weeks later Tommy Bottone and I observed passengers arriving from Mexico, and I observed a bulge in an arriving passenger's pocket. We escorted him to a search room. Looking at him I said. "What's that bulge in your pocket?"

The passenger removed a plastic bag from his pocket and placed it on the table.

I said "This looks like marijuana how much is in here?"

The passenger paused and then said. "About six ounces, but you see I need that for my job."

I cocked my head. "What kind of work do you do?"

He replied "I work at the track, and we use the smoke from this plant, and blow it into the race horses' nose to slow them down during the race."

I crossed my arms. "If you use marijuana smoke to slow down a race horse that is illegal."

He swallowed as he looked down. "Well, I do what my boss tells me to do, cause he could fire me."

My partner and I shook our heads in disbelief. A field test for the substance proved positive for marijuana. The subject was placed under arrest and transferred over to the local police for prosecution.

As Customs Officers, we enforce a wide variety of laws and collect duties that produce revenue, which pays our salaries. Since the Customs search authority is the strongest in the nation, the areas where contraband has been secreted by persons, in merchandise, vehicles, vessels places and things is ever-changing. New methods of smuggling are constantly discovered, so in order to be an effective officer, one must be inquisitive and never become complacent. Working in plainclothes is requires waiting, watching, at times it can be boring. It's all about concentrating and focusing, focusing on the flights and their country of origin and the products that are produced, anywhere from drugs, merchandise, precious stones, gold jewelry, etc.

Tommy and I observed an Indian couple arriving on the Air India flight. The woman was wearing several gold bracelets as she claimed her luggage. It's very common for Indian women to wear several gold bangle bracelets. Bangle bracelets are part of the Indian culture because it signifies long life, good fortune and prosperity. I looked at Tommy. "Let's stop this couple after their baggage inspection."

Tommy mentioned. "Okay, but these people are reluctant to declare their gifts."

I replied. "Those days are over.

I bought this jeweler's loop at K-Mart. It has a light with an on/off switch that I'll use to assist passengers to be more forthcoming and declare their jewelry purchases and/or gifts."

The customs declaration is a very simple document indicated by the statement below that must be signed by all arriving passengers:

"You must declare all items acquired abroad whether worn or new, whether dutiable or not, whether obtained by purchase or as a gift which are in your possession at the time you arrive."

We stopped the arriving Air India passengers.

I said. "Pardon me, folks I'm with U.S. Customs, can I see your passports and declaration. Are you traveling together?"

The gentleman replied. "Yes sir."

I stated. "Did you purchase anything or receive any gifts while you were away?"

He looked at me. "We declared our allowance of one-hundred dollars each in purchases, sir."

I checked out his passport. "What is your profession, sir?"

He said. "I am a chemical engineer."

I replied. "Okay, please take your bags and come with us."

The pat down search of the man was negative. I looked at the woman. "Can you remove the bracelets and rings that you're wearing; I'd like to look at them? When did you purchase these items?"

The woman was silent as the man said. "We had them for long time."

I looked at the bracelets. "These bracelets look new."

The man claimed, "Oh no sir, these items are not new, we've had them for long time."

I turned to her. "Ma'am, how often do you wear this jewelry?"

The man interjected, "She wears them every day, Sir."

I pointed out. "Well, this jewelry has no scratches, or any signs of wear, weighing about three ounces of 22 karat gold." The passengers were silent.

I looked at the man. "Sir, I have this device that I will use to examine your jewelry. The device was made by the Precious Metals Institute of America and is equipped with a sensor that detects new jewelry. When I examine your jewelry if the light comes on, the jewelry is new."

My partner was smirking and turned away. I placed the jewelry under the loop as there were no scratches; turned on the light. Looking at the passengers.   I said. "The light just came on so this … is new, this one… is also new, I'm thinking that all of this jewelry is new."

Staring at me, wide-eyed, he admitted, "Yes sir, they are new."

I advised him. "You failed to declare these items, so we will seize them."

His jaw dropped. "Oh no, oh no, oh please, Sir, don't take our jewelry, they are gifts!"

I pointed out. "The Customs declaration that you signed, states that you must declare all items acquired abroad including gifts. If you pay a penalty of four times the duty now, you can take the jewelry with you."

He replied. "Oh, yes sir, yes sir, we would like to pay."

I said. "Okay."

29

THE BORDER

My assignment at JFK Airport required working afternoon, evening and weekend shifts, covering the peak hours of passenger and cargo arrivals. At that time, my wife and I were living from paycheck to paycheck. Working evenings increased my salary and provided needed income for our family.

After working in law enforcement for a few years I learned that my mother did not approve of law enforcement work because she felt that it posed a threat to her control. Generally, law enforcement officers are independent thinkers and decision makers. My irregular work schedule, at times, prevented us from attending some family functions. I recalled a few events that were attended by the immediate family, and we did not receive an invitation. My mother did not inform us of the event and excused our absence claiming that I was working. Some invitations for my wife and I were coordinated through Mom, the 'event coordinator.' If my work schedule prevented me from attending a family function, my wife did not feel comfortable going alone. Joann was not the chatty type, and her conversations with my mother were generally brief, since she was not part of my mother's inner circle. After I married, I hoped that my mother would accept my wife as a new daughter in the family. Knowing my mother, I knew the chances were slim.

I reported for duty at the International Arrivals Building. Captain Driscoll looked at me. "Hey Kid, headquarters called, you're going TDY (Temporary Duty) to the Mexican border for three months."

With a surprised look on my face I asked. "Are you serious?"

He spoke. "The duty captain just called me from headquarters."

I remarked. "Are any other officers from JFK being sent to the border?"
He turned away. "I don't know, Kid."

I arrived home from work; my wife was sitting in bed. "I don't know how to tell you this, but I've been detailed to the Mexican border for three months."

She looked at me slack-jawed. "Are you kidding?"

I lowered my eyes. "I wish I was."

Two months earlier we moved into the house we had built. I was angered being detailed away from my wife for three months, leaving her alone in the house; our closest neighbor lived a block away.

While seated in the departure area at JFK Airport, I noticed a customs supervisor checking in at the gate. I walked over to him. "John Capelli are you going to the Texas border with me?"

John seemed perplexed. "Yeah, but under duress! I'm a supervisor, and I've done my time in the trenches. I don't know what they thought they would gain by sending an old guy like me to do a young man's job."

I asked. "John, since you work in the office do you know why I was the only patrol officer from JFK to be detailed to the border?""

He said. "Well, Captain Gorasi called the IAB and told Driscoll to pick somebody to go TDY."

I asked. "So, I was Driscoll's first choice?"

John turned away and looked down. "I think so."

We boarded the flight to Texas trading seats to sit next to each other. I said to John. "It's nice to be with somebody you have something in common with when you're sent to work in an unfamiliar place."

He mentioned. "Neil, I'll travel to the border today, but I'll be back home by the end of the week. If I'm still here by then, I'm calling my Congressman."

A few hours later we landed in MacAllen, Texas. John remained TDY in Texas until our assignment ended.

The next day I met Butch, a patrol officer from the New York Seaport. We traveled together to the town of Falcon Heights, approximately seventy miles west of MacAllen. With a population of nearly a hundred, the town bordered the Rio Grande River and consisted of a convenience store, a motel with six small cabins, and some house trailers. This region of Texas was separated from Mexico by the Rio Grande River. The geography of the area had the propensity for smuggling, since the river was narrow and in some areas the water level was low enough to walk across.

Butch and I selected one of the faded pink one-room stucco cabins, furnished with a single bed and chest of drawers. The next day I found roaches the size of my thumb crawling in and out of the chest of drawers. I approached the owner of the cabins. "My cabin is infested with roaches."

He shrugged. "Those insects in the furniture are palmetto bugs."

I said. "Where I come from we call them roaches."

He shrugged. "Instead of the cabin why don't you move into the house trailer?"

I replied. "Sounds good."

Quickly I packed up my belongings and opted for the house trailer. I made an agreement with Butch, "I'll cook, if you clean." He agreed.

Butch and I teamed up as partners and at 4 p.m. we reported for duty at the office trailer located in Falcon Heights. We were part of ten officers that were detailed to this small border town and responsible for patrolling one hundred fifty miles of border. Three officers per shift is not a saturation of an area by any means, but we made the best of it. Headquarters in Washington, D.C. believed that by adding manpower to the area would produce seizures generating new offices in that location.

We jumped into the four-door marked patrol car and scouted the area. Driving along the main road we observed the flat open space and barren land as far as the eye could see. Occasionally there were scattered areas where cattle and horses grazed, but for the most part green grass was uncommon. While driving for miles we observed an occasional farming garage with a rusted steel roof or a rundown ranch style house surrounded by dirt. A paved walkway or green lawn and shrubbery surrounding a house were nowhere to be found. We turned off the main road into a community along the unpaved streets. The standard of living was low, with very little job opportunities for the residents. We entered the village of Rio Grande City which consisted of a few stores, a gas station and one café.

We continued traveling east on highway 83. I pulled over to the side of the road. Butch walked to the rear of the car to relieve himself. Suddenly shots rang out. I turned around and watched Butch shooting at a six-foot long rattlesnake emptying his gun and reloading to finish him off. He was deathly afraid of snakes. Rattlesnakes were all over the place especially at night when they lay on the paved road that had absorbed the sun's warmth during the day.

We traveled down a dirt road toward the Rio Grande River. A black and brown striped bird, two-feet in height scooted out in front of the car. On the way out, the bird dashed across the front of the car again. Butch turned to me. "Why didn't he fly?"

I pointed out. "I think it's a road runner. They run across the road for no reason."

He said. "Now I know how they got their name."

We laughed.

After working ten to sixteen hours a day, six days a week, we didn't feel like cooking our meals. We headed toward Roma, about twelve miles away, where we ate at a local café. The quality of the food was poor. Cafeteria food would have been an improvement. After asking around, we learned that the Waldorf Restaurant, a short walk across the foot bridge located in the town of Miguel Aleman, Mexico, served better food. We parked our car on the U.S. side and to avoid any conflict with the Mexican officials, we stored our wallets and credentials in the car, carrying only a social security card for identification.

At the restaurant, we stood on marble floors as the maître' d seated us on hand carved wooden chairs. The waiters wore white shirts, black vests and bow ties as they set down fine china and silverware in front of us. I looked at Butch. "You sure this is not the Mexican version of the New York Waldorf Astoria?"

He said. "Eating in a fine restaurant a short distance away from the poverty- stricken town of Roma is hard to believe.

I replied. "Look at this menu: T Bone Steak dinner $2.40, filet mignon dinner $3.00. If the food is average or better, this is a home run."

He smiled. "It doesn't pay to cook dinner."

I said. "Tell me about it."

The tension increased during our assignment on the Texas border. We learned that two brother officers were killed in a gun battle with a smuggler along the border, as he attempted to smuggle marijuana into the U.S. from Mexico. We were on full alert. Every suspicious vehicle we stopped, we cautiously approached armed with shotguns.

Our presence was made known to the residents of the border towns as we patrolled in our marked vehicles. The local residents had never observed customs patrol officers before scouting their neighborhood. We set up electronic sensors, widening our areas of coverage to detect movement on the Rio Grande River. Occasionally we'd lay in on the river bank on the midnight shift, adjacent to the melon fields where the farmers irrigated their crops using the water from the river. Every day we noticed how quickly the melons grew. After a few nights of being eaten alive by mosquitoes, we terminated the lay-in method. Saturating this area with officers would eventually produce smuggling arrests, but it would be a long-term commitment.

We entered a dirt road leading toward the Rio Grande, a known crossing point for smugglers, and parked out of sight. Sometime after midnight, a vehicle raced out onto the road. We followed the vehicle out as it entered the highway and then turned on our red light. After pursuing the vehicle for a while the vehicle increased its speed as we attempted to close the gap. I told Butch, "This guy is not slowing down!" We passed the telephone poles at the rate of one per second as the speedometer read one hundred forty miles per hour. We continued our pursuit for several miles, but we were unable to reach the suspect vehicle so we ended the chase. Driving at high speed for any length of time is not worth risking a blowout. There were no back-up units available since we were the only patrol unit working the midnight shift.

On my day off, myself and Jim Zegel, a coworker, headed toward the town searching for anything interesting to snap photos near the Rio Grande River. A Chevy Blazer passed by and a package the size of a brick, dropped out from underneath the vehicle onto the road. When we approached the vehicle, the driver exited and ran into the woods. The package tested positive for marijuana. Search of the vehicle revealed one hundred sixty pounds of marijuana that was hidden in various false compartments inside the chassis of the vehicle. We discovered the driver's wallet and personal items in the passenger compartment, and he was later apprehended.

Back home my wife worked during the day and tended to the needs of the house by regularly cutting the lawn, watering, trimming the shrubs and whatever needed to be done. Worried about her living alone in the house while I was away, I called her every night. At that time, we were on good terms with my parents and siblings. At the end of the first month in a phone conversation with my wife I asked her. "Has anyone in the family invited you or visited you while I'm away?"

She said, "Not really." I spent one evening at your parents' apartment in the Bronx."

I replied. "I wasn't expecting my parents to visit you frequently since they lived in the Bronx. Have they visited you on weekends?

She said. "No"

I remarked. "Has my brother or his wife contacted or visited you?"

She replied. "No, I haven't heard from them. I'm not spending the night at my parents' house, but I visit them from time to time."

I was bothered that my immediate family showed little or no concern for my wife while I was detailed to Texas. I took it for granted since my wife was alone that other family members would at least call her and offer moral support, but there was none.

A few weeks later we were notified that the three-month detail was being terminated after two months. Somebody from up above must have been listening to our prayers.

Upon my return from the border, I spent a week at home trying to make up for lost time. We missed the beach, so Joann and I spent the day at Robert Moses State Park. The beautiful soft white sandy beach was a place that we frequented during the summer.

We sat on the sand close to the water. The weather was clear, sunny, mid 80s, with a slight breeze as the waves curled, breaking close to shore. The lifeguards congregated at the observation chair a short distance away. I asked my wife. "Why, are the lifeguards gathered together, shouldn't they be at their posts along the beach?"

She said. "I guess so."

The waves curled high, as many bather's body-surfed, so we joined in. While we stood in waist high water a short distance from the shore, a tall wave curled and approached us. We dove underneath it to avoid the impact. I remained underwater for a while. When I surfaced, I found myself further out to sea, unable to touch the bottom. I looked around and my wife was nowhere to be seen. I yelled her name. Moments later I noticed her at a distance. I shouted. "Are you alright?" She waved to me. The current had pulled us more than a hundred feet away from shore as we treaded water. I tried to swim toward the shore, but the current was not permitting me to do so forcing me toward the Fire Island Inlet. I remained treading water. Seconds later, I heard a splash. A buoy hit the water. I swam to it. There were several buoys airborne to other bathers toward the inlet. The lines on the buoys were held by the lifeguards on shore as they he yelled, "Hold on, we got you!" I held the buoy with a sigh of relief. My wife was also being towed into shore. After several minutes, we stood up in shallow water and walked toward the shore. My wife and I sat on the sand looking at each other in shock. We were grateful to God, to have survived. The lifeguard walked over to us. I said, "Thank you so much, thank you so much."

He smiled and shook his head as I asked, "What happened to us?"

He pointed out. "You got picked up in a rip current since the beach in this area drops off quickly and creates a strong current. We waited for it, that's why all of us were gathered here."

I replied. "Thank God."

30

PROMOTION

In January 1976, our living expenses increased since my first son had been born a few months earlier. Applying for a promotion was never a consideration as I was content working my current position and assignment. I liked to work, and that's more than half the battle. The old saying, "if you love the work that you do, you'll never work a day in your life." Every day, I worked as diligently as possible, not out of competition nor for praise; I focused on doing the job I was hired to do. But from an economic standpoint, I needed a promotion.

At that time, the government offered retirement incentives, and many supervisors in the division retired, creating vacancies. Among my coworkers for the most part we maintained the same level of experience, since we entered the government during the Air Marshal Program.

There was no testing required in the federal government for a promotion. Most promotions were given based on politics, a few on merit. A good arrest and seizure record did not necessarily lead to a promotion. Aware that my arrest and seizure record was noteworthy, I envisioned one day I'd achieve recognition. But, after observing coworkers that were promoted based on what I don't know, I became disillusioned. When a person is promoted without any accomplishments, it's generally political.

Written testing was not required under the 'Merit Promotion System.' I often wondered why the government used the word 'merit' in the heading of the promotion system, since the dictionary defines the word merit as: The quality of being good or worthy to deserve a reward, good deeds entitling someone to a future reward; one who deserves or justifies a reward or commendation; a commendable quality act, awarded for excellence.

When a position becomes available in the government, the candidates submit their application, evaluation and any other paperwork required to the Personnel Division. A final list of the 'best qualified candidates' is compiled. The list is submitted to the selecting official, normally the head of the division. The selecting official can select anyone on the list.

While on duty in the arrivals area in the IAB I spoke with Dominic Sieni, a legend in the division. Dominic was detailed to the airport from the New York Seaport. A charismatic man in his early fifties, six-foot, stocky build and roughly handsome. He spoke with a raspy commanding voice. He reminded me of the actor Danny Aiello and spoke in the same intonations. Dominic and I leaned over, resting our legs on the metal partition in the arrivals area, as we observed passengers arriving from the Alitalia flight from Italy. Dominic turned to me. "Hey, there's Gina."

I replied. "Gina who?"

He said as a matter of fact. "Gina Lollobrigida, the actress."

From a distance, Dominic called out, "Hey Gina!"

She looked at him with her arms stretched out. "Dominic!"

They ran towards each other and hugged. It reminded me of love scene in a movie. At that time, Gina had starred in almost sixty movies. Apparently, Dominic was friendly with her since she frequently traveled to New York aboard the ocean liners that cleared Customs at the New York Seaport.

Dominic was a seasoned officer, having more than twenty-five years of experience, but he was unable to achieve a promotion. He spoke five languages fluently and never graduated high school. At that time promotions were given to officers with a college background, so Dominic never had a chance.

Dominic looked at me. "You know Kid, over the years, I've made a lot of arrests and seizures, and I can't get promoted. There's guys working here that couldn't find a ham in a refrigerator."

I nodded in agreement.

Dominic said to me, "Remember, Kid, bullshit baffles brains any day of the week."

Laughing and shaking my head from side to side I sort of agreed with him.

I was naïve at that time to think that productivity is the path to a promotion. After a number of coworkers received promotions, I believed that Dominic's opinion regarding promotions was correct.

When I walked into the office, Ray, the supervisor, looked up at me. "It looks like Tommy and Joe are looking good for the next supervisory promotion."

I said. "What have they ever done in their career to justify a promotion?"

He replied. "Well, I heard their names being thrown around at headquarters; they probably have hooks."

I sighed. "You know, it's frustrating when your record, your experience and performance is not a major factor in the promotion system."

He uttered. "Kid, look at how long it took me to get promoted; just hang in there, your time will come."

I looked away. "The promotion opportunities are now, with many old timers retiring and once they're filled, it could be years before any vacancies become available."

At headquarters, I made an appointment to see the Branch Chief, Rick DosSantos. I was not a fair-haired boy. With no special access, no angle and no hook. I had nothing to lose. Early on I met him briefly, but I was unable to form an accurate opinion of him. The word among the ranks was that he was occasionally a hard nose, no nonsense guy, but at times you could hear his loud laugh resonate throughout the office.

He waved at me to come in. "Mr. Buonocore, step into my office and have a seat."

I walked into the office where he sat behind a large mahogany desk. He reminded me of Earl Lewis, the lead singer from the Channels, a legendary

Rock and Roll Doo-Wop vocal groups in the fifties. So, I figured how bad of a guy could he be.

He offered, "Sit down."

Standing in front of his desk I started to speak to him as he sat with a grin on his face.

He said. "Sit- down, sit down. I'm not going to listen to you, unless you sit down!"

I continued to speak. He stood up from the chair, walked over to me, put his hand on my shoulder forcing me down onto the brown leather sofa.

I pointed out. "Look, I'm here because I'm tired of hearing about coworkers that promote themselves with words to management and have no record to back it up. I watched a co-worker boast about his seizure record attaching himself to my achievements and received a promotion. I received a Special Act and a Special Achievement award which would account for some consideration under the merit promotion system. I'm not going to stand by and continue to watch mediocre people promoted in front of me. It's humiliating." While I spoke with him, the smirk on his face changed to a serious look.

I advised. "My arrest and seizure record is notable and I a few Special Achievement Awards.

The Branch Chief rotated his chair and looked at me. "The Merit Promotion System is the only system that I have to work with. I answer to the Director in the World Trade Center. He makes the selections."

I leveled my gaze. "That's true, but you still have a lot to say about who you want working for you at JFK Airport."

He looked me in the eye. "Ha, ha, ha, relax, sit tight for now and we'll see how things go. Next time you come into my office, you'll sit down and calm down."

I replied. "I apologize for my behavior; I don't know what came over me. I feel better now, thanks for listening." After I walked out I said to myself. "He's not such a bad guy."

In the spring of 1976, the Branch Chief detailed Officer Dick Hoffman and me to Long Island, to develop narcotics smuggling information. Dick and I carpooled together, but I didn't know if that was the reason we received the same assignment. At that time, this assignment was a good position so I felt that the Branch Chief's decision to detail me to Long Island would aid in my career advancement.

Our Intelligence information indicated that Long Island, due to its coastal waterways and 25 plus airstrips, was an opportunity for smugglers.

We met with boatyard owners and local and marine law enforcement agencies on Long Island. The information that we provided to them was to be on the lookout for any suspicious activity, where vessels may be offloading bales of contraband in marinas, docks, boat ramps or any area where a vessel has accessibility to ground transportation. At the marinas and airports, we posted agency generated smuggling signs for display to their customers, offering up to a $50,000 reward for information leading to the arrest and/ or seizure of narcotics.

A marina owner asked me, "A while ago there was a commercial fishing vessel that was removed from the water. While the vessel was in dry dock, I noticed four large eyebolts connected to the underwater portion of the hull. Is that what you're looking for?"

I said, "That's exactly what we're looking for. What's the name on the boat and where is it located?"

He said. "That was a while ago. Let me check into it and I'll let you know."

I advised. "Here's my card, thanks."

The Branch Chief called us into the office. "I am assigning you and Hoffman, to work in the Marine Branch at the New York Seaport. Report there on Monday for the four by midnight shift."

I replied. "Okay, boss."

We arrived at Pier 62 on the North River and entered a small trailer that sat at the edge of the pier. The Marine Branch supervisor Rancik greeted us. "So, Dos Santos sent you pricks down here to check up on me."

I looked at Rancik. He laughed. "By the way, Tom, how've you been I haven't seen you since you worked at JFK Airport."

He replied. "I'm doing okay, thanks for asking; put your clothes in the lockers, and change into the jumpsuits. We'll cast off as soon as the boat captain's ready."

I said. "Okay, boss."

Harry warmed up the twin engine 38 foot Bertram patrol boat, outfitted with the latest radar and detection equipment. Harry was a skinny 5' 8," cool, calm and collected guy who spent six years in the Navy. He piloted the customs vessels since the inception of the Marine Branch.

We boarded the vessel and proceeded south toward the tip of Manhattan and passed the Statue of Liberty and Governor's Island. It was a clear autumn evening as we traveled under the lighted Verrazano Bridge. Shortly thereafter, we were at the entrance to the Atlantic Ocean where ships cross the threshold into New York Harbor and entered one of the busiest ports in the world.

During Prohibition, smuggling was difficult to stop since there was a shortage of law enforcement agents. Today, they have a greater presence. There is also an enormous amount of goods imported into the country. The current smuggling methods are more complex via commercial vessels, but the smaller private and fishing vessels have a limited amount of space to hide a large load of narcotics. The same techniques that were used to smuggle liquor during Prohibition are employed by narcotics smugglers today, however the equipment and concealment methods have improved.

We hugged the perimeter of the shoreline where commercial vessels docked in their berths. The marine community and the public were aware of the presence of the patrol vessel; it served as a deterrent. The likelihood that a vessel could or would off-load or transfer contraband in the busy open waterways of the New York Harbor was remote. Utilizing the patrol vessel to observe the piers where commercial ships docked and marinas where commercial fishing vessels are active in and around New York Harbor was a way to detect illegal offloading, that was not always visible from the shore.

The information that we had developed indicated that commercial cargo vessels off-loaded contraband in the ocean, as they traveled through the shipping lanes, or thereabouts, to smaller fishing or go-fast boats. Any vessel that entered the Harbor from the ocean was subject to a search by U. S. Customs. The Customs search authority is the most powerful search authority in the federal government. The U.S. Customs search authority pertaining to vessels is as follows:

Any officer of Customs may at any time go on board any vessel or vehicle at any place in the United States or within the Customs waters or, as he may be authorized within a Customs-enforcement area established under the Anti- Smuggling Act (19USC1701) or any authorized place, without as well as within his district, and examine the manifest and other documents and papers and examine and inspect, and search the vessel or vehicle and every part thereof and any person, trunk, package or cargo on board, and to this end may hail and stop such vessel or vehicle, and use all necessary force to compel compliance.

31

FLORIDA

After my assignment at the New York Seaport, the Branch Chief detailed me to work at the U.S. Coast Guard Station located in Short Beach, Long Island. We maintained an office in a trailer at their facility. The Coast Guard donated a 30-foot vessel to Customs that we updated. After a few months of work the vessel was launched and the Long Island Marine Branch was formed.

Supervisor Tom Rancik walked over. Tom was a retired NYPD detective who worked as an air marshal and promoted to a supervisory patrol officer.

He yelled. "Hey, get your ass in the boat; we have orders to go to Rockaway to gather some information!"

I replied. "Right now."

He ordered. "Yeah, Right now."

I jumped into the boat. We headed south toward the Jones Beach Inlet. At a distance, I noticed high swells curling as the outgoing tide was ripping. I turned to Jim Zegel, the boat handler. "The waves in the inlet are curling high and breaking; why don't you take the inland route?"

He replied. "Yeah, I see that."

Rancik looked at us. "I'm the boss, go through the inlet."

I walked into the cabin, put on a life vest and sat down. I was confident that Jim possessed the skill to handle the inlet waters, but you never know. Jim and I had worked together as marshals, and later he received boat handler and scuba diving training from the US Navy and Coast Guard. Prior to working for the government, Jim spent a good part of his life working on the water, clamming in Moriches Bay to pay for his college education. He lived in a south shore waterfront community his entire life. While harvesting scallops during the winter months, he decided that a government job offered more opportunity than harvesting shell fish.

As we headed through the inlet Rancik with a smirk on his face looked down at me while I sat in the cabin wearing a life vest. "You know, you're a fuck'n chicken, ha, ha, ha."

I looked down shaking my head. We headed into the first breaker as the boat rolled high from bow to stern.

Jim looked at Rancik wide-eyed. "It's pretty dam rough out here."

Rancik was silent. Moments later, a wave broke over the top of the boat. The water poured in from the sides like a giant hose drenching Rancik. He stood there speechless, soaked from head to toe while his eye glasses and hat remained intact and the water dripped from his face.

I sat in the cabin and looked up at him. "Now you don't need a shower." He ignored me, never wiping his face, standing there silent as if nothing had happened.

We continued into the ocean, heading west towards Rockaway inlet. Inside the channel, we headed east towards the Cross-Bay Bridge. Rancik said to us, "The intelligence division is requesting that we designate the areas within the bay that are potential off-load locations by a seagoing vessel. We need to locate any potential off load sites and give the information to the intelligence division."

In November 1976, I was promoted to the position of Supervisory Customs Patrol Officer assigned to JFK airport. The promotion couldn't have come at a better time as my second child Christopher was born. I must have squeaked in under the wire because shortly thereafter, the Director of Patrol, Ed Coyne, informed the ranks that candidates that possessed a four-year degree would be given greater consideration for promotions. At that point, I possessed a two- year degree and was considering returning to college for a bachelor's degree but we just couldn't afford the additional expense.

The following spring, at a family gathering at my home, John, a long-time friend of the family, visited, as we walked through the house together. I explained to him the specifications that were used to construct the footing/foundation for the house which was critical, since we lived near the water. John worked as a civil engineer, and he was impressed that I made the correct decision to construct an oversized reinforced concrete footing for the house foundation. While we walked, he turned to me. "Neil, are you planning to get your four-year degree?"

I replied. "I don't have the money right now to pay for college tuition."

He pointed out. "Neil, it doesn't matter. If you have to beg, borrow or steal, you get your degree."

I stood there shocked, I didn't know what to say. John's insistence that I pursue a four-year degree remained imbedded in my head. Not long after, I enrolled in classes at the New York Institute of Technology in the College Accelerated Program for Police. I registered as a full-time student while I continued to work. College placed a burden on my family but I thought it might be beneficial in the long run.

In 1978, I received a Bachelor's Degree in Criminal Justice with a Behavioral Science minor.

While working in the IAB the phone rang in the office. "Neil, the Branch Chief is on the line."

He advised. "Neil, I need you to go to Miami International Airport and train Customs Patrol officers regarding our search techniques used in the arrivals area at JFK Airport."

I asked. "When must I be there?"

He said. "You need to be there next week"

I replied. "Okay"

When I arrived home, I walked into the kitchen. "Honey, I've been detailed to Miami for two weeks. Why don't you and the kids come with me? It'll be like a vacation."

She remarked. "Okay, maybe we can visit my uncle in Ft. Lauderdale while we're there?"

I said. "Why not."

I added a sheet of plywood on top of the rear seat in my 1972 Ford Galaxie creating a play area for the kids. The following day we were on our way to Florida.

While driving to Florida, the kids were asleep. My wife turned to me. "I'm really getting tired of your mother repeating the story about your childhood to me. How you'd climb all over the furniture in the apartment and your actions drove her crazy."

I replied. "I was an active kid."

She rolled her eyes. "Your mother mentioned again that you fell down hitting your head when you were a child implying that there is something wrong with you?"

I pointed out. "I explained this incident years earlier. I fell from the top of the slide in the park and hit my head on the pavement at the age of five. Maybe the impact knocked some sense into me? Seriously, that event would not have occurred if my mother was more attentive to me, instead of sitting on a bench far away from the play area. I know my mother is up to something when she starts recalling unpleasant events. I'm really getting annoyed with her attempting to create dissention between us. I guess every story needs a villain and I'm the one?"

I have a vivid recollection of this event when I was eight years old:

My Father came to me and said. "Your mother's in the hospital and we need to go visit her."

I asked, "Why is she in the hospital?"

He said, "She doesn't feel well and needs to rest for a while."

Sometime later we arrived at Westchester Square Hospital and walked into the room where my mother sat up in bed. It was an empty single room and there were no medical devices in the room or IV's connected to her. My Father spoke to her for a while and then we left. When you see your

Mother lying in a hospital bed you never forget it. Years later I learned that my mother had a mental breakdown. At that time people were sent to hospitals for recovery of mental conditions since the field of psychiatry was not developed as it is today.

What I learned later was that my mother was having difficulty living in a one bedroom apartment with four people. She didn't drive so it restricted her ability to get out, totally relying on my father to drive her to do her errands.

After my mother returned home from the hospital on many occasions I slept at Nana's house on Saturday evenings. My Father tried to provide some relief for my mother by enjoying a movie or dancing. I guess it worked because the next year my sister was born.

Getting back to my mother's condemnation of my mental stability can be explained as follows:

In the therapy business, this is called pathologizing. In the psychiatric jargon the word pathologizing describes this activity to a T. Pathologizing is a way of making us appear sick when we don't go along with the coercer. Mom has accused me of being neurotic and crazy. She's dissolving the trust that's somewhat accumulated in a relationship by lining up all the unhappy events we've shared with them. How disturbed can I be? After all, I did pass three–hours of psychological testing required to work as an air marshal. I'm not aware of any member of the immediate or extended family that have been psychologically tested, so be that as it may. Maybe if every family member received psychological testing, it might be helpful; then we could sort out the people that need help. While working as an air marshal, the government trusted me to protect the lives of hundreds of passengers in flight and on the ground. I'm not surprised that my mother is attempting to plant a seed of mistrust. I love my mother, but I have very little trust in her based on the experiences I've encountered while growing up. My mother appears to be unable to stop attempting to destroy our relationship.

After my parents moved to Long Island, my wife made several attempts to establish a closer relationship with my mother by visiting her as much as possible, when our children were toddlers. A memorable event was when my wife created a garden for my mother in a small area in the back yard of her home. My wife purchased seedling vegetable plants and planted them for her.

She said. "I'll plant the seedlings, but you need to water them daily."

Mom said. "Oh, okay."

Weeks later Joann visited my mother and walked over to the garden.

She said. "The garden soil is dry and the seedlings I planted are very dry. Have you been watering them every day?"

Mom replied. "Oh yes."

Joann pointed out. "Maybe you should water more frequently, the plants look like their dying."

Mom said.in a lowered voice. "Oh, I… don't… know."

I was happy that my wife was making an effort to create a closer relationship with my mother. I didn't want to be a pessimist about my wife's efforts, but I informed her to be cautious.

After I married, Mom's control issues were always on my mind. I knew that change was not part of her psyche. My wife is the new member in the family, and my mother feels that she has every right to try to shape her up to meet her expectations.

Two days later, I arrived for duty at Miami international Airport assigned to the Customs arrivals area. I met with the terminal supervisor, and he assigned Walt, his best officer, to work with me. As we stood watching arriving passengers, I explained some of the techniques we used to locate smugglers at JFK airport. Near the baggage belt a tall slim male passenger, dressed casually, had just cleared the inspection. I identified myself to him. "Can I see your Customs declaration and passport?" He handed me his documents.

I asked. "How long were you away?"

He answered. "One week."

I said. "Did you buy anything?"

He replied. "Just some souvenirs."

While I reviewed his documents, I noticed he was wearing work boots. I thought that was unusual arriving from a tropical Jamaican climate.

I looked at him. "This is a continuation of your Custom's examination, please take your bags and come with us."

We escorted him to a private room.

I instructed him. "Empty the contents of your pockets onto the table."

I patted him down with negative results.

I said. "Sit down and remove your boots."

I inspected the inside of his boots which were negative.

I told him. "Lift up your leg."

I patted the bottom of his feet and felt an object inside the toe area of his socks.

I ordered him. "Remove your socks."

I turned the socks upside down and four black balls approximately the size of ping pong balls, dropped out onto the floor. A search of the other foot revealed four more balls. The passenger looked up at me as his eyes were the size of lemons.

He looked up at me in shock. "Special investigations?"

I replied. "You know it."

A total of eight, balls, wrapped in condoms. The contents field-tested positive for liquid hashish.

While I reviewed the passenger's documents, I discovered a baggage ticket for luggage that was not in his possession. I looked at Walt. "He's traveling with another person, get out there fast and try to locate a Canadian National arriving on the same flight."

Minutes later, Walt escorted a man into the search room. The baggage claim checks matched. I walked into the room.

Walt looked at me for direction. "We searched the luggage and his person, which were negative."

I replied. "Did you look inside his shoes and socks?"

He said. "Yeah, we checked everything."

I asked. "Did you look inside the radio?"

He replied. "No."

I uttered. "Let's open it."

Examination of the radio revealed ten ping pong sized balls, wrapped in condoms, for a total weight of a pound of hashish oil. The subjects were placed under arrest and turned over to the local authorities for prosecution.

On the weekend, together with my wife and children we left the urban rush of Miami and traveled to the Florida Keys on the single lane Highway 1. While driving along the road as we traveled over the bridges observing the crystal-clear blue and green water was simply mesmerizing. The water and beaches in the Florida Keys are the closest in color to the beaches in the Caribbean Islands.

At one point, we observed the miniature deer, the size of a dog as they grazed on the grass along the highway. We stopped at a park beach in Key Largo where our children played for hours in the crystal- clear knee- high water. We watched the seagulls and brown pelicans diving for fish and the long legged white and blue herons strutting their long-curved necks. Later on, we picked kiwis from wild growing trees in the park. At the end of the day we dined at a local restaurant enjoying the freshly caught fish that has never been equaled till this day.

When I returned to New York I sat in the office talking with Jack Lovett the new Branch Chief at JFK Airport. Jack was a heavy smoker and the ashtray on his desk was filled with cigarette butts. He leaned back in his chair with his feet on the desk as he inhaled a cigarette with the suction of a vacuum cleaner. During the meeting, Jack mentioned several techniques to reduce cargo theft but they were unsuccessful. Jack looked at me. "In your capacity as a supervisor how would you improve the arrests and seizures in cargo?"

I replied. "Jack if you leave me alone, my squad will increase the arrests and seizures." Jack was silent.

After the meeting was over Jack stood up from the desk and looked at me. "Neil, I'm an Irishman and having the gift of gab makes it easier for me to get my point across. It wouldn't be a bad idea, if you enrolled in a course at Dale Carnegie; it could be helpful." Shocked, by his suggestion that I needed a self-help course, I put my head down. Then I turned to him. "Jack, I'm more of a doer than a talker." Jack was silent.

A few months later Officer Ryan, a member of my squad, apprehended an Air Canada employee stealing furs totaling $26,000. The fur seizure was related to an earlier hijacked shipment from JFK airport.

While assigned to the Cargo Theft Squad at JFK Airport. Gary and I sat in our unmarked vehicle while we observed Pan Am employees exit the commissary at the end of their shift. At this location, in-bond liquor is stored for use on passenger flights. In bond items such as liquor are permitted entry into the US without payment of duties because it never enters the commerce of America. The liquor is used on outgoing international flights. Employees that work in the in-bond area are subject to a Customs search because they are essentially working on the border and have access to international cargo and in this case dutiable merchandise. We observed a male employee exit the building carrying two bags. He entered his vehicle. We were unable to stop him before he sped away. Gary stepped on it and turned on the siren, while I placed the magnetic red light on the roof. The subject increased his speed and moments later, he entered the Belt Parkway. The subject weaved in and out of the lanes as he threw bottles out of the window that exploded upon impact. Traveling at a high rate of speed in the passing lane, we closed in on him. We stopped counting bottles after ten. He threw a bottle that hit the grill on our car and exploded. A short time later, we pulled up alongside the driver and convinced him to stop on the median.

We exited the vehicle and identified ourselves. "What are you doing!"

The subject sat in the car and looked up.

He said. "I was scared; I'm sorry."

I pointed out. "You know a bottle nearly missed our windshield and could have caused serious damage to us and other drivers."

Speaking in broken English he looked at me. "I'm a sorry, I'm a sorry. I was a bring'n some champagne home for Christmas."

The debris from the bottles stretched for miles along the parkway, not retrievable as evidence. We searched his car. The evidence was destroyed.

I advised him. "How many bottles did you have and don't lie to me, I will go back and count them?"

He spoke. "I tink they were tirteen or something."

We transported the subject to our office and questioned him at length. The subject was uncooperative in the beginning, but eventually provided invaluable information regarding in- bond liquor theft at the Pan Am commissary.

After debriefing the subject for a few hours our tour ended at 2 am. On my way home, I was traveling eastbound in the passing lane on the Sagtikos Parkway, about four miles from my home. The road was empty as I passed the Bay Shore exit. Feeling drowsy rounding the curve I noticed headlights that appeared to be shining from the opposite traffic, through the tree lined median. A moment later, I was shocked to see a set of headlights in my lane heading directly toward me. Immediately I turned the wheel to the right, barely avoiding a head-on collision, as the car sped by me and the engine loudly roared. The car continued speeding as I pulled over to the shoulder and my heart beat like a drum. Waiting to calm down, I sat there for a while to gain my composure and thanked God for having watched over me. A collision at that speed would have been deadly. At that time, there were no seatbelt requirements.

32

TERRY'S DREAM

The Branch Chief at JFK Airport must have been ahead of his time when he launched an intelligence gathering program regarding narcotic smuggling by private vessels and aircraft. He expanded the marine unit and broadened the scope of our work. On Monday, November 12, 1978, this article was reported by the *Daily News:*

Federal drug officials suspect that $15 million worth of Colombian marijuana and Quaalude tablets were seized in Far Rockaway, Queens were brought in by organized crime.

Investigators are going over their 28-ton haul and the vessel that carried it to try to find links to other major drug seizures along the east coast.

They estimated that 25 drug smugglers slipped past an assault force of city cops, federal agents and two Coast Guard patrol boats.

The raiders led by Coast Guard Group Commander George Johnson were alerted by a caller when the smuggler's darkened 75- foot fishing trawler slid into the Sommerville Basin off Grassy Hassock Channel slightly before midnight.

Agents said the trawler contained more than $150,000 worth of sophisticated electronics, including radar scanners and back-up systems which not only enabled them to travel on the high seas but warned the smugglers of the approaching raiders.

The heavily armed guardsman said they notified city cops and federal narcotics agents. Before going in they found cans of beer, cups of still warm coffee and mounds of cold cuts on the pier of Yan Caribe Enterprises marina at 6201 De Costa Ave.

Nearby awaiting transfer to four trucks and two vans seized at the scene lay 780 bales of high grade Colombian pot weighing 58,500 pounds and worth more than $35 million 15 cases containing 10 million sedative pills worth $10 million.

The more than 38 tons of pot is said to be the largest amount of pot ever seized during a raid in the Northeast. It topped a 20-ton load at Portland,

Maine last May, according to John Fallon the Regional Director of the Drug Enforcement Administration.

Fallon said the trucks were registered to All Rite, Inc. of 1034 East 82 St, Brooklyn. He said no firearms were recovered after the smugglers scattered from the deserted marina.

Jules St. Prix of 53 Beach St. owner of the marina said he had closed the dock at 6 p.m. Saturday and had given no one permission to tie up at his dock.

Fallon said the drug trader's 75 gross ton commercial vessel was registered to Edgar Taylor of Bayou LaBatre, near Mobile, Alabama. A wooden plaque painted with the name "Darlene C" had been affixed to the stern of the trawler, covering the registered name Terry's Dream.

Fallon estimates that the marijuana sells for $40 an ounce on the streets of New York and that Quaaludes sell for $1 to $3 a pill.

In the area where the vessel was seized a dead body was found and the case has never been solved. Sometime later, I met a man who was involved in the offloading of contraband from the Terry's Dream. The statute of limitations expired on the drug smuggling charges but the murder case is still open.

The seizure of this vessel set the ground work for the opening of the Tactical Operations Branch (TOB) office at Republic Airport, on Long Island. The branch was staffed with a group of customs patrol officers, a helicopter, fixed wing surveillance aircraft and vessels. A year later I was transferred to the TOB where I supervised a group of Customs officers, pilots and boat captains. My experience regarding tactical aircraft at that time was non- existent. In order to familiarize myself with our equipment,

I spent time flying in the Customs helicopter and observation aircraft piloted by Ron Morosky. I was honored to be flying with Ron who had served as a Marine pilot and survived being shot down twice during the Vietnam War. On several occasions, we patrolled the coastline of Long Island and far out into the ocean searching for any suspicious vessel activity.

Frank Knapp, our Customs liaison officer to the Drug Enforcement Administration, walked into the office. Frank informed me that a confidential informant (CI) will be working as an off-loader on a mother ship that will attempt to smuggle narcotics into Long Island. I asked, "Who is the guy?"

He replied. "He's a defendant that's cooperating with DEA to help reduce his sentence."

I said. "Keep me posted."

He answered. "Okay."

Since the off-load location was unknown at that time, I notified the troops to be on twenty-four-hour standby, in the event that we need to intercept a vessel offload on Long Island. When the confidential informant (CI) boarded the mother ship, he placed a transponder on board. DEA had been monitoring the suspect vessel that was several miles offshore. When the mother ship approached the southern tip of New Jersey, the transponder stopped transmitting. DEA was unable to track the ship's location and concluded that the bad guys may have discovered the transponder, or there was a glitch in the transponder, or the CI shut it off. I contacted the DEA supervisor on the phone. "Are there any details regarding the mother ship and its destination?"

He said. "Not at this time."

A week later the Tactical Operations Branch Chief Hank Kleinpeter called me into his office. He asked, "What's happened to the DEA informant?

I remarked. "According to DEA, their informant has been found dead in Florida."

He asked. "What happened?"

I answered. "What I know is that the transponder was transmitting but when the mother ship reached the southern tip of New Jersey, it stopped. We were unable to establish a location for the mother ship at that time nor were we able to identify it."

For some reason, Kleinpeter felt I was responsible for the case being unsuccessful. It seemed to me that there was more to this story.

The following week I was assigned to the Middletown New Jersey office which was ninety miles and three hours away from my home.

After the transponder case soured the Branch Chief decided to replace me with his friend Billy Desmond.

After working in New Jersey for one year I received a phone call from Rick DosSantos the Branch Chief at JFK. "Neil, you're being reassigned to JFK Airport, report here on Monday. You're assigned to supervise the aircraft Search Squad."

I replied. "Thanks, boss." When I hung up the phone, I was relieved that my daily six-hour, one hundred and eighty-mile commute had ended.

The aircraft search squad was responsible for examining arriving international aircraft. A small group of specialized officers trained to search all areas of commercial aircraft, to locate contraband. The searching of commercial aircraft was limited by time constraints, since most aircraft were serviced and turned around within a few hours after landing.

The Avianca flight from Colombia arrived and officer Alaimo approached me. "Neil, I'm gonna check the cargo hold. You know the Colombian newspapers are a good place to smuggle drugs because they are expedited cargo."

"Sounds good go for it!" Joe, an experienced searcher. "Neil, yesterday on your day off, I seized two kilos of cocaine on the Avianca flight, hidden in the Colombian newspapers."

I remarked. "Joe, that's outstanding. What do you need me for?"

He laughed.

Several months later, a group of ship searchers were detailed to the airport for a blitz. It doubled our existing manpower, especially targeting the South American flights. During the search of the Avianca flight from Colombia, Officer Selby discovered two kilos of cocaine secreted under a passenger's seat. Sometimes all it takes is additional manpower and skill to produce results.

Selected flights were searched daily by the searchers and the customs canine unit. We waited while the Customs dog handler Charlie, completed searching the passenger compartment of the aircraft. He walked his drug detecting dog named Snifter, a Doberman Pincher, down the aisle of the aircraft. Standing in the first-class section I looked at Charlie. "Why is your dog so hyperactive?"

He spoke. "Well he's less active now since they removed one of his testicles."

I replied. "I can't imagine what he was like before the surgery."

He pointed out. "Even after his exercise, training and reward time, he doesn't tire. They figured surgery would be the best solution for him."

Charlie talked with another officer while I retrieved a pillow that had fallen on the floor. At that moment, Snifter locked on to the pillow. I was unable to remove it from his mouth, as he played tug of war with me, violently shaking his head back and forth. 'Tug O War' was reward time, or 'play time' for the dogs after they locate drugs, but the pillow was not considered reward time for him. While Snifter violently shook his head back and forth, he tore a hole in the pillow and propelled the down feather stuffing into the air. The feathers were very small, having the appearance of snowflakes slowly falling down as they spread throughout the entire first- class section. While exiting the aircraft, the British Airways manager walked in and noticed the falling feathers. He asked, "What going on here?" "Nothing, and then I pointed to the dog." Even after the search squad walked away, the down feathers continued to fall. Vacuuming up the down feathers must have kept the cleaning crew busy for a while. A situation like this was humorous and that keeps the rank and file in a good frame of mind.

33

HURRICANE GLORIA

In November 1983, I received a promotion to the position of Tour Commander answering directly the Branch Chief Jack Lovett. The next day I walked into Jack's office as he greeted me in a lowered voice. "Congratulations on your promotion, but you were not my choice." I was shocked by his honesty and replied. "Thanks' Jack, maybe over time you'll feel differently?" Jack had no comment.

As the Tour Commander at JFK Airport, I supervised twelve first line supervisors and eighty Customs Patrol Officers. The position was short lived. Sixteen months later, due to a reorganization within the Customs Service, all officers in the division were notified to apply for the position of Special Agent. Historically, the Special Agent's position was difficult to obtain since there were a limited number of positions generally requiring a hook (a person that wields influence).

The reorganization created an unsettling environment. Seasoned officers, some with almost twenty years of experience, were notified to apply for a new position and attend twelve weeks of training in the Federal Law Enforcement Training Center (FLETC) in Glynco, Georgia. Older officers like myself, viewed the change as if we were starting our careers over as new recruits, going through basic training at forty years of age. Some officers were concerned that they might lose their job or incur a transfer, if they didn't pass the twelve-week training course. The reorganization placed us in unchartered waters. The word from above was to apply for the position. The answers to our concerns were given to us verbally, not in writing.

I arrived at the office in the afternoon as the day shift Tour Commander

Jack Conti spoke with Barbara, the secretary. Everybody liked Jack. He was very compassionate and understanding, an uncharacteristic trait in law enforcement. But sometimes Jack would feel 'his oats.' I signed in on the clipboard. Jack looked at Barbara. "Look at this left- handed prick, the way he writes with his hand cocked at an angle." Jack returned to his office. I walked over to Barbara. "Can you type this letter for me?"

She pointed out. "Well, right now I'm typing Jack's application for the agent's job which is about ten pages. He needs it right away. Tomorrow is the deadline."

I replied. "Barbara, I need this letter typed now."

Jack approached looking worried. "Listen, she's working on my agent's application right now. This is priority."

Something was going on that day and I was in need of a good laugh, so I said to Barbara. "Can I see what you're typing for him." She handed it to me.

I remarked. "I have urgent government business which takes priority over Jack's job application."

I walked over to the shredder and fed Jack's application through the machine while he stared at me from his office. Jack's eyes popped and his face turned white.

He ran over to me. "Are you crazy, how do I meet the deadline now? That's my only copy!"

I responded. "Well it's too bad. You know better than to take advantage of Barbara's typing skills. You should work on the application on your own time."

I let Jack stew for a while as he paced around the office indiscriminately.

I looked at him. I made a copy for you. Next time don't make fun of the way I write."

He uttered. "You scared the shit out of me, you really scared me."

Shortly thereafter, I was selected for the position of Special Agent in the Office of Investigations. At the end of July, I received notification to report to the Federal Law Enforcement Training Center in Glynco, Georgia, for twelve weeks of training.

When I arrived home from work, I told my wife, "I was notified today that I need to be in Georgia for investigator training."

She responded. "For how long?"

I said. "Three months."

She frowned. "This really came at bad time, especially what's going on in the family."

I replied. "Look, the kids are on vacation, why don't we all go together and then you can return home when school starts. It'll be like a vacation… maybe?"

She agreed.

We loaded the faded, rusted, pea green 1974 Toyota pickup truck with our belongings. I converted the cargo bed to a sleeping area for the kids and we headed to Georgia.

Upon our arrival in Georgia, we rented a hotel room with a kitchenette. While I attended training, my wife kept the kids busy taking them to the different beaches, sporting activities, library and shopping.

The trip to Georgia was sort of a vacation until we decided to travel to Disneyworld one weekend. That part of the trip made it all worthwhile for us. Everyone remembers some of their experiences in Disneyworld, but over the years my children have more vivid recollections of our weekend trip from Georgia to Daytona Beach Florida. When we arrived at the beach I noticed cars driving on the sand. Driving on the beach sand up north was only possible with a four- wheel drive vehicle. I drove my two-wheel drive pickup truck onto the beach, and parked near the water. Everything was at our disposal, since we didn't have to lug all of our items from the parking lot to the shoreline. My sons raced up and down the beach using their skim boards. When they tired-out, they paddled into the surf with their boogie boards in the clear Florida waters. By the end of the day they were exhausted, but happy. When your children are happy, you feel happy.

At the end of August, my wife and children boarded the Amtrak train to New York. It provided time for my wife to get the children ready for the start of the school year. A few weeks later on Friday September 27, 1985, Hurricane Gloria hit Long Island. When I heard that the hurricane would hit Long Island, I immediately booked a flight home to be sure that my wife and children were safe and sound.

I landed at the airport late in the evening and scurried around to locate a transportation service. It was a forty- five-mile ride to Oakdale. Sometime after eleven, the driver entered the neighborhood. The stars shined brightly, the air was still, no streetlights, no house lights, everything was black. We traveled on Vanderbilt Boulevard toward the water, steering around large oak trees that blocked the road. Some trees rested on homes, power lines and cars. It looked like a war zone.

The operator pulled into the driveway. I exited the van and walked- up the steps as the door opened. My children rushed to me. I hugged them and kissed my wife. My son Victor said, "We knew it was you, we heard the van pull up."

I remarked. "Wow, it looks like a war zone driving toward the house. I see you have candles, thank God you're all okay."

My wife said, "We don't need heat but there's no electric. The Fire Department came to the house before the storm and told us to evacuate so we went to the shelter at the school."

I walked into the kitchen. "How are you keeping the food cold and what about cooking?"

She pointed out. "We cook on the charcoal barbecue and I have a cooler with ice."

My wife pointed to the damaged roof.

I replied. "I'll work on that tomorrow. Has anyone in the family made contact to see if you and the children are alright?"

She remarked. "No, but the telephone is working and I have not heard from anyone."

We had not heard from any family member after the hurricane. The next day I traveled through the neighborhood and looked at the devastation. Huge trees were uprooted, lying down, and blocking the roads and some had fallen on homes, cars and power lines. Roofs were torn off and broken windows and debris were scattered around the area.

Hurricane Gloria is best described by my nine-year old son Victor, who wrote this assignment for school:

The Day "Gloria" Came

It all started as a tropical storm on September 27th. After we heard the news report we started bording and taping the windows. We helped our mom pack boxes and furniture. The boxes on the first floor had to be put in a higher place in case of flooding.

We finally drove away, stopping first at the bank. All of a sudden, the car started to move side to side. We were scared we thought it was going to fly away. Next, we drove to the shelter at the Junior High school. For about an hour everything was fine but then the lights went out. Good thing we had flashlights and a radio. We were in the shelter about four hours.

There were so many people waiting with us for the storm to end. The Red Cross people brought blankets, cots and medical equipment.

The Fire Department came after a while. They had a generator on the truck and finally gave us lights.

The wind was so strong. Trees were falling everywhere. Some pieces of the roof broke the skylight and the rain came in. People were scared.

We brought some of our toys. After the eye of the storm came we left. When we saw our house, we were so happy. Only four trees fell.

The worst part was no light for seven days. Even boiling water took so

long. Ice was $4.00 a bag. My father came home from a business trip. He was
so happy we were alright. Can you imagine how the cowboys lived years ago?

There were so many people to help. Sunday was a day we prayed and
thanked God for his miracle. We will always remember Gloria!

Five years after the estrangement from my parents, I was sent a thousand miles away for training, leaving my family to watch over themselves. The ordeal that my wife and children endured before, during and after Hurricane Gloria was an eye opener for me. The fact that not one person in the immediate and extended family inquired in any manner sent a chill up and down my spine, and it reeked of one word 'vendetta.' I read an article that isolation in domestic abuse has to start somewhere. Usually the isolation in domestic abuse begins with the controller inserting emotional wedges between the victim, his family and friends. At some point, the victim finds it too difficult to connect with friends and family due to the controller's embarrassing or abusive behavior and victims' believe that the controller is telling the truth.

In a brief conversation years later with my father, I asked him what prevented you from calling us after Hurricane Gloria? My father said, "We were fighting." After hearing his response, I felt like I was dead in his eyes. His answer reinforced the word 'vendetta' in my mind.

After almost five years since the rift with my parents and they want to assert their grandparents' rights, I had not once cried for having lost my immediate and extended family members. The severing of our relationship with the family was generated as a legal threat causing me to be angered and defensive since the love was gone.

As our attorney had advised us. "Wait and see if your parents proceed against you in court." The family's rejection was hurtful, embarrassing, and humiliating but deep down inside, I knew that our reaction was to seek privacy and avoid situations that brought pressure on us. For us to seek privacy and avoid undue pressure at weddings and funerals that we were aware of, was one way we avoided any derogatory comments, dismissive cold receptions and rejection by any family member. The after-effects from a hurricane are material and mental. The material repairs can be remedied in time with money. The mental effects of a hurricane can be traumatic where panic, uncertainty, anxiety, despair and lack of support, can remain with victims for the rest of their life. But, after reading my son's description of 'Hurricane Gloria,' I cried for them being deprived of family relationships. The content of my son's assignment was a positive display of help from people that they didn't know. The assignment excluded the lack of concern on the part of the immediate and extended family that they knew about the hurricane and chose to ignore us.

Hurricane Gloria was well-publicized, so everyone was aware of the storm's damage. Members of the immediate and extended family cannot claim they were unaware of the storm's impact. The lack of interest and more importantly abandonment on the part of my children's grandparents, aunts, uncles and cousins, is a form of mental abuse which I found to be horrific. If you dislike my wife and me for some reason, okay. But to take out your animus for no reason on young innocent children brought tears to my eyes. Moreover, I could not reconcile in my mind how anyone in the family thought that abandonment/ isolation is going to teach my family a lesson.

Two days later, I flew back to Georgia and continued the remaining four weeks of training. My wife remained home caring for our children and running the house without power for more than a week. Here's an opportunity for the immediate and extended family to show some interest in my family at a time of need, and they did nothing. They chose to ignore us and continue their abandonment which was hurtful. I didn't want my children to be ashamed of their parents because we were unable to provide them with a good immediate and extended family connection which they could be proud of. In times of adversity, we tried to instill in them the positive aspects of events so that they did not become tainted.

34

DOUBLE TROUBLE

Sometime in the late seventies, we were invited to Nick's house for dinner. He greeted us at the door. A handsome man in his mid-forties, six-feet tall, well-built, with dark wavy hair ushered me into the kitchen. We sat at the table, as he rested his elbow positioned for an arm wrestle. He looked at me. "Let's see what you can do?" We locked hands and butted our arms and elbows together. Two seconds later, he pulled my arm down. I was no match for Nick's strength having a slender build at five-foot ten and one hundred sixty pounds. He laughed. "Pretty strong, ha."

I replied. "Yeah, you must be working out."

Nick looked at me. "I like to keep in shape, summer is on the way."

Nick knew how to get his message across that he was better than you and don't mess with him.

I met Nick through marriage. A generous, but calculating man. When he does a favor for you, he expects a favor in return. He worked as a salesperson for a large construction company. His house was furnished with fine marble floors, an oversize kitchen containing fine wood cabinets, marble countertops and tiled floor to ceiling bathrooms.

Nick's wife Sophia walked out of the bedroom strutting her tall shapely body as she greeted us. She wore an aqua-colored tight- fitting outfit, accented with her blond bouffant hairdo. I don't know where she thought she was going. She held out her hand to show off her oversize gold charm bracelet. "Do ya like it, Nick bought it for me?"

My wife looked at the bracelet. "It's beautiful, good luck with it."

She remarked. "Yeah, I'm glad you like it. We're gonna have veal Milanese with gnocchi and asparagus, I had it made at a caterer."

As we sat on the sofa in the living room, my children played with their Lego blocks on the plush carpeted floor. Bobby walked out of the bedroom to greet us, as the strong odor of marijuana followed him into the living room. I clenched my lips and looked at Nick. "Wow, that's a strong odor."

The odor of marijuana reminded me when I was a teenager living in the Bronx:

In 1964, we hung out on the street corner harmonizing to, "A Teenager in Love" by Dion and the Belmonts. Cousin Michael sang lead, while Guy, Mike and I were back-up singers. We weren't that good, but good enough to attract a few listeners. We enjoyed the harmony together. It made us feel good and sometimes a few girls hung around and listened to us. I enjoyed singing after spending a year in the church choir. A small crowd of people gathered around and listened. As the crowd increased, we seemed to improve our sound.

Moe, a neighborhood Hispanic kid walked over to us. "Why don't you guys come over to da club?"

I said. "What club?"

He replied. "See dat door over dare, in back of da luncheonette, dat's it."

We followed Moe behind the strip mall into the walk-out basement. Music played, in a dimly lit room, furnished with an empty makeshift bar, some vinyl covered booths and small formica tables. We sat at a table, while we watched people we didn't know, gather at the bar. Moments later, somebody dropped a large clear plastic bag on the table where we sat, opened it, removed the contents and spread out what looked like dried plants. People walked over and placed the contents into paper, rolled it, lit it up and smoked it. Within minutes, everybody in the room smoked except the four of us. The room was engulfed with marijuana smoke. Even if you didn't smoke, you could get high just being there. The four of us stood up and walked outside. I guess they thought that we'd join in and smoke with them, hoping to acquire future marijuana customers. My friends didn't use drugs, we drank alcohol. Tobacco products irritated my nasal system and marijuana was no different. This was my first experience with marijuana.

Nick said to me. "Yeah, I've been telling Bobby that he needs to stop smoking that shit."

I pointed out. "How do you permit him to smoke marijuana in your house when you know we're coming over? You know who I work for and I don't want my kids exposed to any kind of drugs."

Nick replied. "I'd rather he used it at home than on the street somewhere."

I looked at Nick. "What if he drives his car and gets into an accident under the influence of drugs? How does it make it safer for him to use drugs at home? As long as you condone the use of drugs at home he'll continue to use them."

Nick sat there remaining silent.

I remarked. "Look, I'm not the right person for this. When it comes to drugs of any kind that are not prescribed by a physician, I won't ingest it."

Nick turned to me. "What do you think I should do?"

I pointed out. "If he was my son, I'd tell him that ingesting or smoking a substance that is not prescribed by a physician could result in an unexpected outcome that could forever change his life. Sometimes marijuana is laced with other chemicals causing erratic behavior, aggressiveness or even an overdose. I'm not an expert in this area, but there was this guy Joe, from the neighborhood. While at a party, someone spiked the punch with LSD. I guess whoever spiked it, thought it might be funny, to watch an unsuspecting person's response to a hallucinogen. I learned that the LSD altered Joe's mind. After he drank the punch he was never the same person again."

Nick glanced at me with a worried look on his face. "Well I don't know if Bobby will listen to me."

After we finished eating dinner, Bobby walked over to me "Neil, I read an article in 'High Times Magazine', where these Customs guys were arrested in Arizona for marijuana smuggling. Do you know about it?"

I replied. "The incident had been talked about. Cases like this tarnish the reputation of everyone in the service and you hope that people don't paint you with the same brush."

Bobby did not respond and handed me the article.

I replied. "If it's the same guy mentioned in this article he worked in New York years ago."

Bobby with a surprised look on his face. "So, you actually knew this guy."

Bobby smiled appearing pleased that I knew one of the customs officers that was arrested for smuggling.

I remarked. "Some years ago, he worked at JFK Airport for a short time and later transferred to the southern border."

There was a knock on the door that Bobby answered and immediately walked out.

Nick and I sat in the living room as he thumbed through the newspaper angered over the rising fuel prices. He looks my way.

"President Carter isn't helping us with these rising oil prices, we're really get'n hit over the head. How are you handling your heating bills during this cold snap?""

I pointed out. "Well, I installed a wood burning stove in the living room to help offset the fuel oil cost. I'm always on the lookout for wood to burn, so If you know anyone with a downed tree, I'll haul it away for no charge."

Nick said, "The fuel prices today can really put a dent in the money you make."

I replied. "Yeah, we do the best we can."

Nick said. "You know, one day my ship will come in."

I remarked. "You seem to be doing alright for yourself."

Nick paused for a moment and whispered, "You know, If Bobby

cleaned up, cut his hair and dressed up, would you let him through Customs with drugs?"

I shrugged. "No!"

I put my head down shaking it from side to side, shocked that he would ask me to participate in smuggling drugs for him. I did not want to believe the words that he uttered. A family member asking me to participate in a conspiracy to smuggle drugs was dispicable. Nick may have felt that I owed him a favor for the money he loaned me to buy the cesspools during the construction of my house. I paid Nick for the money he loaned me years earlier. Many people viewed me as an easy mark, a friendly face, easily approachable and Nick was no different. Then he paused, staring at me and laughed. "Ha, ha, ha, " as he slapped his hand on my knee. I was angered by Nick's suggestion to participate in a conspiracy with him and his son to smuggle drugs. Nick wasn't joking because he was always looking for a score, so he tried to soften it by laughing. His suggestion to involve me in drug smuggling showed his lack of respect for me, my family. Integrity was not part of Nick's character.

Sometime later I sat on the sofa in the living room at Nick's house. He yelled to his wife Sophia, "Turn-on the TV, I wanna watch the game."

Nick leaned over and whispered to me, "You know Bobby just got back from Texas, and he said that drugs are cheap down there. He brought some back home, and I'm keeping it in the basement." Being a federal law enforcement officer, Nick's statement that he was storing a quantity of drugs in his house sent chills down my spine. For a moment, I pretended not to have heard what Nick said. Shocked and silent, I stared straight ahead in an effort to absorb his comment. Nick stared at me waiting for my response. I did not respond. Seconds later, he stood up and walked away. I sat alone in the living room, for how long I don't know, running scenarios through my head: Is this a set-up?

Should I ask Nick if I can see the drugs and ignore the fact that I have done so?

Should I confront Nick and ask to see the drugs and then decide if the quantity is sufficient to proceed criminally by arresting him and Bobby?

Should I leave the house and report the information to my superiors or the local police and let them decide to obtain a search warrant and leave me out of it?

Is Nick testing my integrity to see my reaction to a large quantity of drugs in his house?

Is Nick attempting to involve me in a conspiracy with him since I am on the premises and have knowledge that he is storing drugs?

Maybe there are no drugs at all?

Nick disapproved of his son's drug habit, but he approved his son's purchase of a large quantity of drug's and storage in the house. You can't have it both ways.

Nick returned to the living room as he focused on my blank face. When confronted with a serious issue, I have a habit of remaining silent. Reluctant to make a hasty decision, I tried to process as many aspects of the situation as possible. I did not speak. Nick did not know what to say to me as he appeared to be worried. Nick is a salesman, and he presumed that he could read me. Factoring in my appearance and qualities, he decided to try me. Nick may have mistaken my quietness for weakness. He thought he knew me. A few minutes passed and it felt like forever. I decided my best option for the sake of my job and family was to get out of the house immediately.

My wife sat in the kitchen; I walked over to her. "Let's get the kids dressed." Nick stood up from the sofa in his stocking feet with a sullen look on his face as we put on our coats and said goodbye.

While driving home, I focused on what had happened, angered by Nick's flagrant disregard for my integrity. Based on the circumstances, I knew we would never return to his home, and my wife would suffer the loss of her relatives. My wife turned to me. "Why did you want to leave early?"

I responded. "I'll explain it to you after we put the kids to bed."

Later- on at home my wife and I sat in the living room. I told her, "There's illegal activity going on in Nick's house. You know your uncle's a wheeler-dealer.?

My wife raised an eyebrow. "What are you saying?"

I pointed out. "I won't go into it, but if we continue to visit Nick, I can jeopardize my job and put our family at risk. Our best option is not return to his house. If any law enforcement agency is investigating Nick there is a possibility that I could be connected to Nick's activity. My career would be sent into a turmoil. We would be devastated. If the police search Nick's house and find drugs, his family is in trouble. Nick or Bobby could claim that I have knowledge of their operation to reduce their guilt. I'd lose my job and possibly get a jail sentence. The slightest association or inference with drugs would forever tarnish my career. I couldn't live with guilt every day especially when I report for duty. All of these scenarios are strong possibilities and do not place me in a favorable position."

I continued, saying. "For example: Tomorrow If I call Nick and say, listen, we can't visit you anymore because you keep drugs in your house. My association with you might jeopardize my job."

I said. "What do you think Nick would say?"

Nick might respond. "We don't have any drugs in the house. Don't worry, anytime you come over we'll make sure there are no drugs in our house."

"Or: Don't visit us, we'll visit you."

Nick may be part of a current investigation and if he's followed to our house for a visit I become connected to his illegal activity.

"Or: If any law enforcement agency decides to review Nick's phone records and they connect him to me I become part of their investigation. It's too risky, it's going to cause more problems, it's a conundrum."

I could see a worried look on my wife's face so I stopped discussing the situation with her.

I looked at her. "We'll deal with it!"

After the incident with Nick I thought about contacting the Internal Affairs Division (IAD) in my agency to explain the situation, but I realized it might bring needless suspicion on me which I did not need. Knowing how some government bureaucrats work I needed to shy away from the Internal Affairs Division (IAD). Willingly telling my story with the best intentions to an IAD agent cuts both ways. If the agent feels that there is some culpability on my part a few things could occur: a forced transfer, a termination of employment or criminal prosecution. What came to mind was the phrase, 'the road to hell is paved with good intentions'. I recalled from investigator training that the government can terminate an agent for committing nonfeasance and my association with Nick met that to a tee.

Nonfeasance is the total omission or failure of an agent to enter upon the performance of a distinct duty or undertaking, the failure to perform a duty or the neglect or refusal without sufficient excuse to that which is the officer's legal duty to do. From the government's point of view, public service is a public trust. Employees must avoid any actions creating the appearance that they are violating the law. Whether circumstances create an appearance, that the law on these standards, has been violated. An allegation of corruption is enough to taint my career and follow me to my grave.

What occurred at Nick's house is illegal; it's wrong; it's downright dirty. I can't ignore the fact that there was a high probability drugs have been or are present in Nick's house. There is no telling what would or could occur if my family continues to visit Nick's family. I am unwilling to risk my career on the backs of anyone and family members are no exception. Nick and his family are pleasant, generous folks but his behavior has always been questionable as he draws you into his web little by little creating difficulty to get out. I realized my family had one option because any other choice would jeopardize my career, so this choice is the lesser of all the other evils. Abort all contact with Nick's family, it's too risky. There would be the loss of my wife's support base, the glue that holds most families together through thick and thin. I knew this decision would change my family's lives forever. A situation that divides a family hits at the core like a knife going into your heart that cannot be removed. I knew that we would suffer. But what's better - no support base or jail?"

Months later, Nick called me on the phone. "Bobby's been arrested down South in a marijuana deal. What should we do?"

In a stern voice, I replied, "Without knowing any details, which I don't want to know, I would suggest that you hire a very good lawyer for him." After that phone call, I had no further contact with Nick again.

The severing our relationship with my wife's family and the estrangement in my family occurred around the same time. My parents had joined forces with my wife's family to apply pressure and perpetuate the estrangement. I don't believe in coincidences but I do believe this was a conspiracy. I can only describe this situation as 'double trouble.'

Sometime later there was phone called made to our home and the person on the line said to my wife. "You know too much, I can have you taken care of."

35

HEADQUARTERS

On May 26, 1986, Memorial Day, together with my wife and children we rented a small motor boat in Moriches bay. Fishing was something that we all enjoyed doing as a family. We headed out a short distance from the dock, dropped the anchor and lines waiting for a nibble. This was the time of year when flounders were abundant in that area. The thrill of watching my children struggling to land a fish made it all worthwhile.

At lunch time, we headed to the pristine beach in Moriches bay, just on the other side of the ocean to stretch our legs. The boys enjoyed scouring the beach for crabs and shellfish, anything that moved while my wife and I watched them. After lunch, we continued fishing in and out of the protected bay coves. We had a good day ending up catching thirty- five flounders and headed for the dock. There were several fishermen cleaning their catch on wooden tables. While I cleaned my fish, I noticed a man walking from the parking lot, bypassing several fishermen and stood directly in front of me holding a clip board.

He said. "I work for the Federal Fisheries Service, and we're taking a survey. Can you can answer some questions?"

I looked at him. "Do you have identification?"

He pointed to a poorly constructed plastic covered nametag with no photo pinned to his shirt. It looked like it was made by a child.

He advised. "Yes, I have this I.D. I'm wearing."

I pointed out. "A plastic tag with your name on it? That doesn't look like a government ID. Do you have an official government ID? I am a government employee and I'm familiar with official credentials."

The guy's eyes opened wide. He stood there speechless, with a worried look on his face. He abruptly turned around and walked briskly toward his car, started it up and sped out of the parking lot. It seemed odd to me that he had not spoken to any of the other fishermen and never asked me any questions. I walked to the parking lot and copied down his license plate number.

After cleaning the fish, we packed up our gear and headed home. When we arrived at the house, I walked up the steps and noticed that the front door was slightly ajar. I was shocked to see the front door unlocked because I have a deadbolt lock above the entrance lock. Opening that lock requires a high skill level. I walked in, not alerting my wife or children as to what had taken place and thinking it might be better if they didn't know about it. After searching the house, nothing had been disturbed and it didn't appear that anything had been- taken. My inspection before leaving the house has been the same for years, where I systematically check every window and door prior to leaving, ensuring that everything is locked. When you grow up in the Bronx you lock up everything to the point where some people lock their car door before they check their oil. Just a figure of speech.

I contacted a friend who works in private security, and he reinforced my thoughts about the open door. He informed me that, "opening a locked door is a simple task for someone with basic lock-picking skills and/or the proper equipment. Lock-picking is not a common trade, but there are some unscrupulous people that possess the skill. An entry made into a residence without permission is a crime. That act was done to create fear and intimidate you."

I had not mentioned to anyone that my family and I would be away for Memorial Day. Even if someone had been watching the house, that person would not have knowledge of my return. There's a strong possibility the phony Federal Fisheries guy called someone to confirm my location, so that opening of the front door was- accomplished shortly before my return.

A few weeks later, I arrived home from work and walked into the kitchen. My wife informed me, "While driving to the stores today with the children, a guy followed me in a car."

I asked. "How do you know?"

She pointed out. "I noticed him behind me when I drove on Oakdale Bohemia Road. I turned onto Sunrise Highway and into the shopping center. When I left the shopping center, he followed me through the neighborhood. Later on, I drove to the post office and while parked in the lot I noticed he was parked at a distance."

I replied. "It appears that this guy wanted you to be aware that you were being stalked. Did you get a look at him and the license plate number?"

She replied. "Yes."

After the stalking of my wife and children, the previously opened front door, it appeared that someone was attempting to intimidate us.

The vehicle that followed my wife was registered to a man who lived in Central Islip and the description matched the person who was stalking my wife. At the office, I notified my group supervisor, and provided the details of the stalking of my wife by this unscrupulous individual. He said, "If you were working in the Narcotics Division, I could see your concern. Your current assignment in the Fraud Division would not lend itself for us to pursue this matter. It sounds like it's a private matter." I didn't want to inform him of the drug conspiracy that Nick attempted to involve me in because that would complicate matters. Then I would be required to explain in detail my association with Nick and that might trigger an inquiry from the Internal Affairs Division creating more problems for me and my family. So, I decided to drop it. I wasn't happy about my supervisor's reaction to my request.

I filed a complaint with the Suffolk County Police department (SCPD). They informed me that the man had a long arrest record and there was an outstanding warrant for his arrest. Several weeks later SCPD notified me that their investigation revealed that the stalker had died in Chicago. My gut feeling was right, since I learned later that the stalker and the phony Federal Fisheries guy were associates.

When I attempted to verify the death of the stalker, I learned that there was no record of his death in Chicago. My information revealed that the stalker lived in Arizona where the records listed him as deceased. It seemed odd that a man in twenties died at such a young age.

While at work I attempted to maintain an upbeat persona. I constantly tried not let my personal life spill out into my profession. My story had not been told to anyone including co-workers. While working in the office one day, Al Frare, a coworker walked past me in the hall and uttered. "What are you so happy about? Every time I see you you're always smiling." I replied. "Al, I'm laughing on the outside, but crying on the inside." He smiled not believing me as he shook his head from side to side.

From 1985 to 1987 the hang-up calls and harassing calls were increasing and that provided an incentive for us to move. In June of 1987, I received a promotion to the U.S. Customs Headquarters, Washington, D.C. Our decision to relocate was something that we considered due to the estrangement. It's difficult to give up a home that we had poured our sweat and blood into, making it a place where we lived in proudly. The abandonment and rejection from the family provided the incentive to leave and start a new beginning. The promotion to headquarters in D.C. was an important change in my career. Headquarters is the place where policy is made, and that's where field agents must go if they want to move up the ranks. The purpose of the move to D.C. was not to launch my career, but to start a new life leaving the bad memories behind.

While working in Headquarters, I wrote directives for William Rosenblatt, Assistant Commissioner of Enforcement's briefings to Congress.

Our house was up for sale with a local real estate agent. On a Saturday afternoon, Joe a real estate agent contacted me from the Sally Mandell Agency located in Babylon.

He advised. "Hi, my name is Joe and I have a couple that's interested in your home. Could you show it to us?"

I replied. "When do you want to see it?"

He said. "In an hour?"

I answered. "Okay."

I contacted our listing agent on the phone. "I have a couple that wants to see the house in an hour. Did the buyer's agent contact you?"

She said. "No, they did not, but if their agent is present during the viewing, it's okay."

"Thanks."

An hour later, Joe the buyer's agent, arrived at the house with an elderly couple. As they walked through the rooms, the woman opened every cabinet and closet door in the entire house closely examining the contents. She reminded me of my nosy Aunt Rose. Normally, most people open one or two closet doors or ask permission prior to opening any doors. After about ten minutes of examining the house, the woman turned to me. "Where is your wife?"

She spoke as if she knew her.

I replied. "She's out right now. Did you want to speak with her?"

She said. "Oh, oh, I was just wondering."

I finished showing the house and escorted the potential buyers outside.

The man said. "Thank you for showing us the house. We'll think about it."

I replied. "You're welcome."

Uncomfortable with these buyers, I contacted Uncle John on the phone. "Do you know anybody with the last name of Mercuri?"

He immediately responded, "Al and Joan Mercuri, they were friends of the family when your mother and I lived with Nana on St Lawrence Avenue in the Bronx."

I asked. "So, my mother knew the Mercuri's and sent them here to spy on us?"

He said. "I wouldn't be surprised."

After the Mercuri's visit I realized that they were in my home pretending to be prospective buyers, but they were sent to spy on us!"

The Mercuri's did not buy a house in our neighborhood. The visit by the Mercuri's caused me to think about the constant rhetoric from my mother. "We don't know what you're doing; we don't see you." My mother wanted to ignore me, but she wanted to know what we're doing. She couldn't have it both ways.

The alleged potential homebuyers from Babylon snooping through my home bordered on an invasion of personal privacy. I found that disturbing.

Our house had been on the market for a few months, and I kept decreasing the price. I couldn't understand why a mint condition, custom-built home, with a water view of Fire Island, located in a serene neighborhood didn't sell.

The movers packed up the furniture and placed it into storage. We moved to Virginia, just outside the perimeter of Washington, D.C., where I traveled to work every day on the metro. While living in Virginia the hang-up phone calls started-up again, the phone was number was unlisted and I noted the calls.

One day at lunchtime, I walked out of the door of my office building located on Constitution Ave in Washington D.C. Immediately a man walked right up to me as if he knew me.

He said. "Hi I've seen you in the neighborhood, I have the Irish Setter dog."

I looked at him. "I'm sorry you don't look familiar." I asked.

"Where, do you live?' He said. "I live on Cleveland." Later on, I checked my neighborhood and Cleveland Street was approximately ten miles away.

The guy was silent and walked away. He was a stocky black man, about thirty years of age. Being somewhat suspicious, I decided to follow him. He walked several blocks and then entered an office building on Second Street. I waited a moment and then walked in and read the directory on the wall. The building contained several attorneys' offices which reinforced my suspicions about this man, who claimed to be a neighbor was a ruse. That evening I contacted my mother on the phone.

She answered. "Hello."

I remarked. "After we moved away from you I thought that you'd stop playing your games hiring goons to harass my family?"

She replied. " We don't see you, we don't know what you're doing."

I angrily replied. "Just stop with the hang-up phone calls and call off your goons, enough is enough!"

I hung up the phone.

On weekends, I traveled to New York to check up on the house and show it to prospective buyers, but there was very little activity. I couldn't understand why a pristine condition custom built home with a water view of Fire Island was difficult to sell. I wondered if my parents were using their friends to act as potential buyers for my home, could they use their connections to forestall the sale of my home and cause me financial hardship? Anything is possible.

The cost of two residences became burdensome. At the time, I was not eligible for the 'government buyout program' since my position in Washington was a promotion and not a forced transfer or a directed move. Only forced transfers or directed moves met the criteria for the 'government buyout program.' I wrestled with that regulation.

I contacted the Special Agent in Charge at JFK Airport and requested a voluntary transfer back to New York. He responded. "If you pay your own expenses, including storage and travel, we will accept you to work in the Long Island office."

"Okay, thank you."

I didn't have much of a choice so I agreed to the transfer and borrowed ten thousand dollars to cover the cost of storing our household furnishings for one year.

On July 7,1988, my wife and I rented a truck and traveled to Virginia to pick-up our household furnishings from the storage facility. Due to limited space in the passenger compartment, my wife asked her father to care for our children at his home, even though she was not on good terms with him. Her father was the only person that had knowledge that our home would be unoccupied overnight, unless he told someone else.

When we arrived at home, I walked inside and checked the windows and doors and noticed that the back door was slightly ajar. Prior to leaving, I double checked every window and door. After we settled in, I searched the house and found that nothing had been disturbed and nothing had been taken. I did not alert my wife. This was the second illegal entry. I got the message and took measures to prevent that from ever happening again.

In the summer, together with my wife and children we decided to take a vacation. We traveled along the seventeen miles of the New Hampshire coastline. We spent a few days admiring the sights and swimming in the cold northern waters. In the evening, we dined at a local restaurant, and we shared a four- pound lobster.

Two days later we traveled on to Bretton Woods, New Hampshire, the home town of the Cog Wheel Railroad. We bought our tickets for the train that travels 6200 ft. up to the summit of Mt Washington. The temperature at the base of the mountain was eighty- five degrees. We were told by the employees to bring a warm coat since the temperature at the summit was much cooler. We boarded the colorful red train in anticipation of how it would climb up a thirty- seven- degree mountain. The cog wheel train is a rack and pinion gearing system that has been operating since the 1800's.

While we traveled up the mountains, the panoramic view spanning the White Mountains, was like a picture post card, unlike anything we had ever seen. The closer we approached the summit, trees and plant life did not exist, since the year-round temperature prevents plant growth at that elevation. At the summit, the temperature was thirty- eight degrees. The wind blew at over forty miles an hour. At the top of the mountain winds have been recorded well over two hundred miles an hour. While walking around the weather observation station, we snapped pictures and admired the scenic vista. On a clear day, you can see the Atlantic Ocean and six states. The trip was a most memorable experience for all of us.

36

SOUTHERN STATE PARKWAY

In 1988, I arrived home from work.

My wife spoke to me. "While I was in the backyard today, a tan pick-up truck parked on the side of the house. The driver put a ladder against the telephone pole and climbed up.

While standing in the backyard, I got his attention. "What are you doing here? I didn't call for any repair service."

He replied, "I'm just checking the telephone line."

She pointed out. "As soon as I started to talk with him he immediately climbed down and quickly loaded the ladder into the truck. He drove to the end of the street, made a U-turn and drove past the house.

I spoke. "Did you get the license plate number?"

She replied. "I tried to get the license plate number, but there was none on the front and the rear plate was bent, so I couldn't read it."

I asked. "Can you tell me anything else?"

She said. "It was an old pickup truck and there was no writing on it."

I assured her. "Okay, I'll take care of it."

The next day I contacted the New York Telephone Company and inquired regarding any repair at the telephone pole located on the side of my house. I asked if the New York Telephone Company owns, leases or subcontracts any tan colored vehicles, or any pick-up trucks and the type of identification that is required of their employees?

This is the response I received:

"The New York Telephone Company repair vehicles are predominantly white vans bearing the Company name and logo and marked with a number for the fleet. As for identification, all our employees have an identification badge around their neck with the New York Telephone Company logo and the employee's photograph. Based on the information you provided, it does not appear that what occurred at the telephone pole abutting your property was an employee of our company."

I replied. "Thank you."

The phony telephone repairman's actions, was another attempt to intimidate us by demonstrating that someone has the ability to tap into our telephone and that was meant to scare, harass or pressure us.

Early in the evening together with my wife and children we decided to visit my wife's ninety-eight year old Grandmother who was being cared for in a nursing home, located in Rockville Center. My wife was driving on the Southern State Parkway and signaled to move into the right lane. Moments later a vehicle tailgated us and flashed the bright lights. I said, "That's not a police car. Why is this car flashing the lights?"

She replied. "I don't know. Before I moved into the right lane I signaled, and before I knew it, that car was on my bumper."

I said. "Well, I didn't hear any screeching of brakes and no contact so just drive."

Moments later while driving in the passing lane, the same vehicle pulls up alongside us and forced our car onto the grass center median. The driver parked perpendicular to the parkway. A man over six-feet tall abruptly exited the vehicle moving swiftly toward our vehicle. I told my wife, "Close the windows and lock the doors, this guy looks violent."

The driver stood in front of our car yelling at us.

He yelled. "You wrecked my fuckin car! What the fuck is wrong with you! What the hell are you doing!"

We remained in the car watching him. The guy turned away and did an about face, and abruptly leaped toward our car violently striking the windshield with the full force of his body. The impact vibrated throughout the car. It's a wonder the windshield didn't crack. The guy was abnormally strong and I thought he was going to inflict serious harm to us.

My wife was terrified and turned to me in an elevated voice. "What's wrong with this guy? "

I replied. "I don't know, just stay calm."

My children sat silently in the back seat, but I could see they were frightened.

I turned around and looked at them. "Don't worry, it will be alright."

The driver walked toward his car. He opened the trunk and while bent over inside he proceeded to feverishly throw the contents one by one onto the ground. I thought he was searching for a weapon. If I became involved in a one on one situation with him he would have overpowered me. When I'm off-duty I rarely carry my weapon, but on this day, I was armed. Quietly, I unhooked the clasp on the holster, removed my weapon and held it close to the floor, so as not to alarm my wife and children. Minutes later, a New York State Police car arrived on the scene. Thank God. The last thing I wanted was a shootout in the presence of my wife and children.

The officer exited the vehicle and was immediately approached by the driver speaking in a hostile tone. After the trooper listened to the driver he ordered him, "Sit in your car!"

The officer walked over to our vehicle. "What's going on here?"

I replied. "Officer, I am armed and here is my ID."

He asked. "So what happened?"

I pointed out. "My wife had signaled and entered the right lane when this car suddenly appeared driving on the right shoulder. As we continued to drive, he pulled alongside of our vehicle and forced us onto the median. He exited the vehicle and punched our windshield with the full force of his body while he yelled obscenities at us. Then, he feverishly emptied the contents of the trunk of his car. I thought he might be looking for a weapon."

The officer walked over to the driver. "You're under arrest, put your hands behind your back."

The driver yelled. "Oh no!"

The officer asked. "Can you follow me to Meadowbrook Hospital, the driver claims he needs medical attention."

I said. "Sure."

While in the hospital Emergency Room, the driver yelled to the nurses while handcuffed to the chair. The nurse walked over to the police officer. "Can't you remove the handcuffs from him?"

He replied. "No, that guy's violent!"

I signed the police statement that accurately described the incident.

The next day while eating breakfast my wife said, "The guy that forced me off the parkway looks very similar to the guy in the tan pick-up truck that claimed he was checking the telephone line on our house."

I asked. "Can you positively identify him?"

She said. "Not positively, but he looked very similar."

At the court appearance for the incident on the Southern State Parkway, I did not testify. The attacker/defendant had a record of several arrests, so he accepted a plea deal for a lesser charge. At that time, I learned that the subject lived a short distance away from my parents' home.

Uncle John and his wife were home at that time. I visited them as they lived in the same neighborhood as my parents. We sat at the kitchen table.

I asked them. "Have you noticed any cars parked at my parents' home recently?"

Aunt Terry said. "Well, when we're out shopping sometimes we pass by their street. About a week ago, there was a car parked in front of their house."

I asked. "Did you get a close look at it as to the type of vehicle, like an SUV or pickup truck?"

She replied. "All l can remember is that it was tan, but I can't remember any more than that. Let me tell you this, I've seen your mother speaking on the pay phone on Merrick Road, which I thought was odd being that her house is just a few blocks away."

I said to Aunt Terry. "Earlier this week there was an incident. I won't go into the details. Do you see this name and address?"

They looked at the information I had written down. Aunt Terry crossed her arms and with a surprised look on her face. "That name is not familiar to me but that street is near your parents' house.

I replied. "I'm trying to sort out the information right now, and I'll let you know what I find out."

They replied. "We understand."

37

ANNIVERSARY

In 1990, we received an invitation to my parents' fiftieth wedding anniversary party. More than ten years had passed since my parents had abandoned us, and our relationship had not changed. I don't know why my parents sent us an invitation? Knowing my mother, the invitation was sent in case anyone at the party asked about my family she could say, "Well, I sent them an invitation."

My wife did not want to attend. Reluctantly, I decided to attend the party alone, going there without a plan. The event presented an opportunity to observe, first-hand, the extended family's reaction to my presence.

Inside the banquet room, everyone was seated as I arrived late, so that my presence was known. I walked toward my parents while they sat alone in high back wing chairs on a stage. As I approached them, they frowned. This was an opportunity for them to extend an olive branch to me, to meet me halfway, and show their love. I stood directly in front of them. "Hi, congratulations."

My mother held her head down and spoke in an angered low voice. "Why are you here?"

Confused, I said, "You invited me."

My father was silent. They both turned away, as their eyebrows lowered and lips pressed together while I stood directly in front of them for everyone to see. My parents really put on a show for their guests. My mother was the matriarch of the family where her domineering and repetitive dramatic descriptions of events that occurred during the estrangement were believed by the siblings and extended family. Throughout my life, my mother maintained a dramatic posture in our brief conversations. Behind the scenes, when I was young, she'd flare-up over very minor infractions such as challenging her level of punishment. I've never witnessed her punish or flare-up with my brother or sister. Her true personality was restrained in public and during her conversations with relatives. Mom was very cunning and manipulative in her conversations by saying as little as possible and eliciting more information from the other person. My parents sent me an invitation to their party, never expecting after ten years of estrangement, that I would attend. But my parents' love is not about acceptance or tolerance, it's about their own emotional comfort level and image. I had never experienced a public rejection by my parents. Their reaction made me realize their life is dependent on outside admiration and approval.

In the banquet hall, there were several tables that were occupied by family and friends. As I scanned the room, there were relatives I had not seen in years. Not one of them greeted me. Cousin Michael and Aunt Anna were seated at a table. They were the closest relatives to me on my mother's side of the family. I had not seen either of them in many years, but my attempt to visit them had been rejected eight years earlier.

I walked over to them. "Hi, how are you?"

They responded together. "Hi, Neil."

There was no emotion, no embracement or hand shaking on their part and no further discussion. I found their response to be cold. Aunt Anna and Michael's response was hurtful so I walked away. No sense perpetuating the rejection. The old cliché we only see them at weddings and funerals was so true. If a relationship is based on a casual conversation at a wedding or funeral, it begs the question: How well do you really know someone?

Feeling uncomfortable standing alone, unacknowledged by anyone, I looked for a place of refuge. A vacant seat was available at the table where Uncle Paul F. and his family sat. They were the closest relatives to me on my father's side of the family. Prior to the rift with my parents, my relationship with Uncle Paul and his family was flawless throughout my entire life. During high school, I worked part time at Uncle Paul's factory for five years, and maintained a good relationship with him. His son Sandy was my idol when I was child. When I became older, occasionally I visited Sandy at his office when I worked in the World Trade Center. I walked over to Uncle Paul's table and cousin Sandy asked me a question about someone seated at another table, and that was the end of our interaction. He did not ask me about my family and I was hoping that he might talk longer, but that did not occur. Immediately, I sat down beside Aunt Ester uncle Paul's wife and looked at her. "Hi, how are?" She glanced at me and in a monotone voice said, "Neil." She did not express any emotion, or embracement, and there was no further discussion. Uncle Paul glanced over at me and nodded his head. Two years earlier, I contacted Aunt Ester and together with my family we visited with her family at their home. We had not seen each other since the rift and I was curious to see their response to my family. Everyone was congenial during the visit and there was no discussion regarding the estrangement from my parents. The visit was not very long and we left. Obviously, my parents' version of events had taken root in the extended family.

While seated, I hoped that someone might talk with me or ask me about my wife and children, but that did not occur. I recalled the good relationships I maintained with my relatives during my earlier life. The majority of our relatives were Catholics and I hoped that someone would display some moral rightness, but no one did. Maybe some of the guests were not practicing Catholics or maybe atheists. Why didn't any one of them step forward and do the right thing, religion or no religion. The thought of someone, any guest, approaching me never occurred to anyone. Aside from religion I was hoping for some goodness in anyone, but maybe I was expecting too much from the family.

Recalling my childhood and adult life, I had never done anything in my life to disrespect anyone present at the affair. Since I hadn't seen many relatives in years, maybe my expectations of their responsiveness were unreasonable.

After sitting there, for how long I don't know, bearing the humiliation, hoping that someone might initiate a conversation, and it didn't happen. Food had not been served yet and there was no ceremony or activity that was in progress that prevented anyone from speaking with me. The silence was deafening. My head remained straight, but my eyes focused from left and right. It looked as though everyone was frozen in silence. I couldn't stand it anymore. I pushed back my chair, stood up, turned around and walked out the door never looking back. Shunning is a silent and insidious form of psychological torture. It's impossible to describe its effects unless you have felt it yourself. It eats away at your insides in a way that cannot be visible.

On the ride home, I thought of my parents and how they are pained, because the relationship they have created with my family is inexcusable. It's too shattering, too threatening to bear close examination, and it cannot be reversed. I realized that in order for my relatives to ignore my presence, there must have been a deal made, a deal for silence. I'm sure the years my parents spent portraying my wife and I as villains' and their dismal facial expressions bought their silence.

My mother handled the rift as her soap opera. She watched soap operas daily as long as I lived at home and continued watching for years thereafter. I read somewhere that there are people who watch soap operas that possess a personality trait called NFD 'need for drama'. Persons of this type possess characteristics of 'interpersonal manipulation' which is a tendency to control or mess with other people, and victimhood, "a propensity for believing one is a victim in situations that others would dismiss as benign. Those traits fit my mother to a tee.

During the early stages of the estrangement I felt that the family abandonment was a conspiracy, an agreement. Simply speaking, if my mother, father, grandmothers', sister, brother and their spouses conveyed my parent's version of the rift to any extended family members and friends, the story had spread exponentially. On the low end, the immediate family's version of the story outnumbered my version, six to zero. On the high end, it's six multiplied by the number of people that each person told. Not one family member or friend had heard my version of events, it had never been told. My parents used gossip made up of lies, innuendoes and half- truths. Once the gossip has spread it's impossible to reverse it, the damage was done.

38

GRANDMA

Feeling rejected by my parents after four meetings in the therapist's office, I decided to visit my grandmother in the nursing home in St. James, Long Island. Together with my children we walked into her room.

I said, "Hi Grandma, how are you?"

She reluctantly looked at us. "Hi ya." There was no embracement.

I told my children. "Say hello to your great-grandmother."

She looked down at them and said half- heartedly. "Hello."

There was no embracement with me or my children and she was devoid of any emotion.

I said, "How are you doing, Grandma?"

She held her head down. "Well, I have this pain in here, and I take these medicines for different things."

I asked. "Are they taking care of you here?"

She replied. "Oh yeah, yeah."

Then she said, "Your mother and father were here last week. Have you seen them?"

I gazed out the window. "No, I haven't seen them."

I didn't feel it was right for me to burden a ninety-year old woman with the facts surrounding the estrangement. My parents provided Grandma with their version of events regarding the estrangement. Grandma didn't want to see us because her mind was made up, so why tell her the facts.

Grandma frowned. "I can't be talking to you, until you, make-up with your parents." Grandma was reiterating the same words spoken to me by my Nana during her last conversation with me. The family was applying pressure from every angle. My relationship with my immediate and extended family was sabotaged, and we had become radioactive.

The tension in my neck and the pain in my heart immediately increased.

I looked at my children and turned to her. "So, Grandma, you don't want to say anything to your great-grandchildren; they are here to visit you?"

Grandma put her head down, remained silent and turned toward the window with her back towards us.

I said to my children, "Come on, let's go. Say goodbye to Grandma."

For the life of me, I did not understand Grandma's rejection of her innocent great-grandchildren who had done nothing to cause her to shun them. Grandma's actions were difficult for me to swallow and cruel to my children.

At one point, I thought that part of my disagreement with the family was due to the lack of education of my grandparents. Both of my grandmothers' were never educated beyond the sixth grade. On the other-hand there were immediate family members that possessed post graduate degrees. I realized that all members of the immediate family marched in lockstep to my grandmothers' way of thinking: 'our minds are made up we don't want to know the facts.'

Throughout my life, I thought Grandma loved me and at this moment she rejected me. She and Grandpa were born in Italy. When they immigrated to New York in the 1920s, they lived in Harlem and later moved to the Bronx. Grandpa made a living by selling fruits and vegetables from a push cart.

When I was a child, Dad regularly brought me to visit his parents where they lived in a small apartment in Parkchester, a planned community located in the Bronx. It was always the same scenario. My father sat at the kitchen table and talked with his father in Italian, while Grandma busied herself in the kitchen. Bored to death while sitting at the table, I walked around the apartment in and out of the bedroom, looking for something to do, but there was nothing to do there. My grandparents didn't have much, and they were not that attentive to me. After a while Grandma yelled out, "Give the kid a fruit, give him a fruit."

I craved fruit, having a sweet tooth. Grandpa pushed the bowl of fruit in front of me. He spoke in broken English. "Here take, take one."

The fruit bowl overflowed with peaches the size of oranges and plums the size of apples that Grandpa sold from his pushcart. The fruit was unlike what I was accustomed to eating at home. Each piece of fruit was flawless, without bumps or bruises, perfectly ripened and shaped. I guess that was how my grandparents showed their love for me.

When I was a child we visited my father's sister Mary and children at her home in Port Jefferson, New York. I recalled an incident after the visit, when Dad hurriedly exited her house. He entered the car, and spoke in a loud voice. "I just got into a fight with Sal, I don't like the way he treats my sister!" Sal and Mary had divorced a year earlier.

Many years later at a party at Aunt Mary's house, her son John spoke with me.

He said. "I've been accepted to attend the State University at Geneseo."

I replied. "That's great John. Geneseo is over three hundred miles from here?"

He informed me. "Yeah, my father bought me a car, so I can travel back and forth on holidays and semester breaks."

That was the first time I heard Uncle Sal's name mentioned in more than fifteen years, let alone anything good. My parents never mentioned Sal's name after the divorce. If Sal was persona non-grata, why was he so generous to his children? I needed to find out.

In the nineties, after checking the telephone book and I was shocked to learn that Sal lived in Port Jefferson, just one mile away from his children. Something told me to contact him, so I drove to his house and knocked on the door. A woman answered. After introducing myself, I asked to speak with Sal. She directed me to sit on a chair near the garage. Moments later, Sal walked over to me. "Hi, I remember you, but much younger." I smiled at him.

He sat on a chair next to me.

I said, "I'm very surprised to see that you're living so close to your children all these years; I was not aware of that. After your divorce from my aunt, I never heard your name or anything about you mentioned again."

Sal pointed out. "Well, I'm not going anywhere. I'm a retired scientist from the Brookhaven Laboratory. At the lab, we do research in nuclear and high energy physics, science and technology, bioscience and national security. Right now, I take courses at Stony Brook University to keep my mind working. During World War II I was a pilot flying the P47 aircraft. I received a degree in Electrical Engineering from Brooklyn Polytechnic Institute. While I worked at the Brookhaven Lab, another scientist and I were the only tenured employees working there without a doctoral degree."

I didn't know anything about Sal. All I knew was that after the divorce from my father's sister, I never heard his name mentioned again, until Cousin John told me that his father bought him a car. Listening to Sal was a breath of fresh air as he explained his life to me. There was no braggadocio in his explanation of himself, no pretensions, no illusions, very pragmatic and realistic. I had never met anyone in my family with Sal's personality, let alone his background. He was not opinionated and spoke clearly, concisely and to the point; he was absent, of drama. After about an hour of talking with him, it was like a shot in the arm. There was a connection between us, something I hadn't felt with anyone in my immediate family and extended family.

I looked at Sal. "The reason I'm here today is that I'm on the outs with my parents, and I need to ask you this question." Sal nodded.

I said. "When I was child, we visited Aunt Mary at her house. My father returned to the car speaking loudly as I sat there with my mother.

He was raving and said. 'I just got into a fight with Sal. I don't like what's going on there."

I asked. "What was that about?"

Sal calmly replied. "First of all, there was no physical fight between your father and me, only anger expressed between us; it isn't worth our time to talk about it, but your father did have a short temper."

I remarked. "I understand that, but I've never heard your name mentioned by my family since that day."

He didn't seem surprised. "Well, let me say that they didn't like me."

Sal and I spoke at length as he described his travels across the United States in his camper with his female companion. I found it fascinating that he built a sailboat that he kept in his garage. Later during the conversation, he looked at me with a smirk on his face.

"You're not like the others in your family."

I replied. "Well, you're right; I guess that's why I'm on the outs with them."

He said, "Your parents maintained this air about them, as if they were better than everyone else. Sometimes it's good to remember where you came from."

I pursed my lips, shook my head and looked at him. "Well I was concerned for years that my parents would file a case against my wife and I seeking 'grandparent's rights'. There was a strong possibility that we would be involved in a legal battle with them due to my father's connections within the legal system in New York City."

Sal turned to me. "Now I understand how your Aunt Mary retained a shyster lawyer from Brooklyn more than sixty miles away, to handle our divorce."

I replied. "Yes, my father transcribed cases for the surrogates court in New York City."

Sal pointed out. "Years ago, when I worked at the Brookhaven Lab I was asked to interview a prospective employee. When I looked at the application, I realized that it was your brother. Immediately, I informed my superiors that I knew this person, so I recused myself from the interview."

Sal was free of bias, so by recusing himself, he let his honesty, integrity and objectivity shine through. My family was well aware that Sal worked at the Brookhaven Lab. My brother did not get the job. Sal was persona non- grata, with my family, but they wanted to use his influence to help my brother obtain employment. My brother had never told me that he had applied for a job at the Brookhaven Lab. I can only surmise that my brother was attempting to use Sal to gain employment, which might reflect poorly on him since my parents were dismissive of him.

Sal and I spoke for hours, and then we walked around the property as he pointed to the projects that he built over the years. While inside the house, Sal handed me a three-page list of at least fifty titles of scientific writings that he developed while employed at the Brookhaven Lab. I found it difficult to read the titles, let alone understanding the content. Even with my technical education, the subject matter was far beyond my comprehension. While Sal worked at the lab, he was revered by his peers, and shunned by his in-laws. Years later I worked a home remodeling project for a scientist who lived in Stony Brook. I learned that he and Sal were coworkers at the Brookhaven Lab. He and his coworkers lauded Sal professionally and personally.

After talking with Sal for a few hours, I uttered a sigh of relief, as if a weight had been removed from my body and the tension in my neck was released. Sal and I continued to meet periodically for breakfast at the diner in Port Jefferson. He expressed an interest in my children, so on occasion my son Christopher joined us at the diner for breakfast. Sal and my son enjoyed speaking with each other. Sal provided the missing ingredient for me and my children, 'a sincere honest relationship'. After eating breakfast one morning, Sal leaned forward.

Speaking in a lowered voice. "I understand your family situation, but you must know that you're not alone here. Let me tell you a story. After I married your aunt, we lived in the same apartment with your grandparents.

Whenever your grandmother was angered, she'd say. "The women run the family; men are only good for one thing - bringing home a paycheck."

Then he pointed out. "Your grandmother didn't like me, and she didn't want me living with them, so she contacted the landlord and had your aunt and I evicted."

I stopped him. "Are you saying that your mother in-law evicted her daughter and you?"

He uttered. "Yes, she didn't care, as long as I was out. If they could get rid of me, then they would patch things up with their daughter afterwards."

I remarked. "What you've described is somewhat similar to my situation. My parents created hostility to attempt to cause a divorce."

He replied. "Yes, it certainly looks that way."

I sat there in shock. "Wow, wow, you just shed a whole new light on everything."

Sal concluded. "I didn't like the way the in-laws treated me, so the best thing that I can do now, is to outlive them. With a smile on his face he said. Maybe I'll live to the age of one hundred twenty."

I said. "I'd like to see that happen."

We laughed together.

Sal passed away years later. I missed him because he filled a void in my life and relieved a good amount of trauma, deprivation of empathy, good conversation and common interest from the immediate family. He provided kindness, mutual respect, peace, free of guilt and most of all an honest and genuine relationship. I will never forget him.

The poor relationship with the immediate and extended family did not rob me and my family of joy. During the Christmas holidays, we gathered our ski equipment, and together with my wife and children, we traveled to New Hampshire. The excitement preparing for the trip emanated through each one of us. Once we crossed the Throg's Neck Bridge from long Island into the Bronx, we traveled north toward the mountains. After five and half hours we arrived at Pat's Peak in Henniker, New Hampshire. The mountain provided skiing for beginner's, since the slopes were designed for the novice. Even my wife learned to ski. We spent several days there taking lessons which provided the basis for our future ski trips. As we gained our confidence on the slopes, over the years we traveled to a variety of ski resorts including: Loon Mountain, Smugglers Notch, Sugarbush, Sunapee, Sunday River and others, located in Maine, Vermont and New Hampshire. It was a wonderful time to share common interests with our children. The memories of those trips have remained with us forever.

39

RELIGION

After we moved back to New York from Virginia my parents invited us to their home. Together with my wife and children we arrived and sat in their backyard. The visit was an attempt to test the temperature of the water in our relationship. It was our last- ditch effort to salvage the relationship if any, with my immediate family. My sister, her husband and daughter and my brothers' wife and daughter were not present during the visit. It was unclear of my parent's motivation behind this visit, but it presented an opportunity for my children to meet their cousins which did not occur. My brother was present at the visit and appeared to be disinterested in communicating much of anything with me, my wife and children. My mother was still running the show and the absence of immediate family members at our visit said it all.

In 1987, I contacted my sister since I had not heard from her since the rift in 1979. I set up a meeting with a family counselor and she agreed to meet with me. After two sessions, I realized that my sister's loyalty to our parents was more important than her loyalty to me. Aware of my brother's and sister's support for my parent's position asking for their support risked their rejection. So, I avoided contacting them since I felt it was up to them to contact me and learn the other half of the story. I learned later that my decision not to contact them early on in the rift was correct. Additional rejection by my siblings would not be healthy for me. Normally siblings communicate and talk to each other in order to rectify a relationship problem in the family, but they did not.

The wide difference in age between my brother and I did not provide a way to develop a healthy sibling relationship. As siblings, we were raised as if we were totally independent of each other lives, like it was a secret. Whenever my mother punished me, we were always alone, and that's when she'd flare-up. When I questioned her punishment, it brought out the worst in her, because I never observed her display physical punishment toward my brother or sister. They were well behaved. For some reason, my mother resented my opposition to her wrath, viewing it as being disrespectful and challenging her authority.

While growing up my mother maintained a closer relationship with my brother and sister, which she told me. Till this day, I don't know what my brother and sister's likes or dislikes happen to be. Rarely did I have more than a brief discussion with them due to our schedules. At dinner, the family was rarely together. I'd eat quickly and leave to study, play sports, or go out with my friends. While growing up and during my adult years, I was not much of a talker, a much better listener.

I ran this scenario in my mind over and over how my mother convinced my brother and sister not to contact me during the rift. One method my mother used to control my father, brother and sister was her dramatic descriptions and explanations of any event. Secondly, my mother would provide half of the details of an event or conversation. Thirdly, many times while growing up she said to me. "Be nice to your aunt she has money, and when she dies she might leave some of it to you."

I was always bothered by my mother's point of view regarding money.

What I learned later on about my brother and sister is that they had an enmeshed relationship with my mother. Enmeshment is the inability to control one's emotional involvement with another person. If one's identity is wrapped up in meeting another person's needs, then their own goals are thwarted. Enmeshed relationships lack healthy boundaries and we lose a sense of where we leave off and another begins. Our sense of individuality is compromised.

No common ground had been achieved between my parents and siblings in almost nine years. The atmosphere was tense at my parent's home, everyone made small talk and all of us were on our guard. As I sat there, all I could think about was how my parents made no attempt to reconcile our differences at four therapist sessions years earlier. Now that my family was present at my parents' home, along with my brother, and there was not even a half -hearted attempt at reconciliation. Being the older brother, the visit was an opportunity for him to make an effort and intelligently discuss our differences, or at least make a suggestion to come to some common ground, but he did not. My father reiterated to me many times over the years, Richard is the oldest, implying that he has the most experience and he can lead the younger siblings. I was hoping to see a gesture or some sort of compromise, but that didn't happen. While sitting there, I hoped for some miraculous change and dealt with how things are, rather than wishing how they were.

Over the years I never thought ill of my brother and sister but their inaction was actually an action that fueled the conflict which was totally devoid of any love. I can only describe their behavior as 'monstrous indifference.'

Members of the immediate family have one thing in common:

They live their life based on how other people view them. They have allowed other people to influence or determine their choices, trying to please their expectations. Social pressure is deceiving where we become prey without noticing it. Before we realize we lost control of our lives, we end up envying how other people live. If you don't speak up people will continue invading you. If you don't resist you legitimize the agreement and it becomes a social practice Soon you'll start doing the same to others-when you let other people define your life, you want to prescribe theirs too. Not expecting things from others is the first step to preventing people from dictating how you live.

In 1999, twenty years after the rift I still had not had a real conversation with my brother. I decided to set up a meeting at the Catholic Church in my brother's neighborhood. In the rectory, I explained to the priest that my brother and I had been estranged for many years and asked for his help. He informed me that he would not conduct a meeting of that nature and did not explain the Catholic Church's position regarding those- kind of situations. I didn't challenge the priest's rejection. While driving home, I thought that possibly the priest may have had a personal relationship with my brother as a parishioner, and he would be unable to objectively deal with the issues.

After my request for help at the Catholic Church in my brother's community failed, I visited the rectory in the parish where my mother lived. My father had passed away a few years earlier. I met with the priest in the rectory and explained that I had been estranged from my parents for many years and asked him to meet with my mother and me in order to improve our relationship. He informed me that he would not arrange a meeting, and he did not explain the Catholic Church's participation. I was shocked by the priest's response; I did not know what to say to him and departed the rectory.

Being raised a Catholic, I did not understand the Catholic Church's rejection of my request for help. Mediation could be viewed as acting like a judge because God's house is where we gather and pray and celebrate Jesus' sacrifice of his life for our sins. While in the priest's office, I thought he would at least offer or suggest a method of compromise, but he did not. There was no offer by the priest to help me, not even prayer. The priest's demeanor was a cold response to someone who's asking for help. For a moment, I sat in silence; I didn't know what to say, so I walked out feeling guilty.

When I looked into the Catholic Church's position regarding mediation, I learned that Jesus is the only mediator between humanity and God. Christ mediates God's grace to the world in and through him. Prayer is what is needed and the mercy and grace of God's immediate attention. My belief was that the Catholic Church was a place I could go to obtain guidance and help. The meetings with the priests left me in a state of guilt, and later on I questioned the Catholic Church's position regarding help, morality and solidarity. The priests that I approached for help never even offered to say a prayer or a positive suggestion to ameliorate my family situation. My understanding was that the Catholic Church was available to help those in need. I never returned to the Catholic church again.

A friend of mine once mentioned to me that it's been his experience with the Catholic Church:

"Whenever I meet with a priest in the church I provide a monetary donation prior to my request. The church will not ask for a donation, but that is what they want. I think the donation practice stems back from the Middle Ages. At that time, the Catholic Church sold indulgences, a monetary payment of penalty which supposedly absolved one of past sins. The donation is also a way to, 'grease the skids.'"

In other Christian denominations, pastors provide some sort of help and guidance as opposed to doing nothing. In very serious matters the pastors refer congregants to mental health professionals.

After my attempts to reconcile with my brother failed, I wrote him a letter. While growing up we were friendly to each other until he married. The only negative situations I recalled as a child was when my brother called me nicknames, but I never held that against him. As far as I was concerned a derogatory nickname was not a relationship breaker. Nicknames were commonplace when we were children. When I was called a derogatory name by anyone, I frowned and bore it and repeated the rhyme; "Sticks and stones may break my bones but names will never harm me." The rhyme taught me to ignore the taunt, to refrain from physical retaliation and to stay calm and good-natured.

In my case name calling toughened me up. Currently, society feels that name calling can hurt us and stick with some people far beyond the time of their telling.

My curiosity prompted me to contact my brother after so many years, even though he supported my parents' position throughout the rift. There was a remote chance that he may have possessed some loyalty, possibly a small amount of love or interest in my side of the story. Meeting with him presented a possible rejection, but at that point I felt I'd be able to bear it. Prior to the rift, we had a small disagreement regarding the fortieth anniversary party planning for my parents, but that was not justification for his years of abandonment and rejection of my family for more than twenty years.

My brother did not want to meet in a therapist setting, so we agreed to walk and talk in the neighborhood.

The first thing out of his mouth. "We don't like the same things. You like white and I like black."

Then he turned to me and said. "Don't you want your money?"

I looked at him. "My loyalty to my parents is not for sale."

My brother was silent. His comment made me realize that he was more concerned about his inheritance than his loyalty to me.

I asked him. "Are you aware of the reason why the rift in the family started?"

He replied. "I know 'tid bits.' "

I said. "Tid bits! You sound like a 'drama queen.'

My brother nodded in agreement. I couldn't believe that my brother enjoyed participating in family drama. 'Tid bits' are all you need to perpetuate a soap opera.

I said. "What do you know?"

He said. "I know that your wife went to Mom's house carrying a Bible."

I replied. "I'm aware of that. Do you know why she brought our Bible to Mom's house?"

He looked at me puzzled not saying anything.

I pointed out. "Mom asked my wife to bring our Bible for her to look at it for some reason. Did you know that?" My brother was silent. At that point, I felt that explaining my side of the story would fall on deaf ears. His mind was made up why tell him the facts.

My brother admitted he rode his bicycle past my home on several occasions during the feud, but never once knocked on my door to see if I was alright, after ignoring me for many years. My brother rode his bicycle past my house to spy on me and report back anything he might see there to my mother.

My brother lived a few miles away in the adjacent town. I told him. "If I was riding a bicycle in his neighborhood, I would have been curious enough to knock on your door." The visit did not help in our estrangement. At the end of the walk I forgave him for how he hurt me, but I did not forgive him for who he was. Maybe my forgiveness was half- hearted but at that time that's the best that I could offer. What bothered me deeply was the abandonment by his family that have left my sons without an uncle, an aunt and a niece.

Sometime later I visited Cousin Michael at his apartment in the Bronx. We were the same age and we had spent much time together, as teenagers prior to his enlistment in the military. I had not seen him since the fiftieth wedding anniversary party for my parents more than ten years earlier. It was difficult to visit some extended family relatives that shunned me because I was deeply hurt by their silence. At Michael's apartment, we spoke for more than two hours.

I said to him. "So why have you not made any contact with me after all these years?"

Michael replied. "I called your phone number, but I didn't get through."

I asked. "What phone number did you call?"

He looked at me. "I called the number in my book."

Michael opened his telephone book and next to my name, I read my current phone number aloud to him.

I pointed out. "The number listed next to my name is my current telephone number and it's in working order, so if you called, we could have talked."

Michael clenched his lips and turned away, unable to provide a plausible answer for not contacting me. It appeared that Michael stood by the fact that there was rift with my parents and he accepted my parent's version of events.

His mind was made up, why tell him the facts. At that point, I felt it best to leave.

After visiting Michael sometime later, I decided to visit my cousin Vinny and his wife Nancy, who lived in the Bronx. While seated in their house, I could see that they were somewhat uneasy, but after a while, they relaxed realizing I had no ill intent. We traded family stories for more than an hour.

Nancy looked down and said. "Years earlier, your mother told me that your wife visited her carrying a Bible!"

I looked at her. "Are you serious?"

She looked at me curiously. "People don't normally visit each other carrying a Bible?"

I smiled at her. "You mean is my wife some sort of religious kook because people in this area are not 'Bible Thumpers '?"

She clenched her lips and looked down with a bewildered look on her face.

I pointed out. "Nancy let me say this to you, shortly before the rift with my parents, my mother asked my wife on several occasions if we owned a Bible. My wife was getting tired of my mother's repeated interest in our Bible. My wife explained to her that we had been given a Bible as a wedding gift years earlier, and she would be happy to show it to her, to satisfy her curiosity. So, my wife honored her request and brought the Bible to my mother's house. Is that what you're referring to?"

Vinny and Nancy sat there and they didn't know what to say. The Bible story was circulated throughout the family, I heard the same story from my father and brother as it was a story to be condemned to create the appearance that there was something wrong with my wife. My wife and I were well aware that the 'Bible story' gossip had spread throughout the family. That incident did occur, and those that reacted with skepticism toward my wife, shame on them. The Bible story was concocted by my mother to continue the her 'soap opera'. It never occurred to anyone that there are two sides to every story. It reminded me of this story I read where a woman described a very minor conflict to the therapist, saying she had done nothing to deserve such hostile treatment.

She asked the therapist, "What should I do?"

The therapist said. "I don't know; there are two sides to every story."

Without pausing for a second the woman replied, "But I'm telling you both sides of the story."

In the 1970s, the Catholic Church was still revered in the Northeast. Long Island, was not the Bible Belt. While growing up, I was unaware if my parents owned a Bible. Catholics don't read from the Bible; they read from missals, at mass on Sundays and Holy Days, analyzing the epistles and gospels. I never experienced Catholics, Protestants or Jews evangelizing door to door in our neighborhood. At times members of the

'Jehovah Witnesses' knocked on doors spreading their Christian beliefs. Jehovah's Witnesses were looked at with skepticism due to their 1975 prediction that the world ended.

After visiting cousin Vinny and Nancy for a few hours, I departed on a positive note. I wasn't expecting anything from them, such as a future invite or an apology for ignoring my family for many years. What I learned was that they were like many other people in the extended family. They believed a story that they were told and never validated the facts. For the next several days after my visit, we received a number of hang-up phone calls at home. At that time, my mother was still alive.

I read an excerpt from a book by a psychiatrist who had analyzed emotional blackmailers concluding that:

They seem to have a childlike inability to connect behavior to consequences, and they don't appear to give any thought to what they will be left with, once they've gotten the target's compliance. They convince themselves that they are helping others with their punishment. They make themselves feel good and make the target feel bad by drowning them in guilt. Instead of feeling guilt or remorse about hurting someone they care so much about, they can actually feel pride.

My parents constantly spread information to anyone that would listen saying: "We don't see them, we don't know why, they don't see anybody in the family." Why would I want to visit parents who are rejecting me and my family subjecting them to condemnation?

As a parent of my own family I have the following rights:

To protect my family's physical and emotional health
To be treated with respect
To express my own beliefs
To get angry
To raise my children without interference
To make mistakes

To change my mind

To say no

To disagree

To let them know that they have hurt me

To take an active part in the decisions about how the holidays and other special occasions that are celebrated

Regardless of the stories that were spread throughout the family, I was not risking a visit to every extended or immediate family member to present my version of events and plead with them to believe me and disbelieve my parents. Additional rejection was not something I was willing to risk. The damage was done.

During the early part of the estrangement I was involved in a conversation with a friend who I had known since childhood. At that time, I was looking for his support, as I briefly explained to him about the rift with my parents. After talking briefly, he looked at me and said, "Well you know I have my own problems." I was taken aback by his response, feeling somewhat betrayed because we had spent several years together growing up in the Bronx. Later on, I realized that many extended family members had their own problems within their families, and they felt the same way. After all, why should anyone get involved and interfere in my life? Most people choose the path of minding their own business. Well-adjusted and caring people can allow for differences in beliefs and needs, perceptions and attitudes. That situation reminds me of the quote: "Evil survives when good men do nothing."

For example, I could have committed a heinous crime, but I didn't. We didn't visit with my parents, since I challenged their threat to take my children away. Our choice not to visit them was a normal reaction to an abnormal threat. Susan Forward, in her book 'Toxic In-Laws' summed up an interesting point of view regarding behavior: "In their mind Family is the only thing that matters, and you must sacrifice everything for the Family. When the Family whistles, you jump. If you don't agree and dare to want to do something on your own, you get labeled such charming things as 'selfish' or 'unloving.' They treat you this way because they are oblivious or indifferent to how much pain they are causing. They cannot feel what you're feeling because they have this gaping hole inside, where their empathy should be. As a result, they are free to cause suffering without the constraints of such minor inconveniences as guilt or remorse-feelings that would not allow them to go so far without suffering themselves. They battle with you as though they are taking on their own demons. The hidden belief is that in attacking you, they somehow, they're somehow attacking some of their own unresolved problems."

Parents can make mistakes and my parents didn't have blanket righteousness. In their mind, there is only one truth one accurate version, one accurate way to look at any situation: theirs. In psychology, they call this a closed system-a mindset, a way of perceiving events that prevents many people from exploring alternative ways of thinking or behaving - because they don't believe there are alternatives where there are.

40

FEELINGS

My wife and I were raised in different communities but we were taught by our parents to be respectful, responsible and obedient as children. Our parents experienced the 'Great Depression' where they were raised in families of limited means. We were brought up in a strict home environment with rules and if they were not followed there were consequences. When my parents threatened to take our children away I was shocked and bewildered by their threat because that act of betrayal is not attempted without just cause. I searched for answers and learned that subconsciously they were attacking some of their own unresolved problems. My parents weren't born critical, or controlling, or engulfing or rejecting. They learned these behaviors through their own experiences with people who treated them in those ways. You would think that someone who was constantly put down, or made to feel like an outcast would go in the opposite direction as an adult and try to spare someone from feeling the way they did, but the opposite is true, and they become much like that of his or her own problem parent. My parents capitalized on our underlying fear of abandonment, fear of disapproval, fear of loss.

In light of the experiences that my wife and I dealt with during the rift, we never sat down and discussed any long-range plans to deal with it. Since our support base had abandoned us, moving away was an option but the choices were limited as to the locations that were available in the government. We built our own house, our children developed friendships in school. We were coping with the family harassment in a reactive mode, but the culmination of the stresses was unlike anything we have ever experienced. Over the years, we dealt with each situation as it arose, such as stalking, hang-up or annoyance phone calls, harassing letters, shunning, intimidation and violations of boundaries. Attempting to dismiss the issues or shutting them out was only a temporary diversion. We handled each situation from a reactive position causing us to establish a mental toughness, a positive attitude, improvisation and adaptability. At times, I felt like I was in a survivalist mode because we had nobody to stand and support us. But other times the stress was accumulating. Not, to be in contact with parents, brother or sister is a profound loss because our families are so deeply related to our sense of who we are. We feel heart struck about our families when they cannot acknowledge us, love us and support us.

When your family rejects you, there's no way of knowing the direction your friends will take, when they learn that your support base is gone. Being without a family support- system, I always felt as though a cloud followed our family and we were- tainted. Rather than risk rejection, we chose to maintain our silence among our few friends. Rejection by our friends would have been devastating. It reminds me of the phrase 'blood is thicker than water' meaning that a family relationship is more important than your friends. In our case the family blood relationship was toxic.

Years after the estrangement in an effort to seek help, I visited my friend Larry. As teenagers, we had grown up together in the Bronx, and I trusted him. At that time, the level of stress I was experiencing as a result of the rift was overwhelming for me. I needed someone to talk with that I trusted, to explain the issues at hand. My conversation with Larry was disorganized and it did not go the way I intended. Instead of starting from the beginning, I was all over the map. Honestly at this time it's unclear exactly what I said to him. Larry offered his help and I told him that I appreciated his offer but decided to handle the issues myself. Leaving abruptly, I made a fool of myself to Larry and I didn't know why. My only explanation for my behavior was that there was this overwhelming force preventing me from explaining the facts in an orderly fashion. I didn't realize it but I was traumatized, wounded, and paralyzed from the rift coupled with the shame that my parents continued to evoke. Parental love for the most part is unconditional. There was no unconditional love on their part, only division. i learned later that I suffered a stress breakdown, which is a normal reaction to an abnormal situation. The overwhelming nature of events and the inability, helplessness and lack of support trying to deal with those events, leads to the development of Complex Post Traumatic Stress Disorder (CPTSD).

Complex PTSD is where the sufferer suppresses their emotional reaction to traumatic events without resolution either because they believe each event by itself doesn't seem like such a big deal or because they see no satisfactory resolution or opportunity available to them. This suppression of "emotional baggage" can continue for a long time either until a "last straw" event occurs, or a safer emotional environment emerges, and the dam begins to break. One can be experiencing feelings from all of their traumatic exposure, even as they try to address the most traumatic event.

Some years later I was traveling with my friend Dennis as we returned from a retirement party. I trusted him and spoke for a moment.

"I want to tell you that my family has been estranged from both immediate and extended families."

He spoke. "There was a family in my old neighborhood where a situation like you described occurred."

I looked at him. "Well this might be a little different. We are estranged from both families."

Dennis looked at me in shock. "Really!"

I wanted to tell him more but I was unable to do so. I ended the conversation abruptly because the hurt went too deep. I was still suffering from CPTSD.

I had met Dennis earlier while I was employed in the Customs service, but our relationship was that of coworkers. Dennis and I became good friends after the fall of the World Trade Center Towers on 911. I had retired in 1996 and worked full time in the home renovation business. I had lost contact with many of my coworkers. After the fall of the towers I learned that the US Customs Service asked for volunteers to help with the removal of equipment and files that survived in the adjacent building at #6 World Trade Center. Dennis volunteered spending several days in that building wearing a paper mask. These masks were not capable of filtering much of anything let alone the contaminants that were present at ground zero. Sadly, Dennis and other customs agents succumbed to these contaminants. He was a good man and I miss him dearly. The loss of Dennis and others that passed away before their time volunteering at Ground Zero angers me till this day and here's why:

Days after 911 my wife was watching the news and said.

"They are looking for volunteers to work at ground zero; why don't you go there with your all of your equipment and help them?"

I pointed out. "What I know is that the contaminants that are present at Ground Zero are toxic and I wouldn't go near that place without a full- face respirator which will filter 100% of the air. Anything less is dangerous."

The voluntary assignment of Customs agents to work at Ground Zero was unknown to me at that time. Had I been aware that my coworkers were working there, I would have contacted them and recommended 100% respirators or not going there at all.

At Dennis' funeral the church was packed to capacity. There were hundreds of law enforcement officers from several state local and federal agencies. At Pinelawn Cemetery, most of us needed to walk a long distance to the grave site.

At the end of the burial ceremony there was an honor guard of several officers firing their rifles into the air in honor of Dennis' life.

After attending Dennis' funeral I was driving home on the New Jersey Turnpike. It was late in the evening during a heavy rainstorm as I drove in the passing lane at about 60 mph. It seemed like I was the only car on the road. Within seconds I noticed at a distance a car stopped in my lane. I hit the brakes veering to the right to avoid a serious collision. At that moment, out of nowhere a tractor trailer was instantly alongside of me radiating a bright light along its entire length. I could vividly see as clear as daylight the corrugated side of the trailer. Both tractor trailer and my vehicle veered to the right simultaneously as if we were attached. I can't explain the origin of the light because the road was unlit. There were no external lights on the tractor trailer. Seconds later the tractor trailer was gone. I have heard stories about people that have seen bright lights during medical operations but I'm not going to go there. Maybe Dennis was watching over me?

My silence as a result of the rift was partly due to the shaming I experienced from my parents. Shame informs you of an internal state of inadequacy, unworthiness, dishonor, or regret about which others may or may not be aware. It can make you feel as though your whole self is flawed, bad or subject to exclusion, it makes you want to withdraw or hide yourself. Shame is often confused with guilt-an emotion you might experience as a result of shame. It's a wrongdoing about which you might feel remorseful and wish to make amends. Where you will likely have an urge to admit guilt, or talk with others about a situation that left you with guilty feelings. It is unlikely that you will broadcast your shame. In fact, you'll most likely conceal what you feel because shame does not make a distinction between an action and the self. Therefore, with shame, "bad" behavior is not separate from a "bad" self as it is with guilt.

A situation real or imagined, might trigger a shame response when you experience yourself to be inferior in a competitive endeavor; when others might become aware of information that you want to cover- up; or you anticipate being viewed as lacking or inadequate, such as lacking a family support base.

My parents capitalized on the fact that I was raised as an obedient, quiet, private and respectful person and based on that, they assumed that I'd succumb to their demands to obey them. As my mother blurted out in my home, "I'm the mother, you don't question me: and my father's statement. "You obey us or we'll have your children taken away." Those words somehow placed a hold on me and prevented my ability to articulate my side of the story in a clear and organized manner. It's hard for most people to comprehend that any parents would threaten to have their grandchildren taken away because their son visited the in laws instead of his parents on Thanksgiving Day. Secondly, there's got to be more to the story. That is why I decided to write the story from my most vivid recollections. Since the story started as a child it requires much time to explain because there was not one event, there were several events. I was not looking for my friends to be my therapist because in the back of my mind I wondered if my version of the events would be positively accepted by them. I did not want to get into a long explanation of the potential legal issue of 'Grandparents Rights,' family abandonment, letters of rejection, intimidation, stalking, and harassing phone calls, etc. A proper explanation could take many hours. Many years had passed and there was too much information to deliver a well- organized explanation. Not being the chatty type, I wasn't willing to open up, and tell the story to anybody. Being a tight lipped non-gossiper, I was not the type of person in need of sympathy. Raised to be independent, I worked since the age of nine, a self-starter who was not handed anything. Brought up in a strict household where there were rules and if they weren't followed there were consequences. But there were positive aspects during my upbringing that was helpful in the development of my character and helped me survive this turmoil.

Over the years, the subject of my relationship with my parents rarely arose in conversations with friends or acquaintances. The few instances when my immediate family relationship arose, I responded. "It's not that we don't visit my parents, siblings or relatives, they don't visit us." What added to our stress was the fact that society tends to project harsh judgment on people who reject their family, even as disturbed as some families may be. After all, who would think to terminate a relationship with someone that bore and raised you? I wasn't rejecting my family. My family was rejecting me. When a relationship is emotionally unhealthy causing suffering, the victim has every right to stop interacting with that person, even if they are related to you.

When the estrangement started I listed the events that occurred immediately. The hand-up phone calls that pre-empted birthdays, anniversaries and holidays. The dates of those events, were only known by a few people. I viewed the phone calls as constant reminder never to forget that you're missing the celebration of your birthday or our birthday, or your anniversary or our anniversary, Christmas and Thanksgiving with your immediate family.

After attending my parents' fiftieth anniversary, I experienced shunning on a grand scale. It is a silent and insidious form of psychological torture. It's impossible to describe unless you have felt it yourself. It eats away at your insides in a way that can be invisible even to oneself. Having dealt with being shunned by my immediate and extended family, I lost all of those relationships. Those members of the family have cut out my ability to express my love and affection. They have robbed me of my affection and have injured me. Every day I get up, I don't have my family is a day I'm subjected to abuse. It's an ongoing thing. It happens every day. Every day my immediate family chooses to maintain their silence and their distance; means that every day they choose to hurt me. It's a strategy designed to hurt me in the most deep and abiding way. It's a strategy to make me believe that I'm completely unlovable and always will be. It strangles you from within your own mind.

After many years of not having contact with my immediate and extended family, I've mourned the loss of those family members. When any of them pass on, I will not grieve their loss. I have already lost them. That may be cold hearted but when honor, love, and compassion are not expressed and the family member is rejected, over time your skin thickens or you go over the edge. When a relationship is lost, the person grieves the loss of that person as if they had died, so when the grieving is over the attachment is over and a connection is very difficult to regain. Having dealt with being- shunned by my immediate and extended family, I lost all of those relationships. They have robbed me of my love, affection and have injured me. In simple terms, it's an 'execution of the soul.'

41

CASES

I had reservations about writing this chapter because some might consider this as boasting. That is not my intention. This chapter covers some of the cases I worked.

Although my parents didn't value my life, others did. I had some major achievements and accomplishments while working for the government. The comradery at work helped alleviate some of the stresses of the rift. An overview of these cases, are described in this chapter, not for the purpose of adulation, but to provide an understanding of some of the work that I performed with the loyal support of my fellow agents. The friendships developed at work helped me cope with the family rejection.

While working at the Long Island Task Force, I received information that an individual may attempt to smuggle steroids into our area via North Carolina. I boarded a flight to North Carolina and met with my counterparts in the Customs arrival area at Raleigh Durham Airport. We verified that the subject was on board the flight from Cancun, Mexico. The subject approached the customs inspector and placed his suitcase on the baggage counter. The inspector performed a cursory check, closed the suitcase and escorted the subject to a private room. Examination of his suitcase revealed the contents to be filled with steroids except for a shirt, a pair of pants and a few trinkets. The field test proved positive for the assortment of steroids including tablets and liquid injectables. The subject was placed under arrest and advised of his rights. During the debriefing, I suggested that he cooperate with us and he agreed. He informed me that he was a body builder who worked out in a local gym in Long Island. Then he told me that he smuggled the steroids to deliver them to three body builders who worked out with him in the gym.

The local Customs Agents in North Carolina assisted me, as we transported the subject and the steroids to the boarding gate for our flight to New York. Once we entered the jet-way I needed to manage the defendant, the suitcase of steroids and our luggage. I placed a jacket over the subject's hands to cover the handcuffs. Never giving it a second thought that I was transporting a prisoner alone which was against policy. The flight was full. I needed a double seat, in order to isolate the prisoner from the passengers. Unfortunately, the only seats available were in the center section at four abreast. I sat on the aisle seat with the defendant seated next to me. My only concern was not about government policy only the successful delivery of the defendant and the steroids to my office.

I approached the stewardess. "I am transporting a prisoner. Would it be possible to swap seats with two passengers seated at the window for privacy?"

She said. "The flight is full. We're moving right now, and you should be in your seat!"

I remarked. "Thanks for your help."

The flight to New York was not that long, but when we entered the New York area, the pilot made an announcement. "We'll be in a holding pattern for a while due to the high amount of air traffic." The pilot reduced power and turned the aircraft.

The defendant leaned over to me speaking in a low voice. "What's happening?"

I informed him. "The pilot's in a holding pattern while he waits for clearance to land."

A few minutes later, the defendant with a worried look on his face raised his voice. "We're slowing down, we're slowing down, are we going down, are we going down, are we gonna crash!"

I said in a low voice. "Shut... the fuck... up, you're gonna panic the passengers!"

I thought the subject was experiencing paranoia as a result of his drug use.

He insisted. "I'm scared. I'm scared."

The defendant started to sweat profusely as perspiration accumulated on his forehead.

He looked at me and said. "Scratch my head, scratch my head, it's itchy."

I said, "I'm not putting my hands on your head."

He demanded. "You gotta scratch my head now!"

I replied. "What's the matter with you?"

He said. "I can't scratch my head wearing these handcuffs."

I removed a pen from my pocket and proceeded to move it back and forth on top of his head. The passenger seated adjacent to him looked at me with a surprised look on his face as I moved the pen back and forth on his head.

I looked at him and said. "He's itchy."

The passenger turned away. I didn't know if he was aware that the subject was a prisoner or not.

We landed at LaGuardia airport and I drove to our Bohemia office with the subject in custody. When I entered the bullpen area, a group of about twenty law enforcement officers cheered as I walked in with the subject. It was a moving experience of appreciation from my peers.

We instructed the defendant to make recorded telephone calls to the three subjects that were expecting the steroid delivery. Once the arrangements were made, we set-up at the Howard Johnson's Restaurant. The subject was wired-up and instructed to meet each accomplice separately inside the restaurant. The meetings were set-up at half hour intervals while we monitored the conversations from our vehicle. After the third subject was arrested inside the restaurant, the waitress at the counter threw her hands up in the air and looked at the agents. "What the hell's going on? Everybody's getting arrested in here. I'm going home!"

On another occasion, I was instructed to assist DEA with a 'knock off' of a Colombian suspect.

I arrived at the DEA headquarters in Melville for a briefing. The plan was that after the DEA undercover made a two kilo buy from the subject, we would go in for the takedown. Sitting in the passenger seat the DEA agent rolled into the parking lot. The order was transmitted on the radio that the deal was completed. We moved closer for the take down. I exited the car. The subject was a short distance away. While I was in the process of drawing my weapon, at the same time the subject drew his weapon from a shoulder holster. At that moment, DEA Agent Brian Noone pointed a semi-automatic rifle at the suspect's head ordering him to drop his weapon. The situation scared the life out of me because I was angrier at myself for not having my weapon out in time. The suspect was forced to the ground, cuffed and transported to the lock-up. I can't tell you how fast everything happened and how thankful I was that Brian was able to quickly get the drop on this guy. It could have been a bad situation for me. God must have been watching over me.

Near the end of my career, I was working in the Narcotics Group. We received information that a red tractor towing a box trailer was on its way to Long Island carrying a load of narcotics. The information was vague except that we knew the license plate number and the color of the tractor. We narrowed down the route and focused on the Throgs Neck Bridge. Special agent Gerry Sireci, and I proceeded to Queens and set up on the Clearview Expressway. Gerry was positioned at the entrance to the Clearview Expressway near the bridge. I set-up at the Clearview Expressway exit. After observing vehicles for several hours, Gerry contacted me on the radio. "I believe that the subject vehicle has just passed me, although I can't confirm the full plate number it's partially correct."

About ten minutes later, I observed the tractor and confirmed it to be the suspect vehicle as it exited the Clearview Expressway. I contacted Gerry on the radio. "2Alpha2106 this is 2Alpha2107, the suspect vehicle has been confirmed, and he has exited the Clearview Expressway heading eastbound on Horace Harding Boulevard."

I followed the truck for about a half- mile. The driver slowed down and parked at the curb.

I spoke on the radio. "2Alpha2106 this is 2Alpha2107 the suspect vehicle has parked on Horace Harding Boulevard."

Gerry called me on the radio. "2Alpha2107 this is 2Alpha2106, be advised I'm on my way to your location."

I acknowledged. "Ten- four."

While observing the suspect vehicle for several minutes I decided to slip on my bulletproof vest and raid jacket. Minutes later three male individuals exited the tractor and walked toward the rear of the trailer and continued to walk away from the vehicle. "2Alpha2106 this is 2Alpha2107, be advised, three males have exited the suspect vehicle and are walking away, I'm going to stop them."

I placed the magnetic red light on the roof and drove my vehicle directly into the path of the subjects, as they crossed Bell Boulevard. I exited my vehicle and drew my weapon.

I yelled at them, "Federal agent, don't move, put your hands in the air. Move over to the car and spread out on the hood!"

I radioed the communications center. "Sector 1, this is 2Alpha2107, this is a 10-13 officer needs assistance at the intersection of Bell Boulevard and Horace Harding Parkway. I'm detaining three suspects in the street!"

I contacted Gerry. "2A2106, this is 2A2107 I'm here alone."

Gerry responded. "I'll be there momentarily."

I said. "Ten Four."

Waiting for back-up felt like an eternity. Gerry finally rolled up, and walked over smiling.

"You didn't think I'd ever get here did you; felt like forever, huh?"

I replied. "Boy, am I glad to see you, let's get these guys out of traffic."

A search of the trailer revealed 1,500 pounds of narcotics. All of the subjects were placed under arrest and the vehicle was seized.

A few months before I retired, I was awakened after midnight by a phone call from the Customs Aviation Branch located in Ronkonkoma, New York. The pilot informed me that an aircraft that departed Colombia, South America is currently under surveillance by the Customs Air Branch from Florida and is heading into our area.

About thirty minutes later, I met with Customs pilots Bob and Joe at the Aviation Branch at Islip McArthur Airport. Minutes later, inside the hangar, I sat in the rear seat of a King Air twin-engine aircraft. After the pre-flight check was completed, the co-pilot locked the door and said, "This is a nasty rainstorm. It's going to be rough. Do you get sick?"

I said, "If you don't crash, I won't get sick."

He did not respond.

We taxied out of the hangar into a torrential downpour. Flying was not new to me since I had flown many times while assigned to the Aviation Branch years earlier. The pilot taxied down the runway and minutes later we were airborne. When I looked out of the window, the rain poured, and I was unable to see anything. We headed directly into a strong wind, coupled with exploding thunder and lightning that shined through the torrential rain. The aircraft vibrated as I bounced around in my seat while my stomach rose up to my chest. Forcing the seatbelt against my stomach, I knew if I survived this flight, it would the one I would never forget. Placing the hood on my sweat shirt over the top of my head, I drew the string tight creating complete darkness. I put my head down and prayed to God to guide us through this storm. The aircraft continued to bounce and vibrate as the rain pounded against the fuselage. Several minutes later the pilot yelled out. "Bear with this for a little while; we'll be clear of the storm shortly." A short time later we were beyond the heavy rain, in the clouds heading due north. We landed at a private airport in Knox County located in Rockland, Maine.

While we waited on the ground, Joe spoke in a concerned voice. "If the suspect aircraft lands and off-loads, we're only equipped with handguns."

I asked. "This aircraft is not equipped with long guns?"

Joe looked at me helplessly. "No."

I replied. "My office doesn't supply us with long guns, so we'll do the best we can if a confrontation arises."

I was just as concerned as they were.

Bob looked at the aeronautical charts. "This guy's 'fly'n Lindberg!'" That's aviation terminology for flying from point A to point B in a straight line; Colombia, South America to the northeastern United States. When Charles Lindberg flew the first solo flight non-stop from Roosevelt Field, New York to Paris, France, he flew practically in a straight line. The suspect aircraft departed Colombia, South America flying a DC 3. The aircraft was designed to fly approximately 2,100 miles with the existing fuel tanks. In order to travel non-stop from Colombia to the northern United States the aircraft would be equipped with bladders, providing the extra fuel needed to travel greater distances than the aircraft was designed for. The trip from Colombia to the northeast is roughly 2,800 miles. Smugglers prefer flying over water because it's a route where they can avoid or limit their detection by law enforcement.

We received a call from the chase aircraft, a Customs High Endurance Aircraft. The suspect aircraft was located by an Airborne Warning and Control System (AWACS) aircraft which patrolled the southeastern United States. We received an incoming call on the radio from the chase aircraft.

"2lima141, this is Omaha .....45. We're about 15 minutes from your location, over."

Joe responded, "We'll be airborne in a few minutes."

In five minutes, we were up and shortly thereafter we were behind the suspect aircraft. Omaha.... 45 dropped off and we assumed the surveillance point. Without giving details, smugglers rarely, if ever, detect they are being followed due to the counter surveillance techniques employed by law enforcement.

After about 20 minutes, Joe contacted the communications division. "Sector 1 this is 2lima 141."

They replied. "Go ahead 2lima 141."

Joe ordered them. "Contact the Canadian Air Force, and inform them that we are tracking a suspect aircraft that has entered their airspace."

When the suspect entered Canadian airspace, he changed course traveling in a westerly direction. The sun peeked through on the horizon, and when I looked down all I could see was endless undeveloped forest land surrounding numerous bodies of water. A short time later the pilot yelled out. "He's dropping altitude; he's a couple of hundred feet off the ground and slowing down! There are no landing strips or airports in this area."

A few minutes later the suspect aircraft descended just above the tree line and dropped cargo into a long narrow lake. The suspect quickly ascended and continued in a westerly direction. The Canadian Air Force pursued the suspect aircraft. We circled the drop area and observed a power boat depart a dock and retrieve the floating cargo. "Sector 1, this is 2 lima 141, contact the Royal Canadian Mounted Police and give them these coordinates. Inform them that a suspect aircraft has dropped cargo into the water which was retrieved by a power boat and returned to shore. We will remain airborne as long as possible until law enforcement arrives."

When the boat retuned to the dock, the cargo was loaded into a four-wheel drive vehicle. A short time later we observed the vehicle depart the area at a high rate of speed, as the dust followed the vehicle along the road. "Sector 1, this is 2lima141, be advised that the cargo has been loaded into a light colored four-wheel drive vehicle heading eastbound from the coordinates we provided." Later on, we observed law enforcement stop the suspect vehicle before it was able to reach a paved road. We later learned that the Royal Canadian Mounted Police arrested the subject and charged him with transporting several hundred pounds of cocaine.

While at home, at 2 a.m. on Saturday morning I was-awakened by loud music, outside. I looked out the window where a black SUV parked adjacent to my house with an open tailgate playing booming music from large speakers located in the rear of the vehicle. I wasn't in the mood to go outside, so I called 911 to report the noise, but the driver departed the area before the police arrived.

Two weeks later on a Saturday at 1 a.m., I was awakened at home by loud music that played outside. The music from the restaurant down the street sometimes awakens me. Myself and the neighbors had ongoing complaints with the restaurant owner for several years, so noise on Friday evening was not uncommon. When I walked into the street, the music stopped playing. A black limousine was parked adjacent to my house, so I approached the driver and tapped on the window. The driver lowered the window.

I looked at him. "Were you playing loud music?"

The driver rolled his eyes at me. "No, I'm not playing music!"

I stared at him, perplexed. "The music originated from this location since there were no other cars parked here."

The driver's voice increased. "Look, I told you I didn't play any music!"

I frowned at him. "You know you're parked in a tow away-zone?"

The driver sarcastically responded. "If you don't like it, what are you going to do about it? What are you going to do? Why don't you get your gun?"

I looked at him. "I know what I'm going to do." I turned to walk away.

At that moment, the passenger door opened in front of me. I thought the limo was empty. A stocky man in his forties stepped in front of me. Speaking in a friendly voice, he said, "Hey, hey everything's alright, it's good, just a slight misunderstanding."

The guy put his hand on my shoulder while he spoke to me. Seconds later two guys exited from the other limo door, followed by three guys as they all walked towards me. One guy was the size of a refrigerator. Being outnumbered my heart dropped. I envisioned myself being ushered into this limo and driven off somewhere never to return. Looking at these guys, I was no match for any of one of them, let alone six of them. They were non-corporate types, casually dressed, wearing expensive clothing and shoes with classy gold jewelry and nicely styled hair. The guy with his hand on my shoulder must have been the leader of the group as he continued to talk to me. My instincts suggested that they were members of the 'bent nose crowd.'

He said. "Every ting is ok, don't worry bout a ting ear. We're just out for the night, every ting is good, every tings ok."

The more he told me that everything was good and okay the more I worried. Feeling that I was seconds away from a car ride to never land.

I pointed out. "If you don't mind, let me tell my wife to cancel that 911 call."

The leader cocked his head back with a surprised look on his face. "That's not necessary, we were just leaving."

The six of them hurriedly entered the limousine, and the driver sped away before I returned to the house. Thank God. I really didn't know what to make of the incident.

After 26 years of federal service I filed my papers to retire from the U.S. Customs Service. At that time, I had built up a clientele in the home remodeling business that would provide steady work for almost a year. Under the circumstances, I felt that retirement would place my family in a better financial position.

I surrendered my government issued revolver and purchased a fully automatic handgun. Having maintained and trained with a revolver my entire career, I never paid attention to semi-automatic handgun training. After purchasing a small caliber weapon, I inserted the loaded clip into the gun and pulled the slide back to chamber a round. That action required an unusually high amount of strength for a small caliber weapon. I was unaware that small caliber automatics utilize springs that require more force that larger caliber weapons. When I pulled back the slide, to chamber a round, the weapon rotated 180 degrees pointing it at my chest. Had my finger been on the trigger I could have shot myself. Miraculously it was not. I took a deep breath and sat on the bed in shock for a few minutes and thanked God for watching over me. I realized I had no business owning a weapon without having the proper handgun training, so I decided to sell it.

There was an incident I recalled while working alone in Huntington remodeling two bathrooms. A leak sprung in the bathroom from a faulty water valve. The water was shooting up to the ceiling. I ran downstairs toward the basement to shut off the water main and in the process, I struck my head on the dropped ceiling above the staircase. I felt like I had cracked my skull. Staggering from dizziness and seconds away from passing out, I struggled to turn off the water main. I laid on the floor for a while to regain my stability. It's a wonder that I remained conscious. In the kitchen, I placed ice cubes into a towel and held it against my head for about an hour. It's a wonder that I survived that accident.

42

THERAPIST

In December 1991, I arranged a meeting with my parents at the clinical psychologist office, and they reluctantly agreed. We sat together in the office as the therapist looked at them. (This meeting is verbatim)

"Do you have any desire to reconcile your differences with your son?"

My father responded in a derogatory tone. "No comment."

The therapist said to my parents, "What is your reason for coming to therapy?"

My mother replied, "Only because he asked us here."

I pointed out. "In 1979, both of you came into my house, and you told me, 'Don't you question me, I'm the mother.' Following your comment, my Father threatened to have my children taken away."

My father sat there speechless. My mother looked away uttering. "The only reason he said that, was to get back at you because you don't act normal."

I asked. "What do you mean by that?"

She said. "That thing about having the children taken away was the result of the letter sent to you by your Uncle Paul B., from Florida and that's how it came about."

I pointed out. "Uncle Paul's letter was sent to us in 1983, four years after both of you came to my house ordering my obedience and Dad threatened to have my children taken away. Uncle Paul's letter was not responsible for my father's threat four years earlier. What you're saying is an absolute lie. Oh, by the way I called Uncle Paul and he does not recall ever sending the letter we're speaking about. I think you and Dad concocted the letter to cover up for your threat four years earlier."

My parents sat there unresponsive for a long time. Then the therapist spoke up. "My understanding of this situation was that your parents were not visiting the children as frequently as they would like, so your father used those words, 'We'll have your children taken away.' To get back at you, because you did not visit them at Thanksgiving. Your parents were very upset that you did not visit them for Thanksgiving and as a result, they had tremendous difficulty in dealing with the fact that you were spending time with your wife's family."

I pointed out. "When the isolation started with you and Dad, why is it that on holidays, birthdays or anniversaries we receive a hang up call, an arrogant phone call or correspondence to ruin the occasion? I have the cards and letters right here. I don't need any of those goons you hired to follow my family around. What were you attempting to gain?"

My parents sat there unresponsive and did not contest any of my accusations.

My father spoke, in a condescending tone. "Who is friendly with you in the family?" He spoke very proudly that he and my mother had isolated and sabotaged our relationship with the family.

I said to my mother, "What have you said to members of the family to make us feel un-wanted?"

My mother spoke, in an innocent voice. "We don't know. We don't see you. You're crazy."

My mother sneered at my wife. "I didn't know that she was going to be here; we didn't need her to be here. I don't want to talk to her; I want to talk to you!"

I crossed my arms. "I'll bring my wife to anyplace I want, and I don't need a permission slip from you."

The therapist glanced at my mother. "Don't blame Joann; everyone is involved!"

I informed her. "My wife had opened up her life to you and explained that she did not want to have any problems with you. She embraced you and brought you into her confidence and you betrayed her, and now you're annoyed that she is here tonight."

My mother turned to me. "I had a good relationship with your son Victor."

I crossed my arms. "You never had a good relationship with my son. You rarely visited us, and when you did, you spent little or no time with my children. "

My mother got stubborn. "You're going to live with this and you'll regret it!"

I replied. "My sons are here right now; would you like to say something to them?"

She asked. "Why are they here now?"

My parents walked into the waiting room and stood away from my children. My mother looked at them. "Oh, you've grown." They stood there silently for a moment and then walked out never talking or embracing their grandchildren. So much for reconciliation and grandparents' rights.

One of the grievous things a parent can do is to leave a child an orphan. My parents and relatives have cut my ability to express my love and affection where the attachment and a connection cannot be regained. I felt embarrassed for my children as my parents were unexpressive of any empathy for them. The rift was a sham, and my parents were embarrassed that they got caught, but not ashamed that they lied to perpetuate a bogus story. In their mind, the end justifies the means. Their behavior was utterly disgraceful.

About twenty years after the rift, I sent a short letter to my mother asking her to send photos of my youth. Weeks later in the mail, I received two wallet size photos and two regular print size photos. My Father was an avid picture taker and we had several photo albums. He maintained the photos that were not in the albums in an organized filing system in legal size portfolios, for as long as I can remember. When I lived at home he filed the photos in sequence and coordinated the negatives with every developed roll of film. If pictures were not placed in photo albums, the information was written on the print packages. He'd write the location and date on the back and front of many of the photos. That information was invaluable over the years. To deprive me of photos of myself as a child and while I grew up, reduced my ability to share with my childhood. Since the relationship with my parents was estranged, I could not understand their reasoning to hold onto photos of their son that they have no relationship with. If my parents didn't want to give up photos to me, then perhaps they might have provided me with the negatives, and I could make the prints, unless they were discarded. Photos show important memories of birth, marriage, anniversaries, holidays, new house, places that we visited and events that were important to my life. It's a personal story, a timeline of my life of good memories. Their punishment is unending.

In October in 2012, the weather bureau predicted that Long Island, would be impacted by Hurricane Sandy. Since hurricanes were not uncommon to us, we started to prepare the house by taping the windows and boarding up the large windows and doors. My son Chris purchased several five-gallon gas containers, which he fueled up for the generator which we positioned on the second-floor deck. We rented a truck and loaded the furniture and household items from the first floor placing them in storage. All loose items on the outside of the house were put away or secured. The area was evacuated and my wife and son Vic stayed with friends as I remained in the house with my younger son to cope with any damage.

The height of the storm surge hit at approximately three in the morning. All electrical power was terminated at midnight. The storm surge for Sandy was rated at a 5.8 out of 6. I was very concerned, since storm surges are dangerous because they flood low lying areas and have been known to take many lives.

At three in the morning, I stood on the front porch in total darkness. I was unable to see anything on my property as if a giant black cover was placed over the entire community. Not a light shined anywhere. Using a high-powered flashlight, I observed the water level against the house to be a foot and half in height. We tried to reduce the water level inside the house by using two sump pumps that were submerged below the level of the garage floor. By 9 a.m. the seawater had drained away from the house as the tide receded.

The street remained flooded for almost two days since the ground was saturated from the tidal water. The next day we looked at the devastation, where trees and power lines were down in the neighborhood. The thirty-foot by twenty- foot deck in the backyard had been lifted off its footings, damaged beyond repair. There was a house that was lifted off of its foundation and a forty-foot floating dock sat on my neighbor's front lawn. Debris was strewn everywhere on the property and in the street, that been carried in by the flood-water.

We fired-up the generator and it ran continuously for fourteen days.

The cleanup was started immediately to prevent mold. My sons and I immediately started the cleanup by removing the rugs and the entire wood flooring. Four feet above the floor, we removed the drywall and insulation around the entire first floor. After we removed the debris we had enough to fill a forty-yard dumpster. I notified the electrician to check the wiring and replace any wiring that was affected by the flood water.

Many years of our life consisted of an emotional storm that wiped out any hope of reconciliation. Hurricane Sandy hit and caused wreckage to our home, and that damage we were able to repair.

My wife and I endured the rift with the family because we were not being met anywhere near half way. We are satisfied with the decisions we made over the years during the estrangement and hoped that our efforts could have ameliorated the feud. My family broke my heart.

Hurricane Sandy was the second major hurricane we experienced. Our days of living near the water were over. We decided to move out of New York leaving the past behind us and start a new beginning.

BIBLIOGRAPHY

Customs Today Magazine 1974

Wikipedia

T.J. Labinsky

Emotional Blackmail by Susan Forward Ph.D

Toxic In-Laws by Susan Forward, Ph.D

ACKNOWLEDGEMENT-
SHAWN POALILLO

Words cannot express my gratitude to Shawn as he inspired me to write the book. A few years earlier I would have been unable to coherently put the words on paper, due to my attachment to the story. Frequently Shawn said to me. "If you don't like what you have written, write it again and again, until you can't get it any better." Shawn provided constant guidance and support that I needed to complete the book. Being technically oriented I struggled at times with the writing process. When I was unable to solve an issue Shawn would say, "writing is an art and It's not like you can research problem areas in a book to help you solve your problem, so try it from a different point of view." All I can say to you Shawn. "Thank you, thank you, thank you!"

Printed in the United States
by Baker & Taylor Publisher Services